I AM MAINE

STORIES FROM SMALL TOWN MAINE

JEREMY FLAGG

For the cast of characters who made me who I am.
Mom. Dad. Jason. Mimi. Mam.

PREFACE

We are not merely Mainers; we are family, joined by this giant chunk of land. We were either born to or like myself, arrived kicking and screaming. We have family members we cherish, and those considered black sheep. Underneath the surface, we have a bond uniting us despite our differences. You are also my friends; the people who have grown with me. Some of you grew with me before I.Am.Maine, and some of you are new to this reflecting on the stories composing the man I am today. Yes, family.

    I wasn't sure how I would measure the success of I.Am.Maine. Would I assess it by the number of people who visited a website? Would I look at how many people left comments? Early on I tried to fight how to do this, but now, as I conclude a segment of this journey, I think I've figured out how to assess the success of my writing.

When the blog went live, I received more views than I expected. I assumed friends of my mother, and of mine, would read and then be on their merry way. However, something unsuspected happened; people started leaving comments and sending me emails. People told me their tales of Maine. I've been gifted stories about how people loved and hated Maine and how they escaped only to want to go back and vice versa. I could tell that each word I read was filled with the same emotion I hoped to convey. I was, and am, glad to share in these heart-filled moments. Each one makes me more and more proud to say I am a Mainer. It washes away any negativity created from living in a small town and leaves only those cherished moments.

This book is the exploration of conflict in a place I loathe and long for. It is filled with sorrows and hope. It is an attempt to reach inside a town and extract its essence and unravel a tightly knit community. But more than that, it is a struggle to put into words what it means to be from a small town in the heart of Maine.

On these pages, I hope I inspire as much as it has inspired me.

FROM THE SHADOWS

We were not the first.
    Maine has a variety of classifications for the towns within the state. In the South, it's more common to hear the term "city," but once you hit those long stretches of roads, they are few and far between. We commonly refer to everything as a town, but even that isn't the truth. Brownville Junction is a village belonging to the town of Brownville. We have our own post office, but other than that, we operate as one community. However, in my school district, we also have Lakeview Plantation, a small step down from a village. Beyond that is Barnard Township and

the former Williamsburg, now dissolved into Northeast Piscataquis. Together, this handful of towns fall just shy of two thousand residents. But even they dwarf the hidden gem found just north on Route 11.

T4.R9.: an uninhabited section of Maine.

Once colonized, they divided Maine into a grid. Six miles by six miles, these plots of land were labeled by cartographers and would evolve and dissolve into what we know today. But there are still parts of Maine that have not only remained ignored, but for the most part are uninhabited. Only identified by slender green post next to the mile marker, these are the passages from and to civilization. Most wouldn't know they exist, giving them the label of "wilderness". But of course in Maine, we find a charm in living close to these empty expanses.

As a kid, I spent hours riding my bike up and down the streets. One day, I found myself next to our small ice rink and noticed an unpaved road leading away from town. Determined to leave no inch of Brownville Junction unexplored, I peddled into parts unknown. The road came to a dead end, but continued into the woods as a snowmobile trail. However, unlike our normal trails, this had once been an actual road, despite being overgrown and unused by wheeled vehicles for decades. Curious, I followed.

For miles, I found myself at the edge of our town. Tacked to a tree was a sign marked "Indian Land," with no further details. At the time, I was too young to understand the implications of the sign. I stopped exploring once I reached a rickety bridge made for ATVs and snowmobiles. Nearby, somebody had once erected a fence between the trees, along with a stable for horses. Like many similar structures in this area, it had been neglected and nature attempted to reclaim her footprint on the land.

In school we are taught Maine is the twenty-third state admitted to the union. Inhabited in 1604 by the French, and would later be occupied by the British in the War of 1812. Originally part of Massachusetts, it declared secession, and on March 15, 1820, it declared its independence. To say our education is lacking is an understatement. For a people with a symbiotic relationship with the land, we ignore the people who came before us. All that remained of our predecessors was a single sign, hand painted, and tacked to the trunk of a tree.

Our education not only offered an enormous gap regarding the indigenous people, what little we were taught was trivial and even harmful. It's an unfortunate and horrific truth I've had to face when exploring the origins of the place I once called home. Long before my town formed, the land belonged to the Eastern Algonquian Native Americans, part of the Wabanaki Confederacy. It wasn't enough to cohabitate, or even isolate their tribes, but as I stared at that sign, what little we learned vilified the first people. I found it disheartening. While we learned to recite each county, Maine's first people were ignored. Only once did they enter our history lesson, and that was to invoke a misplaced pride in their appearance in "Last of the Mohicans." I was coming to grips with the realization that the pride I hold in being a Mainer comes with a stain that is impossible to scrub away.

I talk about T4.R9 and tell the tale of many areas of the state uninhabited and left to its natural splendor. However, it comes with an asterisk. These "empty" lands in central and northern Maine might not have a government or occupants, but there are those who still call it home. The People of the Dawn came long before we labeled thirty-five thousand square miles with the name "Maine". It adds to the melancholy as I explore what makes us Mainers, a term that I find goes beyond the rose colored memories that surface in moments of nostalgia. It's a hard pill to swallow, but on this journey, I am finding that my definition of a Mainer grows and evolves. I only hope that as the next generation emerges, they acknowledge and broaden their views.

We are all Maine.

BLOODY SKI BUNNIES

I have no athletic ability. Unless there is a sport, where being bulky, uncoordinated and techno-savvy are required skills, I will be the last picked for a team. Despite these shortcomings, somewhere, deep inside, I wanted to believe that every Mainer is gifted with a hereditary trait granting them something that can only be considered a superpower. With our winters extending for half the year, I assumed it would be related to snow. I might not run, jump, catch, or throw, but I must be able to ski. Right?

In 1995, the school offered a rare Saturday field trip. Because of the long periods of indoor isolation due to sub-zero temperatures, the school thought it a good idea to mix physical activity with one of Maine's most well-known activities. Having never participated in a winter sport, I thought it would be an excellent opportunity to unmask my true potential and fast track my way to the Olympics. In no time, I would be a household name and uncoordinated children would have a role model. I put aside my dislike of the cold, focusing on the future generations I would inspire.

We loaded onto the bus. It was obvious that there was a divide between those who were frequent skiers and those who preferred reading books inside until the snow melted. We journeyed to Sugarloaf; an internationally renowned ski resort two hours west of school. On one side of the bus, students dressed in colorful fluffy jackets and wearing pants that made a swish noise when they walked. They slid their snowboards, skis and poles into their seat, in a manner that said they were ready to dazzle us with their skill. More than one person had a helmet, and I couldn't fathom why that would be necessary when zipping through powdered snow. The rest of us, however, we wore whatever hodgepodge assortment of clothing we believed would keep us warm. I would later discover that wearing jeans and a pair of long underwear isn't the insulated attire required for hours of downhill skiing.

My clothing choices might have been suspect, but I discovered my superpower is immunity to the arctic winds.

Because of the gale force winds coming down the mountain, little more than the bunny slope was open when we arrived. There was a sigh of relief. I didn't want to over exert myself by taking on the black diamond trails. Instead, I decided it would be best to coax my latent talents to the surface by going through an instructional ski orientation. The gentleman in charge used words like "dangerous" and "warning" thinking we were Flatlanders. Holding onto the rope as we practiced our balance, I had learned everything he could offer. It was time to begin my speed trials and zip through the slalom with a legendary accuracy.

While he focused on the rest of the group, I pushed off, heading toward the bunny slope. I expected lightning speed, but let's be honest, I moved slightly faster than a car accident victim and with as much grace. As I reached the bottom, I hopped, putting all my weight on one ski, expecting a flurry of shaved ice to spit into the air. They must have neglected that area of the mountain because my attempts to stop resulted in smacking my face on the ground.

I hear skiing is excellent exercise. But it can't compete with the boxing match between me and a mountain, in which I constantly lost. If my future as an Olympic skier fell short, I could always create a new revolutionary workout called "Be Lucky You Still Have Teeth."

I still fared better than many on this trip. The gene that creates skilled outdoorsmen must be recessive. Over a six-hour stint on the mountain, our chaperone spent more time in the back of an ambulance than he did on the slopes. Each time the white truck arrived, red lights flashing, I assumed it was another classmate being rushed to the emergency room. Unfortunately, on the bus ride home, it was obvious this was dangerously close to the truth.

A student had jumped from the lift, for reasons unknown, leaving both of his lower legs in white plaster casts. Another had a broken foot from a ferocious tree that sprung from the woods and assaulted him. At least these were related to the act of skiing, a leisurely activity that should come with terms and services that clearly notes the potential for death. Even the flagpoles scattered about the mountain had bruised a groin or two. But the weirdest trip to the emergency was a girl who decided, at the top of a mountain, her clothes were a hinderance. After lying naked on the ground, she discovered that frost bite does not discriminate. There were plenty of lesser injuries, as well. More than a handful of us journeyed to the end of the bunny slopes, where it narrows into a tunnel under a walkway. The massive sign hanging over it saying, "Duck!" should have been more specific about *when* to duck.

We groaned on the trip home, a collection of ski veterans trading war stories. Once we arrived, the chaperone helped our injured to their waiting parents. There were shocked faces. He tried to explain the bruises, the icepacks, and the casts. It would be the last ski trip hosted by Penquis Valley High School.

The people of Maine are many stereotypes. But never think we are naturally gifted with dominion over the slopes. The bus left before the sun came up, filled with students eager to feel the wind in their hair and the snow beneath their skis. Upon return, we weren't the innocent group of hopeful youths who left with the rise of the sun. We had seen things, horrible and terrible sights that would haunt us every time we crossed a sign directing us to one of Maine's many ski resorts. Maine distills many traits into its residents; gold medal ski abilities are not amongst them.

A LAND OF POVERTY

Maine requires all students to take US Government and Maine History. These classes are a mix of lessons meant to teach us about how the government functions at both the national and state level. We learn about how our state came to exist, its role in the French Indian, Civil, and Aroostook Wars. It blends civics with politics and infuses us with pride in our heritage. Today, a Wikipedia search could replace the class itself.

At Penquis Valley High School, both were taught by one of the "good old boys" from my hometown. My parents had been classmates with many of my teachers, and neither had pleasant things to say about this instructor. At this point in my high school career, I put in minimum effort and it showed in my grades. Not caring for my teacher's sense of nationalism and blatant racism, I sat near the window counting down the minutes until class ended. When he offered a chance at an extra credit project that required more creativity than memory recall, I jumped at the chance to ensure I passed.

Define poverty.

Growing up, I never thought about the economic situation of my hometown. Brownville Junction had a wide gamut of residents from differing financial backgrounds. Much of our community was composed of retired individuals. They had spent their younger years working and now they were enjoying the fruits of their labors. The generation beneath them were working at shoe factories, paper mills, forestry jobs, or they were hauling goods via big rigs. But there was also a large contingent of our community who struggled to make ends meet. These families relied on government assistance, only identified by the students who received free or reduced lunch.

Compared to other families in the Junction, mine was well off. My father retired from the Marine Corps, and for a while, we had the additional income from him, my mother, and my grandmother. This allowed us to maintain our home, put food on our table, and buy a car from the dealership. Beneath the surface, we had barely paid off my brother's medical expenses and when my mother returned to school, we tightened our spending habits. We weren't rich, but we weren't left wanting. But like many people in our town, we were only one disaster away from emptying our bank accounts.

The assignment by my teacher was to show "poverty." His questionable exercise in turning down our noses at community came with a mild warning - be aware that buildings or homes might belong to our classmates. I remember thinking it was a very curious statement to make. He opened my eyes. In a class of twenty-five students, more than half were on reduced lunch, meaning that they danced near the poverty line. It didn't change my actions toward them, but it brought a sobering reality to where my family sat in the financial hierarchy of our tiny town.

Determined to complete my junior year, I accepted the extra credit. Brainstorming with two of my classmates, we decided that if we were to thoroughly tell the narrative of our town's struggle with poverty, we'd approach it as a photojournalism assignment. We crafted a story that would show the disparity in our towns. Armed with a story and a camera, we met on a Saturday, ready to delve into our expose.

Our conversations about the assignment remained inquisitive, yet positive. None of our families were rich, and all of our parents were busy working as caregivers, nurses, or in the prison system. We discussed our classmates, and there was a sense of sadness as we quickly discovered most of the students in our class fell beneath the poverty line. What started as a weekend of fun and adventure turned into a need to gain a better understanding of the hardships our community faced.

Parking in a sandpit, we searched for something to start our story. We were nearly about to give up on our first location when one of my friends dropped to her knees and picked up a fist full of dirt. Coating our hands, we snapped photos. We wanted the start of our project to show that the journey we were about to undertake was shared by all the hardworking laborers of our town. Not scared to get their hands dirty, we opted for the literal interpretation.

Stopping at a massive metal building in LaGrange, we discovered it had once been a chicken coup. With enough room for thousands of chickens, it had gone into disrepair. Half the building had collapsed before we were kids. Our discussions turned to how people struggling to make ends meet frequently have to walk away instead of rebuilding. This idea of being forced to abandon and move on became the connective thread of our story.

Just up the road, we committed the first of many crimes that day. Trespassing on private property, we ventured into the car graveyard. From the street, a passerby could see the rusted frame of a long forgotten vehicle. As we walked further, we found dozens of similar skeletons. They had been stripped for parts, and once they served their purpose, the owner allowed Mother Nature to do the job of burying them. It left us questioning the untold tale of the person who had to walk away, leaving the metal to crumble in the forest.

As we drove to the city to find more buildings falling apart due to the elements, we passed a small church. I turned around my car and we stared at this tiny chapel, windows boarded up years ago. Finding the plywood covering the door had been pulled loose by hooligans, we couldn't resist slipping inside. The dust was thick enough you could see it floating about in the air. Illuminated by a broken rose window, the floorboards hadn't seen traffic in decades. It had long since been abandoned, proving that hardship wasn't for individuals alone. We treated it with respect, and continued our questioning, developing theories about what left these structures standing but empty.

We passed more than one house where we debated stopping and taking photos. Once we discovered they were inhabited by classmates, we drove on, focusing on abandoned properties. These empty properties litter Maine, left to the elements to decay until they collapse in on themselves. While the teacher had asked us to show demonstrations of poverty in Maine, we opted to tell our own story about the working class unable to make ends meet. The somber reality gave us a newfound respect for families determined to persevere.

I do not know what happened to the scrapbook, but I've never forgotten the photographs. The image of the hands is burned into my memory. They no longer denote poverty. Now they speak about the working ethic of Mainers and their willingness to get their hands dirty. The church reminds me of the grand things that once were and how quickly they can fade. Even the car graveyard showed how the people of Maine cling to a utopia as it once was. I don't think we ever found poverty in our gallivanting, but I think on that Saturday afternoon, driving down back roads, we glimpsed the reality endured by those who call Maine home.

CAN YOU FEEL THE LOVE

I was never a kid with a lot of money; I don't think many of us were. While this seldom played into our lives, it created a conundrum when we wanted to celebrate birthdays. Because of our financial limitations, we relied on creativity. We gathered at somebody's house, made a cake, and exchanged gifts. With my group of friends, it took little to leave an impression, and it was as much about the intention as it was the actual gift. Thoughtful always trumped flashy.

But there were those amongst us that pushed this idea further. Instead of any gifts, they'd make demands for baked goods, a night at the movies, or a large potluck dinner. None was more notorious for making demands than Hillary Roberts. With her flair for the dramatic, she insisted that her birthday be a celebration that relied on no budget. We gathered at a friend's camp, with the one intent of celebrating Hillary's birth.

This was no ordinary birthday. She had reached eighteen, a symbolic number denoting her ascension into adulthood. Because of this milestone, she made a single demand: poetry must be written and recited at the gathering. It allowed those of us without money to join in, and since each of us partook in creative endeavors at school, it worked. Some poems were drafted ahead of time, others only a moment before arriving, but we each came armed.

It was the usual band of misfits. We had been friends since middle school and at some point, we shifted from friends to found family. There was the core group of us, but over time it grew and on this particular day, there were at least a dozen of us gathering to commemorate our friend's exit from childhood. We goofed, we laughed, and like always, we sat and talked. Full of cake and punch, eventually our queen for the day announced it was time to deliver our presents.

She nestled herself onto the couch on the porch, draped in afghans, as we waited to be called upon. Each of us stood, paper in hand, awkward and nervous at being put on the spot. Ultimately, she pointed at me, commanding me to the front of the porch where I'd blush awkwardly. Years later, I can't recall the poem. It was most likely something touching, heartfelt and filled with admiration. Even amongst our closest friends, there were those too embarrassed to read their works aloud. Being a benevolent queen, she read them silently, cheeks flushed as she said, "Aww" at the end of each.

These gestures weren't uncommon. Since we had limited options for locations to host these special moments, they forced us to use our imaginations. Some parents might host a party for their kid, but by high school, we relied heavily on our friends to pick up the slack. One person would take the lead, finding a house without adults, and from there, they planned the snacks, beverages and who would supply the cake. They were like any other gathering except for the inevitable round of singing and blowing out of the candles. Of course, some of us always insisted on a second round of celebration in a more intimate setting.

A year before, for Hillary's seventeenth birthday, like always, I had no money to spend on a lavish gift. While this might have created a bit of awkwardness with her, a gift only required making her feel special and the center of the universe. Anything to be done, was going to be creative and rely on the adage "it's the thought that counts." In my younger years, I was a romantic and lived for these brief moments.

With the phrase, "I have a surprise for you," her eyes lit up. Conflicted between wanting to know, and the building tension of a mystery, she couldn't wait for the gift. Blindfolded, we drove, an event not uncommon for us. Between her grins, she tried to guess our destination, never once coming close. Going through parts of town I never drove, hopping onto dirt roads, I thoroughly confused her. I parked my car, and she continued speculating, unaware of what I had in store for her.

In Lakeview Plantation, there's a secluded wooden dock sitting twenty feet out into the water. I opened her door and led her down the path, across the boat landing and onto the dock. The wind had stilled, leaving the lake like glass. When she opened her eyes, she was greeted by candles littering the small platform. Having spent many afternoons splashing in the water at this location, I think my intent confused her. Of all the places I could take her, this was one we were all too familiar with.

Holding up my finger, I rushed back to my car. Rolling down the windows, I shoved a cassette into the radio. Turning up the volume, Elton John's "Can You Feel the Love Tonight" filled the air. I returned, and with a slight bow, held out my hand, asking her for this dance. For a teenage boy with no money, this was going to be the only way a candle lit evening would take place. After a single dance, the gift had ended.

I never wasted an opportunity to remind a friend that they made the world a little brighter. It was one of those instances, a creative romantic gesture you tell later in life, giving you the title of Casanova. A four-minute, lifelong memory.

JE ME SOUVIENS

Unlike many parts of the United States, Mainers view their roots as coming to life within the boundaries of Maine. To ask them where their families are from, you might get a more complex answer featuring countries across the world. However, for a good majority of my town, our heritage begins with Canada. People ventured outside their home countries and for a time, took resident in the great northern country. After several generations, they migrated south. In the town of Brownville Junction, many of our stories started in the French-speaking providence of Quebec.

Despite growing up in a Francophone town, it is uncommon to hear the locals speak in their native tongue. There might be an occasional accent while checking out at the store or neighbors shouting the obligatory "merci beaucoup." None of my family acknowledges their Canadian heritage. We viewed it as a pit stop, as our families traveled from Ireland, England, Scotland, and France before settling in the northern stretches of Maine. For somebody who has never had roots, I wanted to connect with my ancestors. At the time, I didn't realize that longing would become a source of motivation and teach me to step outside my comfort zone.

My junior year, I found myself outside the country for the first time. At Penquis Valley High School, they rewarded those who survived their first year of French with a trip to Quebec for a long weekend. This excursion allowed us to test our Quebecois and immerse ourselves in the culture. Having grown up with a father who has seen the better part of the civilized world, it offered a chance to see beyond the borders of Maine.

We boarded the bus and headed north. I was taught that Brownville Junction is considered northern Maine. While it might be part of the North in terms of population, the hours on that bus proved that we are closer to the center of the state. Once we reached Jackman, crossing from the United States into Canada, we had only reached the half-way point of our journey. A few hours later, we entered Quebec, a vibrant modern city, unlike anything we have in the northern half of Maine.

These modern buildings, stretching into the sky like monoliths, were unlike anything I had seen since moving to Maine. But they quickly gave way to something even more beautiful. Old Quebec City maintains the charm of an era long passed by. The buildings have more in common with castles and the boardwalk stretches around the fort, peering down on a seaside village. In the middle is the Le Chateau Frontenac, a medieval looking manor built by the same railroad that once breathed life into my own town.

It wasn't the architecture, or the trip to the Basilica of Sainte-Anne-de-Beaupré, or even the waterfalls at the Parc de la Chute-Montmorency that resonated with me. As the night settled and they allowed us to wander free of a chaperone, I found myself enjoying the view of the Saint Lawrence River from the boardwalk. While that might have been majestic on its own, it was only when I turned to the roar of clapping that I discovered the buskers. These street performances ranged from solo guitarists, to violinist, to fire breathers, and even acrobats. I walked the wooden path, watching as the performances started, people gathered, and eventually applause erupted. Having performed in band for years, I never considered standing alone and putting on a show. For me, it was a frightening thought, but watching as they took bows, I wondered if someday I might be brave enough to do it myself.

This would stay with me until my second trip to Quebec City. Unlike before, my mother wanted to us to partake in a family vacation, something we hadn't done for years. Relying on my questionable French, we stayed across the street from my first visit, and wound up seeing many of the same sights. However, this time I managed enough bravery to pack my saxophone. Part of me wanted to live the life of a bohemian and stand in front of an audience and put my soul into my music. I wouldn't get much further than this. Unsure of the culture, and more importantly the legalities, I opted for safety and wandered back to the boardwalk without my instrument.

The night had cooled and high up on the cliff overlooking the bay, people clutched their jackets. I splurged on handmade ice cream and expected to spend my evening reveling in this change of scenery. While watching the ferry move across the river, a man started strumming his guitar. As he sang in French, I did my best to translate, but I learned I will never be multilingual. The man was young, not much older than me, and as he paused between songs, I couldn't help but be frustrated that I had wiggled my way out of performing. When he started playing Billy Joel's "Piano Man," the power of his rendition surprised me. I wasn't the only one moved by his words. Only a few benches away, a man dropped to one knee, and reached into his pocket. As he produced the ring, the singer quieted, and the audience waited for her reply. As she cried, grasping the sides of his face, even I could hear her repeating, "Oui."

Moved, I promised myself I'd use the emotion of that moment to overcome any fear of performing.

The following summer, Brownville Junction celebrated one hundred and fifty years of incorporation. They had a huge craft fair while street vendors sold ice cream for kids. For such a small town, this was the biggest event since my family moved there. Gatherings such as these were a rarity, and because of that, the entire town emerged from their homes to join the festivities. People stopped on the lawn of the Alumni Hall, one of our few communal buildings, to gossip and reconnect with people they hadn't seen in years. For the day, it was easy to forget our worries and see our town as the vibrant community it had once been.

For weeks, I made the joke that it would be my chance to redeem myself. I would join the festivities, my saxophone in hand, and remember a vow I made to myself on the boardwalk. It might not be as majestic, or as grand as Quebec City, but here in our small town, I was determined to connect with the magic I witnessed that night. Setting up my stand and opening my case, I decided this had little to do with anybody other than myself. What started as a trip to Quebec, hoping to uncover some sense of who my people were, I learned a bit of who I was, and am.

My sheet music blew in the wind, clipped to my stand by clothespins. With nobody to impress but myself, I played. After the song, my first patron tossed loose change into my open case. I played for almost an hour and at the end of that time, I had made just shy of six dollars. I packed up and gave the money to a couple of kids at the ice cream cart. It wasn't nearly as majestic, but it embodied the spirit I witnessed on the boardwalk overlooking the Saint Lawrence River.

Mainers might not always admit to our lineage, instead speaking in absolutes about where our people first migrated. But what started as a French class, hoping to one day converse in fluent Quebecois, left me appreciating the many destinations that brought us to where we are today. Someday, I will return, no better at speaking French, but more appreciative of my ancestors and their Canadian blood.

THAT'S MR. CLAUS TO YOU

It is easy to speak about the dangers that come with winter in Maine. The ongoing snow, early thaw, and power outages make it a struggle. But as the first layer of snow covers the ground, removing the sea of yellows and greens of dried grass, the state transforms into a wonderland. The air turns crisp and the pine trees bend low, covered in fresh powder. There is a battle ahead, but in that moment, Maine looks like a Hallmark movie. With Christmas around the corner, we prepare for the impending festivities. Lights spread along our eves and we place plastic reindeer on the roof. At my house, this had an additional level of irony.

My father was Santa Claus.

No, I'm not kidding. In every child's life, there is that moment when the fictitious beings evaporate. I discovered early that my parents had been signing Santa's name to the presents under the tree. It changed little after that. When my parents remembered to put labels on the presents, they still include gifts from the big guy. Had I known that my father was not only forging Santa's signature, but impersonating him, I'd have fodder for my therapist. The emotional confusion would be uncanny. What I didn't know as a child, the mantle of Santa is passed from father to son.

Each year, the man behind Santa, also known as the chosen one, is responsible for bringing Christmas cheer to the town. With the closest mall an hour away, it made it difficult for families to take their young ones to get photos. The role was as much for the kids whispering their wishlists as it was for the parents armed with cameras. So in a community with few activities to celebrate, we turn a simple chore into town-wide event.

I assumed this responsibility my senior year of high school. My father had to work at the last minute, and with the event planned, my mother roped me into this charade. I'm not sure if it was because I'm of the "jolly" physique or because of my overly sunny disposition. I assumed there'd be a ceremony, perhaps a coronation as the King of Christmas. But as she thrust the black trash bag in my hands, I understood this would be a questionable affair.

Adjusting my stomach padding and combing the knots loose in my wig, I transformed from bored teenager to low-budget Santa. This isn't like the mall where I would preside over a makeshift winter kingdom in the food court. Based on the cheap material of the suit and the spotty beard, we were under-funded, and I'd have to do without my elf helpers. Our version couldn't afford the rent on his workshop, the reindeer had been turned into dinner, and my sleigh had been repossessed.

I arrived at the volunteer fire department. They had taken the single truck from the garage and the engine was running. My mother had neglected to elaborate the duties of Santa. I thought I'd say a few Ho Ho Ho's and pose for photographs before tapping the side of my nose and disappearing. Instead, they helped me into the back of the fire engine, promising they'd keep it under the speed limit. I'm not sure the

North Pole offered insurance plans that would cover being thrown from a fire truck, but I decided to go along with this scheme.

Down Main Street, I rode my chariot, wind whipping through my luscious white locks. My majestic red sleigh, even without reindeer, moved at a brisk thirty miles per hour. Forget calling for Rudolph to light the way; this Santa knew how to travel in style. Should somebody's house burn down while I travelled from Brownville Junction to Brownville, it would not deter my mission. Dammit, I would bring glee to the four kids who braved the arctic cold to sit with a Santa. As we zipped through town, people stood on their lawns, pointing at the small town spectacle. I waved back as if I were the Queen of England shouting seasonal greetings.

They housed my winter wonderland in the bay of Brownville's firehouse. My mother joined, and by her expression alone, I could tell she was enjoying my discomfort. She offered brief coaching. Make no promises. Keep the magic alive. Eye the parents for visual cues. Had I known the level of acting they'd demand from me, I'd have asked for an Oscar nomination.

Children arrived, excited to occupy my knee. Moms held their cameras, determined to capture their crying offspring as they sat on a strange man's lap. I squirmed, uneasy with the proximity of children in general. It didn't get any easier as they wiped away their tears, determined to empty Santa's bank account with their lofty demands. The requests started simple, and I offered a jolly laugh. At any moment, I would be infused with the spirit of Christmas and filled with joy. But as their demands grew increasingly difficult to accept, I lost control of the situation. Let's not forget, children can sense fear.

The only thing that filled that red velvet suit came in the form of urine, as a child disagreed with my, "I'll see what I can do."

The day didn't end there. It wasn't enough to satiate the wonder of children. We still needed to make a stop at the elder community in the middle of our two towns. Climbing back into my sleigh, I bid the station farewell and we continued on our Jolly Man tour. While I might not be skilled with children, I spent much of my time around senior citizens. Carrying prepared meals, I knocked and waited patiently for them to make their way to the door. As the doors opened, their faces lit up, far more delighted than any child. Wives shouted for their husbands to see who stopped by to wish them a good day. I attempted my best laugh, making sure my belly bounced. Hugs were exchanged, and the firefighters gave me another tray and I continued my visits. Watching from the windows, they waved to their kin, happy for change to their routine.

I was honored to help the community who couldn't find a better fat man with a mother who wouldn't let him say no. With the looming reality of short frigid days, we make our own cheer and spread it as far as we can muster. I was delighted with the smiles of the children, both young and old, but not so much the empty bladder of one. Despite all these life-changing epiphanies, I couldn't help but feel I should drive by that child's house and hurl coal at his door. You know, because that's what Santa would do.

OUR FADING NAMESAKE

My town once had a vibrant industry.
Originally named Hendersonville for our founder, we transitioned to Brownville Junction. The word "junction" in Maine denotes importance on the trains coming and going in our town. Once the tracks had been laid, the Canadian Pacific Railroad would carry passengers between the two countries. The boom created more jobs than residents. Between upkeep, the station, and the repair yard in nearby Derby, it gave us a sense of pride and purpose.

It might sound foolish, but trains are an essential part of our identity, then and now. The whistle blowing as they crossed the bridge meant fathers were coming home. Watching the trains moving in and out of our station signaled money flowing through our town. The boom spawned growth, allowing us to expand. Hotels and recreational centers were erected, and for a while, it seemed there would be no end. In our community, they were a way of life.

One day, the whistles stopped blowing.

Our industry, absent for so many years, is talked about as if it were a legend akin to Bigfoot. Our elders talk about the days when the rails were nothing more than scribbles on a plan. Their eyes go out of focus as they recount memories of better days gone by. The possibilities return, and reality is pushed aside. They talk about laying spikes into the ground, or people stepping off the train with a sense of wonderment. When they finish, there is an uncomfortable silence as we try to connect a prosperous past with a grim future.

Our lifeblood slowed, but we clung to a dying dream. The train arrivals went from hourly to every few days. But when they arrived, they brought with them a rush of nostalgia. When I was young, I was both terrified and fascinated by the mammoth metal monsters. But to a toddler, they were like toys come to life. Mimi took me to see them cross the road, forcing me to cover my ears and wave to the conductor at the same time. He'd lean out the window with a smile and pull on the chain that let loose a howl that had me cowering against my grandmother's leg.

Then, with the love and determination only a grandmother could muster, she would pack me into her Skylark and speed to the next crossing. We'd repeat this until we watched the speeding machine pull into the train yard. This continued for years, until the stretches between arrivals became so erratic, it was impossible to predict their schedule.

Our way of life became a thing of the past.

The hustle of the station vanished. It ran with a skeleton crew who worked on the trains. For my generation, it was a giant building next to the dozens of empty tracks. There would always be a vehicle parked next to the building, but rarely would we see anybody coming or going. More and more decommissioned cars found their way into the yard, turning it into a graveyard.

Returning now, the memory of our once flourishing industry is fading from view. The weeds have crawled along the station, working their way into broken windows. Cars have gone abandoned, forgotten by their owners. Even the untraveled tracks seem to have disappeared, covered by the elements. We count down the minutes until a new generation has no connection to our namesake. Now Brownville Junction is a community hoping for an industry that will never come.

This became one of the many reasons my parents decided their time in the Junction had ended. Before they left, there were talks of a luxury resort taking over our side of Sebec Lake. Everybody said, "Once the resort is built..." Based on our history, I think it was false hope and the residents knew it would never happen. They did not build the resort. It was not the first time a solution had been presented and ripped away. The same was said about the Casino and a new highway.

A small town with nothing is left with only their hope for the future. But after having that stepped on year after year, their hope has turned to cynicism. The reality is, Brownville Junction is a dying town. In a community where there is no future, the populace survives on the memories, preferring to dwell on a rich past instead of confronting a bleak future.

THE INSULTS WE TAKE IN STRIDE

Mainers have many nicknames, most of them jabs. What the rest of the world thinks is derogatory, we consider a banner of pride. The most common name is redneck. While it is true, we have our fair share of hillbilly stereotypes, we also don't mind the ramifications of working long hard days in the field. Another common nickname is white trash, a slur used to divide the classes of Maine. Some shrug off the comment; some treat it as a rallying call. The phrase can be considered slanderous, or it can be viewed as an anthem for a younger generation determined to prove the world wrong. Behind the slander or pride is the question, "Are we?"

I often speak of the dire financial situation seen in my hometown. Many struggled to make ends meet. I'd like to think my family didn't look down on those with needs, but I can't say the same for others. While the town had its own classification of what was successful and what was not, this question always lingered in the back of my head. It was answered by the time I reached high school.

My prom was in a gym.

Our neighboring towns had the luxury of banquet halls or hotels they could rent for this special night. However, we didn't have a space big enough for the high school within driving distance. It might be possible to transform a space given enough money, but we saddled the decoration committee with only a few hundred dollars to make the night memorable. I'll give them credit, they tried.

Let me paint the picture, because only detailed and slightly over-exaggerated commentary can offer the full image. I will attempt to pierce the romanticized veil of young men in tuxedos and women wearing wildly expensive dresses. For us, prom wasn't a miniature wedding, where tiaras sparkled and men strut their stuff. It was an opportunity to break the monotony of life, a social obligation that came with a long list of rules on etiquette. Scared of violating the rules of social conduct, each year as prom approached, we followed the same formula.

Step 1: Find a Date

Being a gay man in Maine, I had women flocking to my side. I had to beat them away with a stick. Maybe this is a *slight* recoloring of historical events, but my sophomore year, Tasha Granger allowed me to wine and dine her. We even managed an awkward dance or two. Junior year, Tonya Eaton won the pleasure. Granted, I think she may have been suffering from delirium, but it was a majestic evening. Last but not least, Amanda Wardwell had the honor my senior year. I was jazzed she said yes. She was a younger woman, and I'm pretty sure if anybody gave me grief over my boutonnière being crooked, she'd knock their clock. Yes, I was a ladies' man. Dates were never a problem.

Due to the size of my school, we invited the entire student body to the event. While we paired off, it wasn't uncommon for people to go stag. This occurred because of the limited options and because going through the motions could be a costly affair. Putting aside fifty dollars for a single night, for something as foolish as a tux, is a luxury that not all families had. Thankfully, we were an accepting group of students and we welcomed even those in jeans and a button down.

Step 2: Transportation

The first year we had to rely on Corey Bradbury to be our chauffeur. I wanted nothing more than to sit in the back of his Bronco and yell, "To the Prom, my dear sir!" I think he would have left me in my tux on the side of the road. The second year we arrived in the swankiest of fashions - a party boat. You think, going down the river on a party boat is impressive. But of course, no. We arrived by land. The father of one of our social circle drove his truck with our party boat in tow. Yes, it was majestic. The last year I drove. My car, frequently called, "the boat," served as our chariot.

Why no limos, you ask? At Penquis, they weren't allowed. The administration bluntly told us no limos, and almost nobody questioned the decision. In a school where tuxes were handed down from father to son and dresses were often bought at thrift stores, they hoped to bridge economic divide. Even if we had the money, few companies would have been willing to drive to our small town for a quick trip down the street.

However, to give us the experience of a grand limo arrival, administration provided one for us. We took the limo from the front of the building, around the parking lot and back to the front door; they even put out the red carpet. I hate to admit it, but it was quite spectacular.

Step 3: Food (Optional)

Now, some people include food as a requirement for prom, but considering there was no place to eat without booze, we avoided it. I mean, I wouldn't have minded sitting in the local pizza joint in my tux, but my dates wouldn't have been as thrilled. Even more so when I told them we were going dutch.

In our school district the locations available for dining were so few, that even the local bar offered a "prom meal." They hid the liquor and provided a three-course meal early enough that we could rush to the dance. However, these filled up quickly and with limited seating, most of us opted for snacks in the car. We're thrifty like that.

Step 4: The Dance

The gym itself was spectacularly decorated; black trash bags covered the gym windows to hide the splendor from the outside. Inside, balloons hung from bleachers. A DJ on the stage and round tables littered the edges of the dance floor. I might be wrong, but I'm not sure they used tablecloths. The gym was transformed into, well, a gym looking like it had been a victim of a New Year's Day parade (but the day after). Streamers were hung from the top of the bleaches toward the middle of the gym. Had it been a small space, the committee might have transformed it. But the square footage proved too mighty for the dollars at their disposal.

Just to add to the splendor, they provided a photographer so that we might capture the event and look back fondly. Down the hall and into the gym that served as our cafeteria, a lone photographer stood with a backdrop and props placed here and there. While we looked quite dashing, the addition of the Roman pillars in the photograph was a bit too much, even for us. Thankfully, my mother, the photographer, had already required several hundred photos be taken before leaving the house. There is a chance she chased us down the street as I sped away.

This is a prom in small town Maine. Again, I pose the question. Did our inability to splurge on over-the-top outfits and stretched limos make us trashy? As a youth I'd have said absolutely, but now as an adult, I think we made a lot out of a little. We wouldn't allow our lack of finances to set this rite of passage out of reach. So while it might have been low rent, I was in a tux, so of course it didn't matter.

THROUGH THE WARDROBE

In Maine, we learn solitude. The distance between houses can be measured in feet, or it can be measured in miles. In school, our area code grouped us to prevent making long-distance phone calls to complete group work. Seeing friends required scheduling to ensure the lengthy drive was worth the effort. With many of our neighbors nearing retirement, even playing with the local children grew increasingly rare.

In a world separate by these vast distances, our imagination conjured our best friends. We spent days outside building forts in the woods, or creating ice palaces in the snow. While this lack of socialization could be seen as a downside to our way of life, we learned to be self-sufficient, even if it was only befriending ourselves. With long days spent in our heads, we gain a masterful understanding of our inner workings. We know ourselves.

Out of necessity, most of my days played out behind our house near the river dividing the town. People used to go into the woods and have bonfires and drink until dawn. As a kid, I built forts and secret club houses for an occupant of one. I fancied myself like Max in "Where the Wild Things Are." It was a different world. Unlike the house I lived in, there were possibilities out there amongst the trees. It was one thing to play "make believe," but here, I stood as the king of a fantastical world.

These adventures continued until high school. Playing "make believe" was replaced by thought, contemplation, and reflection. Day after day, I'd follow the path from my backyard into the woods. In the forest's solitude, I learned myself. While many might balk at the isolation, it gave me a chance to slow my adolescence and explore who I was and more importantly, who I wanted to be. Living on the fringes of civilization allowed time to move at a crawl.

I look back at it now, and it reminds me of the wardrobe to Narnia in "The Lion, the Witch, and the Wardrobe." Even as the snow fell, it didn't prevent me from entering this world untouched by mankind. As the sun dipped below the horizon, it'd be time to emerge. Each venture left its mark, imbuing me with more maturity than when I started. Wiser, I'd leave for brief time, counting down the minutes until the next trip started and I could return.

Even as an adult, this world still exists. If you tilt your head just right, you can see through the surface to something almost magical. I find myself stopping and enjoying the solitude on a quiet night. Nowhere have I ever felt more myself than where the pavement ends, and the tree line begins.

THE TIE OF BLOODLINES

In my youth, I was an outsider. Maine is my home. I spent my formative years in one of its many small, charming towns. But truth be told, I am a foreigner. I was born in North Carolina, leaving my heritage in question. As an adult, people will take my statement at face value. But that wasn't always the case. Moving homes is part of being family to a Marine. It wasn't until we returned, ready to make it our forever home, that I felt as if I didn't belong.

Kids, in their naïveté, can be cruel. I have always been a storyteller, and I often told stories about Philadelphia or North Carolina or my father being in the military.

I must have shared one too many tales about the South when Janie-Leigh Stearns yelled, "If you like the south so much, why don't you go back?!" I was the *other*, that scary boogeyman that lurked beyond the borders of our state. While solving a math problem, she thrust me into a dark headspace that would require years to understand. One careless, frustrated proclamation and the magic of my new home evaporated.

While my father served, I experienced more cultures than I can recall. Being young, we didn't ostracize based on creed, color, or nation of origin. We giggled as we learned accents came from Cameroon, Greece, and Ireland. Kids would come and go, stationed and then given new marching orders. There wasn't time to discriminate; we had games to play, and adventures to discover. But in the far north of Maine, I lost my diversified social circle and found myself confronted with years of history. They knew one another well enough that they were like family, and I was a stray dog begging for handouts.

In Brownville Junction, I don't introduce myself as Jeremy Flagg. There is an order to greetings resembling the British Monarchy. I am the grandson of Gloria Cowing. It is a declaration that bypasses my birthplace. In this one statement, I stake my ownership as a member of the community. Great grandchild of Hazel Wright. Son of Susan and Phillip Flagg. To any local, these names carry weight. No matter my where I came from, my lineage is grounded in this town. While I can't do it for my given name, our surname provides a seat at the table. While this respect for our blood line grants me access to the community, it comes with a dark undertone.

We carry the sins of our forefathers.

While I wanted to belong, to be considered one of the inner circle, I had to rely on adults drawing connections. But at the mention of these names they thrust their history onto my shoulders. To say I'm a Cowing or a Flagg gives me social status, but it also leaves a complicated and lengthy brand. The stories, true or not, come rushing in and with pursed lips or a slight nod, I am judged.

My mother's father left her mother creating a scandal. My father's mother and father are vile humans who the townspeople adored. I am the kid with a brother in the ground. Whispers follow every significant event and they etch the rumors on our bodies, unable to be hidden by clothes. In Maine, family isn't a choice; it's a legacy. We are the culmination of all our families were, are and will be. To assert myself as one of those who belong, I am required to accept a burden as heavy as the memories are long.

My mother's single mother worked the cash register at our grocery store. My mother's brother coached the little league baseball team. My fifth cousin had a ferocious dog who bit a neighbor. A man, to whom I am far removed but share a last name, shot a man. In a small town, there is little distinction between an individual and their family. It creates a bias before we can be known for anything of note.

These burdens can be enormous enough to make newspapers or be discussed over the police scanner. But there are also the small matters, and for those in close proximity, it becomes game hunting for gossip. A suspicious nature lurks behind every good-natured gesture. Questions asked to know a neighbor are used to know dirty secrets. Fences are erected to keep a distance between neighbors, but every neighbor peeks over. It showcases your mistakes and your wrongs of the past. Whispers hush as you pass. Every small town thrives on gossip, no matter how small it may be.

Because of this close familial connection, our gossip is rarely about individuals; instead it focuses around entire clans. In Brownville Junction, Clan Flagg is small, but we aren't without our scandals. Our surname includes messy divorces, children out of wedlock and extramarital affairs. While little of this relates to my household, it still weighs on our identity. It would be much later in life that I would meet many of these fellow Flaggs. I would become the focus for their misgivings. Each of us carries the burden of our heritage, confronted with scornful and disapproving glances.

Because of this, I look beyond my living relatives and focus on those that fill our cemetery. My brother loved baseball. My mother's mother was known for her knitting. My mother's grandfather's name elicits smiles and fond memories. Our clan is from McAdam, New Brunswick, settling there for a generation before moving to Maine. Our heritage takes us to England and Scotland, where we once went by an unfamiliar name. I think us to be the sum of our progenitor's, but I often forget that there is a story stretching past the borders of Maine.

I am the son of Susan and Phillip Flagg. I am the grandson of Gloria Cowing. I am the great grandchild of Hazel Wright. In small town Maine, I assume the burdens of my family, by choice or not.

HUNTING & SEX

Maine's education system follows some unique rules. They require us to take the standard math and sciences. To expand our cultural appreciation, we require students to take several years of a foreign language. But they also require us to take a year of Maine State History to give us a somewhat glorified depiction of our home. The most awkward class, however, comes during your freshmen year. Under the guise of "Health," this class is unlike any other in the United States and demonstrates a unique set of needs by our people.

We are required to take a semester of health.

It starts like one might assume. There are lectures about the human body, the definitions of health, and approaches to leading a better lifestyle. There are conversations around food, exercise, and mental wellbeing; all topics that would help prepare us as our bodies underwent the brutality of puberty. We would transition to substance abuse, a topic confronting many of my classmates at the time. We learned the terminology and the effects of these drugs on our innards, and mostly, it remained clinical.

Eventually, we reached the most dreaded topic of my freshman year: sex. The teacher of our class had given the same talk to my parents a generation before. To hear one of my grandmother's classmates discuss penetration in an educational setting might have been one of the most horrifying moments of our youths. As he passed out condoms, we uncomfortably tore open foil packages and stared at the gooey latex. Nobody made eye contact. While we might joke with our friends one-on-one, in a classroom filled with twenty-five people, nobody could muster the bravado to poke fun at the situation.

Normal, right? But of course there's more.

We ended the unit on sexual health, the class scared to death by the number of diseases ready to pounce whenever we kissed. The final chapter of this class would be even more important than knowing how babies were made. We had learned how to sheath our rifles, but now we'd learn how to fire them. No, not like that. Freshman year of high school, we were all required to take a hunter's safety course. Yes, the same class that taught me about stress management, the dangers of binge drinking, and how the fallopian tubes functioned, also granted me a hunting permit.

Those who had already received their hunting license vacated the class, leaving us with a small handful who had never stalked a deer through the woods. It started with a prompt history of hunting in Maine and the game our people are permitted to shoot and eat. It moved into the mechanics of a rifle and then turned into a tutorial on the best practices while out in the woods. Each year, as hunting season opened, the newspaper filled with stories about people being shot due to careless behavior. In response, we were taught that pointing a gun at another human is frowned upon. How this didn't fall under common sense eludes me.

Guns and hunting had entered my life before. My father had taken the time to show me how to use firearms, a lesson given to many of the young people in our town. He often got his hunting license, allowing him to kill one of the many deer that frolic in Maine. However, rarely did he go hunting. Instead, we'd receive a call near sundown from a friend who had made more kills than the state allowed. My father would arrive, claim the deer as his own, then generously "give" it to the hunter. While this might seem as if we cheated the system, those he helped relied on hunting season to fill empty freezers. For those struggling to make ends meet, hunting allowed them to bridge the gap and put food on their table.

I killed my first deer when I was a junior. Nothing I learned in my hunter's safety course turned out to be relevant. I didn't need to fire a gun. Late one night, after dropping a friend at his house in a nearby town, I struck a deer on the road. To say it's common is an understatement. I'm sure each of our parents expected the late-night phone call. The impact happened with a loud thud, my brakes screeching as my car came to a halt.

The closest house was a mile up the road, and I'd need to make the trek to alert my father and the authorities. Concerned less about the legalities, I grabbed my flashlight and bound into the woods in search of the deer. Many think of hunters as ruthless, but you'll more often find they only shoot when it will be a clean kill. Our goal is survival, not suffering. Once I found the deer had died, I ran to a house with darkened windows. I knocked, frantic. When the man opened the door, I didn't have to explain myself. He grabbed the phone and thrust it into my hands.

Our police officer arrived, inspecting the damage of my car for the insurance report. Just as my father showed, he asked if I wanted a tag for the deer. There are always those interested in receiving the meat. We did what comes naturally for Mainers. I reached under my driver's seat and pulled out the buck knife while my dad grabbed the tarp from my trunk. One might think it odd to have these items in a vehicle, but like I said, it's not a matter of if, but when.

Thanks to the extensive chapter on dressing a deer, my father and I went to work. In front of his headlights, we cut into the animal, removed its entrails and had it sitting in the trunk of my car within minutes. This part didn't bother me, it was only when we returned home and my father strung it from the garage rafters to bleed the animal I found myself getting queasy.

People think poorly of the hunting population in Maine, like it is an act of savagery where we only partake for the thrill of the hunt. For many, it allows a family to eat when the budget gets tight. We would later donate my first kill, filling the icebox of a family in need. I was always happy knowing this bit of misfortune would benefit others. In a place where money is scarce and refrigerators are seldom full, our unfortunate deer became dinner for a family of five.

I would never kill another deer. But thanks to Maine's unique high school class, where I learned how to both wield and sheath my rifle, I was prepared for the inevitable.

OUR INSTITUTIONS OF EDUCATION

University of Maine Orono.
    To speak this name in front of any Northerner will elicit a long list of responses. The first being, "Go Black Bears!" Like any other town in the shadow of a monolith institution, we rallied around it. This university, with nearly ten thousand students, continued to breathe life in a town that had once boomed because of the lumber mills. UMO (also called oo-moe) was not only our highlight of collegiate sports, it was also the destination for the majority of graduates from my high school. Only forty-five minutes away, it offered proximity, quality programs and the security

of nearby home.

Nobody in my family had gone to college. However, my mother stole my thunder and pursued a degree in higher education to become a librarian. She joined the Onward program for non-traditional learners and flourished during her stay there. While she was busy showing me just how dismal my grades were compared to hers, I spent countless days on the sprawling campus. Because Onward housed older students, it wasn't unheard of for the kids to hang out while our parents were in class. My cousin and I spent our time discovering the fairly new world of the Internet. Later this would be the pivoting point turning toward a career in graphic design.

As I got older, I'd opt to spend the day on campus rather than watching television. When she took a position at the university library, I'd wander aimlessly for hours, taking in the grandeur of such a large building. When I grew bored with exploring, I'd busy myself at the arcade in the student union. For years I lived in a world with little to do, and while it might not seem impressive to the students, the campus awarded me activities. Nothing amazing or memorable, but the boredom had been washed away. It gave me a glimpse into the world outside of our small town, something to strive for.

My mother made it out just shy of a 4.0. Let's emphasize *nearly*. Let's rub it in. Through oh so many report cards, she would decimate my barely average grades. My mother never swears faster than when I remind her of the B+ she received in French. Thankfully though, her being a student and exposing me to the university at Orono left me disenchanted. This doesn't demean the fact it's a great school and turns out amazing students, but after spending middle and high school around within its boundaries, I had seen enough. Like my mother, my tenure at UMO had ended.

The end was made official during the middle of the science fair state competition taking place at Orono's indoor track. As I finished my presentation for science, I ran to attend my mother's graduation. Packed in a room with thousands of other graduating students and their families, my mom walked across the stage and received her diploma. She had done the unthinkable, and by sheer will, pulled herself from the depths of what they expect in our town. While I was proud of her accomplishment, it would be my last time to UMO.

I wanted away from the Junction, to forge my path without the baggage created by small towns. I needed to try something new and different. Ironically, I applied to the University of Maine Farmington (UHMF), a school that had the same small town charm and sense of community that mine did. I traded one rural town for another. At least this one had a Wal-Mart that didn't require a day trip to visit. I traded Black Bears for Beavers; the overwhelming amount of lesbians known to attend only made this amusing mascot funnier. Much like Brownville Junction, there were no secrets and your every success and failure was on display for the masses. Thankfully, this vulnerability meant that we had to get along on some level.

There was no easier way to see this than during Spring Fling. My RA, who hated that I always unscrewed the hallway light shining under my door, would take out her aggression on me in a mud-wrestling pit. True story. While I thought I stood victorious over my peers, she grabbed me from behind, hurling me into the brown muck. I'm surprised she didn't put a foot on my chest and roar at the crowd.

My stay there was brief. I only made it through a year and a half before I found myself suffocated by the same sensations I experienced in Brownville Junction. My classmates grew too familiar, and it went from an institution of high learning to feeling like an ongoing family reunion. I longed for a new adventure, further from home. For the next year I would live in Portland, Maine and have a short stint in Charlottesville, Virginia. I didn't know what I wanted until a friend offered me a chance to work with him developing websites. The lessons I taught myself sitting in Onward came rushing back, and I found a trade that touched upon several of my passions.

It was time to correct my wayward course. I found a new home in Salem. Larger than my previous school, I found it a balance of knowing my classmates, but not knowing their business. Nestled in a historic city, I could spend my days on campus studying or wandering the streets of downtown. After five years, much like my mother, I held my diploma. Only then did I see the road she paved, and how hard she worked to adjust her ambitions to make a dream come true.

THE ORIGINS OF EVERY STORY

They asked, "Where did the idea for this book come from?" There are many things leading me to write this. Foremost is the fact I'm homesick. I addressed these nagging emotions last week as I spent several days meandering physically, mentally and emotionally through my childhood home. What I came to realize is, I'm not homesick for a location; I'm homesick for the invigorating, delightful, enriching memories that were made.

What's the second reason? After I worked through the emotional side of things, I realized the basis of this journal and "field guide to small town Maine" comes from a class I took my senior year. The classroom always smelled of freshly brewed coffee, and students arrived early, eager to begin. It served as the one class my senior year where I could ignore the grades and focus on the creative process.

Creative writing class.

Penquis Valley High School had little in the way of extra-curricular classes. With little money to spare, they focused on maintaining the core academics. But through some miracle, my freshman English teacher managed one class of creative writing. Being a slacker, my schedule was nearly empty, and I decided this was worth arriving first period each day. It was an academic risk after putting the teacher through her paces my freshman year. With many friends taking the class, I threw caution to the wind and arrived early on the first day.

Andrea Lumbra, our teacher, served as the guiding force for this band of misfits. Unlike the first year in her class, the rules were few. She didn't demand we raise our hands or keep quiet while working. Instead, she focused on us putting our thoughts to paper, requiring us to fill the pages of our spiral bound notebooks. Her goals were modest, and I needed to buy a second, third, and fourth before the class concluded.

Her methods of inspiration reminded me of elementary school, before our imaginations were put on hold for academics. We set aside vocabulary words in place of guide meditation and soothing music. Five paragraph essays ceased to exist as we paired off to practice our dialogue writing. The class focused on expanding our storytelling skills and less about the minutia of writing. Each day she entered with a new activity, seeking to get our creative juices flowing, and then she'd leave us be. Deep in thought, the ring of the bell always jolted us back to reality, reminding me it was time to undertake another lecture in history.

Of all the classes I ever took at Penquis, creative writing blurred the boundaries between cliques. We had band geeks. We had hippies. We had a basketball player. We had gays. We had straights. We mixed men and women. We had the sheltered. We had the outspoken. We had the conservative sitting next to the liberal. We were a pretty odd crew. But at the front of this train was Mrs. Lumbra. Four years earlier, I cursed her name as she assigned a wretched "autobiography assignment" in which I wrote as little as possible. At the time, I didn't care about my story. The irony isn't lost on me.

One memorable exercise was having us close our eyes, urging us to connect with all our senses, while she held an unknown object in front of our noses and instructed us to inhale deeply. Once our imaginations took hold, she'd give us the class to write. Of course, I was clueless about the object she hid away in her desk. I went on a tangent; maybe about Playdough? We shared our tales. In this group of awkward adolescents, we had grown comfortable with one another, often fighting for the spotlight, oblivious of how we exposed ourselves. When she revealed the box of freshly opened crayons, I felt foolish. It was okay to be foolish. To this day, I keep a box of crayons on my desk, and whenever I'm stumped, I take a deep breath and let the waxy smell guide me.

Unlike much of our teen lives, the angst of being young rarely entered the class. We had our moments of laughter. Heather Webb fought valiantly against Mrs. Lumbra and rallied the class in an effort to have a coffee maker in the classroom. Her reasoning? If we brewed our own, she wouldn't be late to class because of her morning pit stop. Surprisingly, it worked. I also remember, in a breakout session, Josh Decker's story bordered on the erotic and we listened, waiting for the climax. It wouldn't have been awkward, except for our youngest member, Amanda Kahl, a 7th grader. Gifted far beyond her years, her presence kept us honest, and mostly kid friendly. Josh blushed a little, but he still turns red at the mention of his steam filled pages.

I can accredit my list of published works to this class. And still, there are more novels waiting on the shelf to be edited. There is no shortage of stories to be written. I understand each of these projects ties back to one class. Each of them is born from an idea that we are creators. Even more so, they're rooted in a classroom belonging to Mrs. Lumbra. Between my autobiographical tales or my need to conjure unique worlds, I still refer to the notebooks from her class.

I think living in Maine allowed me the space to flex my creative muscle. Whether it be in the boredom of class or walking in the woods behind my house, I found the only person keeping me entertained *was* me. While the time for pretend and make believe seemed lost somewhere between childhood and being an adult, Mrs. Lumbra reminded us to never completely shut the door. I still play make believe, except now imaginary friends have become characters and I'm there to record their adventures.

READY FOR MY CLOSEUP

For a time, I worked as a photographer. I became a slave to the women in my life, specifically the brides. I found a bit of magic in being able to take memorable moments and freeze them in time. My mother always had a camera within arm's reach. When she took a photography class in college, I often joined her on trips around the state taking photographs of nature. When Penquis Valley High offered a photography class my senior year, I audited the class.

I spent hours in the school darkroom, pulling negatives, creating contact sheets and developing images. Outside our automotive shop turned art classroom, we posed one another against brick walls, attempting to take new and innovative pictures. It's comical to see our fledgling art. The two dozen students believed they were breaking boundaries, and for our small community, we were. Armed with cameras, we sought snapshots that depicted our world and people in our lives.

Amanda Wardwell, a long-time friend, joined me for many after school darkroom sessions. Her father was a respectable photographer, and it showed in her approach to framing an image. When our assignment required models, she begrudgingly offered to serve as my muse. I found her beautiful. She was a tomboy in demeanor, but I always saw her in a much softer light. We spent several years as friends and as an on-and-off-again couple, giving me more insight than the casual buddy. She presented this rough exterior to the world, but beneath that, she was a young woman that rolled her eyes at every comment before a smile lit up her face. She was nothing less than stunning.

After the busses dispersed, we spent an afternoon working in the darkroom. Needing more photos to develop, I begged her to be my model. She resisted, but my determination resulted in an annoyed, "Fine, let's do this." I remember the photograph as if I were staring at it today. She rested her back against the brick wall of the shop. The sun high in the sky flushed her skin in light, forcing her to squint. Her head tilted slightly to one side and her chin dropped. To be ironic, she held a flower, barely more than a weed. The curves of her face opposed the intensity of the thought dancing across her eyes. It took an entire roll of film for her smirk to fade. By the time we finished, she thrust her middle finger in my direction. Had I photographed *that*, I think I would have captured this amazing person.

I wish I could find the photographs.

Hillary Roberts, our resident aspiring actress, was another favorite model. Unlike Amanda, who accepted the position with reservation, Hillary thrust herself in front of the camera at every opportunity. As I raised the camera to my eye, she conjured a character as if I had handed her a script. Of the many personas she brought to the table, Olivia Faye was one of the most alluring. Ms.

Faye was the only one prepared to bare more than her soul for the camera.

Being a senior in high school is almost as awkward as the rise of puberty during freshman year. You're rushing toward the finish line to enter adulthood. By age, you're considered a grown-up, but still being in school, you're forced to deal with the watchful eyes of your teachers. We might have to play by their rules, but we pushed every boundary possible. This rang especially true in photography class.

After school, in my parent's living room, we hung sheets and set the stage for Olivia's debut. As Hillary, she was nervous, rambling to herself about mustering the courage to go through with the shoot. It turned into her repeating, "I can't believe I'm doing this." Once I created her stage, the doubts vanished and Olivia came to life. With her back to me, she undressed, making it a sensual revealing.

The shoot lasted twenty minutes.

Hillary, a girl, vanished, replaced by Olivia, a woman. Knowing we were blurring a line, we ensured we wouldn't be called out for making pornography. Her body, conveniently covered by fabric, gave only hints of her sexuality. The photoshoot stopped being about the amount of skin. As she covered her face with locks of hair, she stared up into the camera. The bold and sultry image held a hint of sadness. While she might have thought Olivia was stealing the spotlight, it was the vulnerability on Hillary's face that made the moment a keepsake.

As soon as I set down the camera, Hillary shook her shoulders, stepping back into her own skin. With quick gasps of air, she panted, "I can't believe I just did that." The next day, I developed the photos. I hid my work from classmates, making it clear I was up to no good. The art teacher stepped into the cramped space, catching me, quite literally, red handed. Swiping my negatives, she asked, "Who is that?" I had to reply with, "Olivia Faye, she's from... uhm... Dover." She squinted in the dim light. "That looks like Hillary." Hillary, without missing a beat, chimed in with, "She does, doesn't she!"

There was an awkward conversation, and I was dismissed from the class for the rest of the term. I promptly turned the negatives over to Miss Olivia Faye, keeping the only set of prints. While I had no ability to draw, and my paintings look like the work of a toddler, I found my creative side in photography. It wasn't the darkroom, or the actual taking of photographs that I missed. While holding the camera against my eye, I was offered a new perspective of people I had known for years. We spend our teen years discovering who we are and building personas necessary for survival. But for a moment, I got to see the reality of Amanda's inner-self and Hillary's vulnerability.

LOVE UNDER MOONLIGHT

We can see the evolution or our town in the surrounding industry. The generation before had the slate quarries. Mined for the material that protected our roofs during the winter months, these transformed into swimming holes. My parents would spend their days jumping from the sides, into the questionable water below. I can't believe they used these dangerous locations for recreational activities. While our parents before us gathered around slate quarries, we, however, were a generation of gravel.

Between Brownville Junction and Brownville, the "pits" litter the sides of the road with massive gaps in the tree line. Upon first glance, they appear like hand crafted dunes in the desert. These pits harvested one of the most important natural resources for northerners: sand. Separated by density, there are signs with methods to purchase rocks for your driveway and sand for your pickup truck. Owned by Bishops, these unnatural areas of our landscape served as the primary provider for the sand/salt slush that keeps our roads safe during the winter months.

Each location had a narrow opening from the road. It was difficult to see the massive machinery used to sift through the soil. As a kid, I'd recede into the woods behind my house and eventually the trek would lead to one of the larger pits. Sliding down the hill, sand filling my sneakers, I'd treat the areas as a personal playground. This particular pit had been harvested and left alone for years, evident by the many campfires and empty beer bottles. If I continued on my journey, I'd find myself face-to-face with bulldozers, rock crushers, and large metal contraptions I couldn't identify. In my younger years, it felt as if I were on an alien world, abandoned by its previous inhabitants.

My perspective changed when I got my driver's license.

On the weekend, the sandpits transformed into gathering locations for teens with nothing to do. Pulling off the pavement, and slowly navigating the makeshift roads, we'd journey to the furthest pit. Here, we'd park our cars in a circle, leaving our lights on, or we'd build bonfires. One vehicle would roll down its window, pop in a cassette, and blare music while we socialized. Most of the gatherings were fairly benign. Somebody might have stolen a six pack from their parents' fridge, but mostly we talked away from the prying eyes of our elders. Of course, there were always those who used it as an opportunity to connect with their wilder selves.

We laughed, we loved, and then we "loved."

I spent many nights in the sandpits near my house. In a world surrounded by trees, it felt like a wide-open expanse covered by a black blanket with tiny shining dots poking through. Even if I were alone, I enjoyed the solitude and reveled in the near infinite stars. While most of our landscapes were cut off by the tree line, from here you could see further than anywhere else in town. On nights when the moon cast an eerie white light on the ground, you could listen to the sounds of wolves and coyotes as they called out to their packs. It served as a reminder of how northerners cohabitate with nature.

My house was always filled with people. Between my parents, grandmother and uncle, it seemed as if there was never enough space of privacy. Eventually, I'd start bringing friends to the sand pits to partake in these therapeutic sessions. There were many who didn't understand my affinity for nature but one friend, however, enjoyed sitting on the hood of my car while we listened to the only radio station capable of penetrating the piles of sand.

I spent much of my teen years confused about my sexuality. My affection for this young man as a friend developed into a crush. I'd be forced to make peace with my unrequited love. But he more than happily spent hours captivated by the tranquil setting. Only inches from this handsome man, the knots in my stomach made it difficult to focus on nature.

With my back pressed against the windshield, I could see him out of the corner of my eye, staring off into the sky. I was tense as my nerves fired like an electric current running through my body while we admired the evening. In a fairytale ending, this would have turned into a confession, leading to a romance. But in small town Maine, my affections would have turned into a scandal. So instead, my feelings were left unspoken.

In this sandpit, far from the closest house, I want to say we loved, and then we "loved." Except we didn't. I loved in silence. I suspect he always knew. In hindsight, he returned what he was capable of: our friendship, built with these many nights captivated by the peace. Over a decade later, I still think lovingly of the boy sitting on the car who would help define me as a man.

Eventually, the owners of the sandpits caught on to our clandestine meetings. We'd be chased away, threatened with legal action if we started another bonfire. We'd trade in these outdoor spaces for family camps or campgrounds. For the teenagers in my area, it further limited our options to gather in a space without adults. But when you consider the amount of untapped forests around us, we'd find a way.

The sandpits are still there.

They have mostly shut down, concluding the generation of gravel. On one of my many days photographing, I decided to see if it they still maintained their magic, or if it was the victim of nostalgia. Parking my car in the wide open spot, I turned off the lights and was amazed by darkness. Unable to see my hand, I climbed onto the hood of my car and laid back. With the windows rolled down and music blaring on the radio, I found that some magic transcends time.

On a chilly summer night, the sandpit still feels like the place where I first discovered love.

LOOPING LOOPING LOOPING

In the world of Maine, you weren't somebody important until you had your license. The moment that piece of plastic found its way into your wallet, a world of possibilities opened. Considering none of the teenagers had anything more than a babysitting job, we begged our parents for their keys. While many teens across the country use it as an opportunity to cruise to the mall, or go on adventures to distant lands, we had one destination in mind.

Anybody who went to Penquis Valley High School is familiar with CJ's Variety. Not because they were the sketchiest gas station in town, but because they stayed open until eleven. In a town that goes to sleep by 8:00PM, this was an oasis. While it remained a fifteen-minute drive, for the vast majority of my school district, it served as a central hub. We scrounged what money we could and after topping off the tank, we'd begin a cultural phenomenon known as Looping.

Very few teens had cars that allowed them to brag. We drove hand-me-down vehicles that wouldn't pass inspection. The doors of our rides might not match, and more than one had a trash bag duct taped to keep out the rain. Even though our cars were barely operating "shit boxes," we spent the evening treating them like status symbols. The car itself meant little, but the fact we had our licenses and the disposable income to waste gas, that meant you were somebody.

Piling in as many friends as possible, we travelled from the parking lot of the high school to the parking lot of the old Dexter Shoe factory on the other side of the town. The entire journey through the center of town was roughly two miles. The route would have you cross the bridge, stroll through downtown, around Napa Auto Parts, past the gas station, and to the factory parking lot. Because of the short distance, nobody sped, and most often there'd be a brief honk if we passed the police officer staked out at the station. If somebody had a loud car, you might have them rev their engine to wake anybody that had fallen asleep watching the evening news.

Looping came with rules.

Many of my classmates had older siblings, which meant they had been backseat Loopers. For those like me, I had to stop and watch before learning the nuances of the Loop. There were two times Looping was socially acceptable; before school and late evening. Outside these specified times would label you a loser, and we often mocked those who ran to their cars after class to begin Looping.

As you turned around in each of the parking lots, you had to wait in line before you could merge onto the road. There were no cuts, and definitely no pulling up alongside a car. No matter the length of the queue, you respected the order of cars. If you wanted to talk with friends, you'd frantically wave while passing and you'd meet further back in one of the parking lots. There was also an unspoken rule for the darkest area of the parking lot. Those parked there were not to be disturbed, for reasons I feel should be quite obvious.

One may question the environmental hazard or even the socio-economic impact of spending twenty dollars a night on gas, but no, this was our social activity of choice. Just knowing that these drivers had the money to spend on such a frivolous activity assigned them a status. Their cars might look as if they would fall apart at any moment, but they *had* a car. In a poor community, the bar for impressive can be quite low. This abundance of spending on gas is why my mother often gave me grief about driving to and from school. And if she caught me Looping, there would be hell to pay.

Of course, I Looped.

I can't say I was skilled at the art form. Frequently while driving the circuit, I'd take a random side road or even forget to turn around in the parking lot. In the morning, it allowed me to avoid arriving at school early and sitting in a vacant classroom as I waited for friends to arrive. Two rounds of the Loop allowed me to chat with a friend while I finished a cigarette before school. Thankfully, neither of my parents passed through town at that point or I'd come home to one of them demanding my keys.

To explain the importance of the Loop to our town, it even had a theme song. Put looping, looping, looping to the melody of "Rawhide." I admit, we might not be the most creative bunch.

There were fond memories of me driving my two shades of shit brown '76 Oldsmobile Cutlass Supreme affectionately called "The Boat." In the morning, I'd pick up friends for school or, if the weather were extremely frigid, pick up wayward students shivering in the cold. Then it was time to do the morning Loop. It was like male peacocks showing their plumes to impress onlookers. But inside the car, we listened to music, talked about life, and avoided the stresses of being a teenager.

Eventually, my days of Looping would come to an end. While I made one last circuit before heading to school, one of my classmates sped up, passing me. To break this golden rule of the road, arms waving in the window, made it clear something was amiss. As I pulled into the parking lot of the shoe factory to turn around, she frantically pointed at the front of my car. Slowing, I could see the billowing of smoke. The Boat prepared its last lap, black clouds filling the sky. As I pulled into a classmate's driveway and popped the hood, a grim reality set in.

Fire consumed the engine. The hand-me-down car had sprung a leak and now, I watched it burn. Had it been a simple fix, I'd have climbed under the hood and gotten to work. But when your car is filled with flames, all you can do is watch in horror. My days of Looping had ended. Its death left us unable to make it to class, but more importantly, unable to Loop.

CLOTHING OPTIONAL

Modesty was not part of our vocabulary.
    Our school was small enough that every student had a certain amount of familiarity with their classmates. We were tight-knit enough to know siblings and birthdays. At the start and end of every relationship, it only took a single passing period in school before it turned into common knowledge. In my group of friends, we had become so comfortable that there were few secrets to be kept. We were like open books, mostly out of necessity. If you wanted to keep something from the others, you were out of luck. We considered no subject taboo.

My friends enjoyed being naked. I can't help but laugh when strolling down memory lane. The majority of our time together in high school involved one friend or another disrobing. While none of our gatherings involved alcohol, you'd be surprised how often one of us sat in the group completely nude. Amongst this crowd, we were more like family, and apparently our stance on body positivity removed any self-conscious barriers.

Because our towns offered little in the way of entertainment, we gathered at whichever home had the fewest adults. This wasn't because we wanted to misbehave, but more as a courtesy to our parents. This rotation prevented keeping them up late at night or having them endure the mess in the kitchen. When we couldn't find a place to congregate, my father would give us access to the American Legion.

Once we finished playing video games on the big screen television, or shooting pool, every party ended the same way. Somebody inevitably slapped a deck of cards onto the table. We'd stop doing our individual activities and drag chairs to the table, prepared to enter a vicious game of poker. The first few games started innocent smack talk as we sized up the competition. We never had money to gamble, but we had food. Once the stakes had been raised, or our food vanished (eaten or lost, whichever came first) we'd start a new game: strip poker.

Once the dealer distributed the cards, people's ruthless personas emerged. The noteworthy players? Corey Bradbury, the bloodthirsty shark, Josh Decker, the whimsical bluffer, and Catie Joyce, the subtle cutthroat. Living in Maine meant we always wore enough layers to keep the game going for some time. Hoodies and socks were gambled away first, then shirts and jeans. Eventually it came down to bras and underwear. In any other setting, it might have been embarrassing, or perhaps we'd have tapped out as we sat shivering in our briefs. But with this group, it was all or nothing.

The poker skills ranged from expert to novice. Somewhere in the middle, I gambled away my jeans, thinking I had a winning hand. The clothes piled on the table, and without warning, I found myself defeated by a flush. My dreams of becoming a professional poker vanished as I debated the value of my underwear. It didn't take long before most of the table sat in a similar state.

While we danced the line between clothed and nude, the tone of the game never turned sexual. Despite us being a group of hormonal teens, sexual tension never entered the equation. The first person naked, leaving ass prints on the chair, was always Josh Decker. You'd think it was because he didn't grasp the game, but he was most likely our most talented player. Once we discovered he continued throwing hands, betting one article of clothing at a time, it was clear he raced to naked. We became suspicious when we flipped his discarded hand to see three sixes. He shrugged, replying, "But it's the Devil's hand!"

Josh was more content naked than clothed. The rest of us cheated, stole and flat out lied in an attempt to beat the two powerhouses. Catie and Corey glared at one another, locked in a bitter rivalry with our clothes on the table. While the rest of us traded cards, trying our best to cheat, it always came down to the two. Eventually we'd walk away from the table, skin bared for all to see.

Of course, somebody outside our pact discovered this unusual familiarity. The American Legion required an adult to be present because of the alcohol on the shelves. Knowing that none of us drank, it granted us more flexibility than the usual occupants. Instead of my father hovering in his office, attempting to work as we yelled at one another, he sent a fellow veteran to do random check-ins. He had barely cleared the stairs, peaking around the corner to see a table filled with half naked teens shouting obscenities as we lost another hand. Never have I seen a man turn around that quickly. Serving in two wars didn't prepare him for this.

Some may think it odd to be that comfortable around friends, but it provided an odd safety. We were all shapes and sizes, and never once was there mocking or whispers. Considering it is an awkward time for any adolescent, this fostered self-confidence and pushed away our insecurities. Who knew that a game of poker would allow us to feel comfortable in our own skin? Things turned awkward when our two card sharks started dating. The friendly game of "Who can get naked faster" went from innocent to foreplay. At this point, we most often bowed out and relied on more harmless games. Like true geeks, we set aside our gambling and moved onto more wholesome games like Pokémon.

Leave it to us, there might have been stripping involved.

THE FAMILIES WE CHOOSE

In small town Maine, it is rare for outsiders to move in and take up residence. It means that after generations, the many individuals are part of clans. Due to our limited pool of suitors, these families merge and now there are a handful that make up Brownville Junction. Once we include cousins, it's hard to discern who is not related. Because of this extended network, we rely on our families. They serve as babysitters and handymen, but more than that, they help us survive the isolation that comes from living in a town far from civilization.

My family does not get along.

When somebody asks about my family, I acknowledge my parents, grandmother and brother (deceased). While I have an extended family (five uncles and two aunts), the baggage involved makes it impossible to explain who is in our good graces and who's trying to kill the other; I avoid them. My grandparents' fiftieth anniversary is where I caught an uncle snorting cocaine in the bathroom. My paternal grandparents are vile humans, and I think given the resources, they would have been evil incarnate. I respect my lineage to a point, but I'm not "of them." In a small town, I couldn't shake the stench they left on my youth.

While I always wished for those happy whole-family moments, they never came. Thankfully, in high school while I was dating Amanda Wardwell, I came to understand what extended family meant. Every year clan Brown met at camp for a weekend family gathering. Along with Amanda would be her cousins and my childhood friends Bert and Derek Brewer. It wasn't a small gathering. The number of family could be seen by the many tents pitched. While the adults took to the beds in the camp, the kids resigned to our more rustic accommodations surrounding the small building. It was an ordeal.

I joined them for three out of my four years in high school. We arrived at camp, greeted by a brown bath towel raised high on the flagpole, the Brown Family Flag. Nobody in this clan lacked a sharp wit. I was a foreigner here, but with such a large gathering, it was easy to blend in. Eventually, it would come out I wasn't related by blood. They jested, "Why would you join this crazy bunch?" But of course, they welcome me with open arms.

Now, if my family is nontraditional in its difficulties and overall disdain for one another, the Brown's were the other end of the spectrum There would always be a group of elders telling stories. They celebrated additions to the family, whether by birth or by marriage. They'd recount the trials and tribulations of their year, ending it with the victory of arriving at camp. I believe more than once, I saw a chart of lineage used as a visual aid.

The children were glad to see their cousins. They would play tag and chase one another with water pistols. The general feeling of mirth occurred regardless of age. Even the adolescents in the group found common ground. Taking to the water, they'd swim across the lake, finding a respite on a large rock protruding from the water. Bert's father often tried to teach me how to wind sail. Needless to say, I spent more time falling than standing.

While the day was fun, what I always remembered were the meals. There would be long tables with dishes prepared by every family within the clan, and every year I looked forward to grape jelly kielbasa prepared by Bert's mother. It looked like a school cafeteria with families gathered together, mingling and taking care of their young. At every table, you would introduce yourself, how you were related, and stories flowed. And while spirits remained high, family members took the time to check in with one another. Despite some not being seen since the last reunion, their family listened, chiming in to offer help where necessary.

As with any family gathering, there are bound to be traditions. Of the many unique and off the wall customs, the one that always stood out to me was the auction. If members of my family wanted something, they stole it. But the Browns turned it into a fast-talking whimsical event for whatever was available. They sold kayaks, along with snowshoes, and toys amongst a slew of other homemade items. The bidding wars added to the fun as playful competitions broke out amongst the family.

This is something great about Maine. I didn't partake in "family" activities with my family unless it revolved around a funeral. However, it was only an invitation and some pleasantries before I became brethren to another clan. In Maine, tight-knit communities adopt faster than they disown. In small towns there is always a sense of, "We're in this together," that binds us. I wonder today if they still fly the Brown Flag and have fast moving auctions? Of course they do. I bet the only difference is, the kids have gotten older, and the clan has gotten bigger.

THE SPIRIT OF OUR COMMUNITIES

Summers in Maine, at least for the students, are a lazy time. For the youngest, there was always the opportunity for sports such as little league baseball. However, as I grew older, and they took away the ball holder and required us to catch throws, I realized my prowess as a tee ball champion didn't translate. Thankfully, as puberty made me more awkward, I fell in love with being a musician. This meant that during the summer months, I dove into my passion without the worry of grades or teacher oversight.

Enter the wonderful world of Community Band.

During the school year, band pandered to competitions and spectacles in the gymnasium. It also meant being seated along with newer musicians who took the class to get out of taking an English elective. We had little to no say in what we played and more often than not, it turned into a disaster as our conductor was forced to deal with misbehaving tweens.

Community Band had no grades. In truth, it had no conductor. The age of the members ranged from ten to seventy. There were formal musicians, beginners, seasoned veterans and those who simply loved to perform. This hodgepodge of personalities blended together in a way that frequently resulted in mentoring, camaraderie, but most of all, laughter.

Community Band was four weeks of practice. The music was easy enough; a collection of John Phillip Sousa marches mixed with show tunes and Disney songs. At first it was simply fun to be in the group of trombones who couldn't take anything seriously. Later, it would be a chance to sit as the first chair of the Saxophone section (when there was more than one of us).

The practices took place at Dover-Foxcroft Academy, which on its own meant those of us from Penquis Valley High entered enemy territory. The drive there became tedious. Frequently, we would diverge from the pavement and take one of the many dirt roads connecting our towns, driving far more quickly than the limit allowed. By my junior year, it had become the routine and on one back-road trip, I saw a cop car and slammed the brakes. The noise of my skidding was enough to not only to turn the cop's head, but to lift the head of his mistress from his lap. She was trying to help him tie his shoes, I'm sure.

After our rehearsals, as the summer days got hotter, we would stop for ice cream at a roadside stand. This small kiosk, only capable of holding a few employees, was the embodiment of small town America. Cars gathered in the parking lot and the lines grew long as patrons waited for their locally sourced ice cream. The world slowed in these moments. Strangers talked to one another about the weather, about music, and about their big plans for the summer. Years later, I'm not even sure if that small shop, no bigger than most people's sheds, is still standing?

Once performance season started, we took part in a concert every week and a parade every Saturday. We performed our shows in the parking lots of local businesses. Each performance was the same. We unloaded folding chairs to a nearly empty parking lot and started to play. At first, it might seem sad, or even desperate to only have a handful of attendees, but this is where Maine weaves its magic. The audience grew. Cars pulled into the parking lot and patrons rolled down windows or gathered as they set up camp chairs.

By the second half of our show, we played to a crowd. The percussionist who led our ensemble would share stories and then cue our next song. Unlike the gymnasium where our parents watched in silence, the crowd responded. We started our show with patriotic members and the retired veterans standing. We played them a love song, and the people sang their respects. As we moved into more jaunty tunes, they clapped, cheered, and more often than not, they danced. In towns that had nothing, we gave them a night of entertainment.

During our Saturday parades, the Community Band, traveling in style, hopped on a trailer pulled by the percussionist's husband. It was exactly what you imagine. A group of ragtag musicians wearing white shirts playing with every bit of energy we could muster in the heat. Littering the side of the parade routes, entire towns lined the street. American flags waved as we launched from one march into the next. The elderly sat in their cars, honking their horns as we passed. Children sat on dads' shoulders, cheering at the sound of music.

At the time, I puffed my chest as a king of the world. We might be one of three bands playing, mixed with muscle cars, marching veterans, or local Boy Scouts. These people, some long-time citizens of Maine and some only for the summer, basked in the wonderment that can only be mustered by the liveliness of a small town. For a brief time, we came together to celebrate the best of who we are as a people and the rest of the world melted away.

Now, in hindsight, I think this is what it means to be a community. Writing this, I find myself choked up, longing for that sense of togetherness. For a moment, as the music played, there were only happy times. Only a small town could take a tiny affair and treat it like the Macy's Thanksgiving Day Parade.

Small towns foster the biggest spirit.

WE ARE THE MOUNTAIN FOLK

There are nuances to Maine, near impossible to describe to the civilized world. Like any other culture, we have traditions that seem to have no origin. There are mannerisms shared by the people that often raise eyebrows and leave onlookers asking questions. When I tell people about how students were let out early from school to go hunting, it is met with disbelief. Showing pictures of our pickup trucks in the school parking lot filled with rifles, it becomes apparent that we are unlike many parts of America. People laugh and dismiss these idiosyncrasies, but they are part of a secret language we share.

Our differences aren't unique. There are a thousand small towns speckling the landscape of this country that offer similar tales. Maine offers a majestic backdrop for many of my memories. Folks will accept that Maine is ninety percent beautiful forests, but when I say my town consists of an intersection of Main Street and Route 11, it is easy to sort out those from the country and those raised in the cities.

Once we talk about the population and the sparse homes along long stretches of road, the ironic humor leaks in, as we discuss the afternoon required to reach McDonald's or how a grocery shopping trip turned into a day-long excursion, the reality pushes aside beautiful mountains. The lack of take out, the closing of shops at sundown, or searching for trails to snowmobile to school aren't the images that come to mind when people from out-of-state think of Maine. Because of this, we have a playful name for anybody outside our borders. We call them Flatlanders.

While attending college in Salem, Massachusetts, I found myself outside my element. Making friends involved telling stories of our hometowns. The more I shared these outlandish realities, the more they asked questions. No, I never picked potatoes. Yes, I've met Stephen King. No, we don't eat lobster for every meal. Yes, my yard had a car on blocks. The more I talked about this world only three-hundred miles away, the more they wanted to see how it differed from their imagination.

The trip came on without warning. It was decided that, for spring break, we'd stay at my parents' house in Brownville Junction. The distance is exactly three hundred miles. As we neared the end of our five-hour drive, their civilization vanished and they found themselves in the boondocks. Houses were scarce and roads continued on for miles without signs of life. They joked about how we'd eventually wind up on *dirt* roads. Much to their surprise, I found one just to prove a point. Transported from the densely populated Massachusetts to the unpopulated areas of northern Maine, they could never have imagined the reality to which they'd agreed, "That sounds fun."

As my car spit up a cloud of dust on barely formed roads, they questioned their decision.

When they discovered my town consisted of a single police officer, they decided they wanted to risk driving. Handing over the keys, I thought, what could be the harm? One of my classmates had a license and had done more than enough driving on her own. As she found the intersection of Main Street and Route 11, she blew through the stop sign. Flying, she escaped the wrath of an eighteen wheeler. I screamed. Slamming the breaks, she didn't hesitate when she said, "I didn't think your town had stop signs!" I took offense; we have plenty. When she inquired about stoplights I responded with, "We have a blinking yellow light, does that count?" No, apparently it does not.

Once we reached "up town," the grim reality set in. They smiled, and I'm pretty sure the term "quaint" was uttered several times. At one point, the inevitable question, "Where's the rest?" Yes, the town store, gas station, function hall and post office served the exciting area of Brownville Junction. Standing on Main Street, you can easily see the entire town. On one side is the train station, and the other half is a collection of run down homes. In-between, there is little more than the essentials.

"Where's the mall?"

I couldn't help but laugh. I had warned them. But despite the ongoing list of things to expect, they thought I used hyperbole. For them, small towns hugged major metropolitan areas. Small in their heads meant forty-thousand residents and a vibrant collection of small shops. I explained the nearest mall was an hour away. The movies theaters? Forty-five minutes. McDonalds? Thirty minutes. Eventually, one guy asked, "Is Canada near here?" Yes, it's down the road, two hours away. A beach? I'm not even sure how to answer that question.

Tourism is one of the primary industries in Maine.

Our postcards show wonderful destinations. Mountains, beaches, campsites, a lone man fishing in a lake that appears infinite, they are very real aspects of Maine. If you were to lie out these images, they would show the splendor of our state. But if you were to spread them out by distance, they'd hardly seem to exist in a single place.

We gladly welcome those who want to partake in our simple way of life. However, those who journey into the far north often underestimate the size of Maine. We have repeat visitors, the ones who come into the state with realistic expectations. When they say they're roughing it, they will hide away in the isolated cabins and spend their days fishing. But more often than not, we are overwhelmed with people expecting a vibrant night life and shopping.

Our license plates might read "Vacation Land," but we have a love/hate with outsiders. Even in tourist-driven Bar Harbor, the moment a shop owner hears a local speak, their demeanor softens. We need their money, but we will exchange grins or a mutual eye-rolling at the tourist browsing their wares. Dependency on the spending of tourism creates a tolerance we endure, but we remain skeptical of southerners.

We call them Flatlanders: it is not a term of endearment.

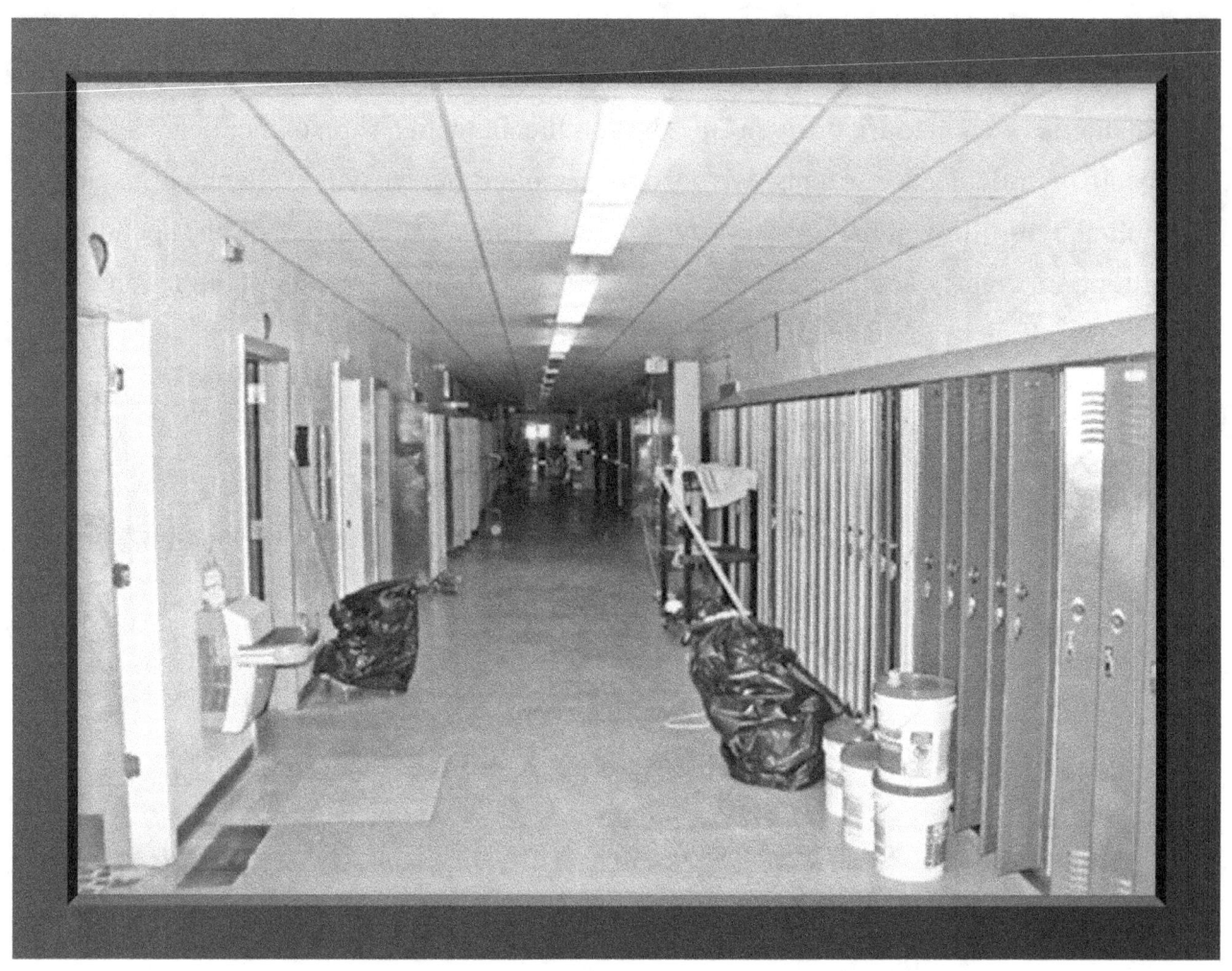

WE FILL OUR CASKETS

My brother, Phillip Jason Flagg, was born on September 25th. Eight years later, I was born on Sunday, September 13th. Jason died three weeks after my birth, days after his birthday. His death occurred during the first of two tours at Camp Lejeune. This meant our family celebration came to a halt, drowned by the death of a child. I would only realize once the impact of this on our family when we retired to Brownville Junction.

I've spent my life as a little brother, but also as an only child. To say it caused a sense of confusion would be an understatement. I associated Brownville Junction with death. Moving to our family home, generations had come and gone, filling caskets. My mother and I visited Pine Street Cemetery often, cleaning tombstones and placing flowers on graves. In a neat line, my brother, great-grandmother, and grandmother occupied space in the middle of the cemetery. Despite my brother passing before my existence, his influence ripples through time, helping mold me into the man I am today.

Living in a small secluded town keeps you connected to the dead. Because of the large demographic of retirees in Brownville Junction, the obituaries are filled with the grandparents of classmates. Knowing the name of every individual in a six-mile radius means that when somebody passes, it connects to a member of your social circle. Because elderly neighbors may pass in the night or the dead outnumber the living, there is a sense of mortality hovering over our heads.

This inevitable life event didn't create a sense of dread. While my family had an intimate relationship with the reaper, I've never experienced a fear of dying. In fact, it provided an appreciation for the time between birth and death. Living with an elderly grandmother, I never understood why she started the morning by reading the obituaries. Often she'd sip coffee with my father and say, "So-and-so is in the obits." One more photograph in her yearbook, having lost the fight against time, received a giant red X. The acknowledgement was a simple nod, and then they'd move on, finding less grim topics. I grew up in a household respecting the dead, but seldom mourning their passing.

Nearing ten years old, I discovered I had a deceased sibling. Photos of him hung on the walls, marking him as a person of note. My parents didn't remove him from my life. They waited until I could comprehend the entire story. In my mother's bedroom, there were small frames showing him in his wheelchair wearing a baseball jersey. It was one of many and always featured a smile. From one to the next, the photographs showed a vibrant life, not without complication, but always emphasizing the joy. In hindsight, Jason had always been present in my life. I grew up with an older brother, physically absent, but never forgotten.

When I reached middle school, I remember asking mom for stories about who he had been. She'd clear a spot for me on her bed, and she'd started with how much he loved me in our short time together. The images she painted left him as quite the character in my head. He couldn't pronounce "faucet" and instead called it a "fuckit," a tale that quickly colored my view of him. Of course, not all his stories are straightforward. Born with his spine outside of his body, he faced more challenges than many will their entire life. Undergoing more than a hundred surgeries in eight short years, he spent much of his life within the walls of a hospital. She recited the names of his favorite nurses, ignoring the fact a child should never have a favorite medical professional.

Eventually the conversation trails off, inching toward the pneumonia that took him. Instead, she explains how Jason, unable to say my name, referred to me as Germany. Flipping through the albums, it's difficult to find an image of him without his trademark goofy smile. But more than that, the people occupying the photographs by his side share in the infectious joy. My brother left an impression on many. He might have died, but there is a legacy of a child who overcame countless obstacles and never let it diminish his light.

I think for many families living in Brownville Junction, it's easy to map our lineage. We speak of our forefathers as if they were legends, choosing to remember better times. We live with one foot firmly planted in the past, dispensing memories to our youth until they someday will do the same. It's not a somber affair and often ends in a shared laugh as we celebrate a person's life.

I think it's only in a small town that we explore our lineage while walking through the cemetery. Chiseled into the granite are stories. "Brother of...," and "Child of..." They lead us to the next chapter and tell a complex and winding tale of our predecessors. You can see a family who had a child at a young age and see who died before their twilight years. As you reach the older sections of the cemetery, messages are written or sigils belonging to the Navy, the Marines, the Masons, or the Order of the Eastern Star. These messages become clues to the jigsaw puzzle creating our family history. For some, this connection to our past is the only context revealing where we come from and who we once were.

For me, I was born on September 13. I am the youngest child of Susan and Phillip Flagg.

DEPARTING WITHOUT GOODBYES

I dropped out of college in 2000 and moved home for a few months while I regrouped and sorted out my life goals. I had left a hippy, liberal, diversified community and thrust myself back into the world of repressed homogeny. The free thought and openness of living in the land of academia had spoiled me. However, leaving the diversity of campus and returning to the wilds of Maine meant connecting with individuals like myself proved difficult.

During this educational hiatus, I started talking online to an older gay man who lived in Milo, a short ten-mile drive away. It surprised me that he had purchased a friend's childhood home. We met for coffee at his place. There was no romantic affair between us. We were the only two gays in the town at this point, so we enjoyed each other's company. In fact, we had very little in common with the age gap. However, this single commonality was enough to spark a friendship. I was relieved I was not alone, and that somebody lived out of the closet. Beyond that, our only connection was being raised in the northern reaches of rural Maine.

Once, while visiting, I excused myself to use the bathroom. When I saw the number of needles and pill bottles littering his bathroom, I was shocked. He must have sensed my curiosity when I returned to the kitchen. Without emotion he uttered three shocking words, "I have AIDS."

Being young and removed from the hustle and bustle of city life, the world of HIV/AIDS had yet to factor into my reality. Other than a few brief mentions on the news or a side character in a television show, he was my first exposure. In our secluded town, few would understand the reality of the statement and the weight that came with admitting your status. I felt cheated that this friendship had an expiration date.

This disease, this *gay* disease, hadn't reached our health classes. I remember in sixth grade I asked the librarian about the disease. Within my school, only a single pamphlet offered any information, and then it relied heavily on stereotypes. Later I found the school nurses' guidebook and protocols for infectious diseases. I absorbed it at an alarming pace. In hindsight, I wonder if this was brought on by subconsciously knowing I was a target demographic. While the information was clinical, the media portrayed it as a death sentence, and without the opportunity to ask questions, I feared it would be the inevitable outcome for my life.

Filled with questions, he answered them honestly. He had long since crossed from HIV to AIDS and took part in studies as one of the longest living patients. There was no sadness in his voice, just simple facts. He contracted it through unprotected sex, and he promptly made sure I wasn't partaking in "risky" behavior. Over the next hour I learned more than I had through the media, teachers, or even the internet.

For the next few months, I brought dinner and prepared meals in his kitchen. We'd have tea or coffee and watch "Wheel of Fortune." I'd go for walks with him and help him take his dog to the vet. Our conversations rarely discussed the future. Most often, I told stories of growing up in a small town. Having lived his younger years in the city, he found it endearing. He'd frequently say, "You need to get out of here."

Like a true Mainer, I extended myself to help in any way possible. He didn't have family nearby, and having only recently moved, the locals shied away. For me, he bridged the gap between our small town and the life I had in college. We found solace in each other's company.

I took his advice.

I left for school in Massachusetts and not too long after, we lost touch. On a trip to visit my parents, I decided to make a detour and catch up. It was like old times. He asked about school and if I had found any cute guys. He laughed as I recounted my blunderings in the dating world. However, afflicted with this disease for so long, his body started to fail him. I cut my visit short as a nurse arrived. Even she paused before discussing his daily routine. The countdown rapidly approached zero, and it had stopped being about treatment and become more about comfort.

He wished me luck at school, and I returned the sentiment, not knowing how to respond. During my next trip to Maine, I made it a point to visit him. This time, the familiar truck wasn't in his driveway, and I drove past. The time after, another vehicle had appeared, and I comforted myself by saying he had traded in his car. Fear prevented me from stopping. The thought of seeing him on his death bed wrote a happier narrative I refused to disprove. I continued driving.

I know now, he passed during the semester. Between our horrible attempts at solving puzzles on the television, he instilled an important life lesson. He showed me you could be yourself and live as you are and make no excuses. A disease had ravished his body, but it never touched his spirit. He lived in a community that wouldn't approve, but he offered no regrets. During a turbulent period in my life, he offered a bit of stability, eating soup before his dog took up residence on my lap.

Even all these years later, I'm angry. I missed my opportunity to say farewell and confess the impact he had on my life. But that isn't the part that stings my heart. For all this man shared with me, I can't remember his name. Without family or friends by his side, I imagine only the nurse stood at his bedside as he passed in his sleep.

The legacy of man slid away in a matter of seconds.

My memory is spotty but this one leaves me racked with guilt. I write this to keep his memory alive, a beacon in an otherwise dark period in my life. However, without his name, a piece of the man I knew has faded.

I wish I could remember.

DATING IN A SMALL TOWN

My town is just shy of one thousand, and my entire high school only held four hundred students. Dating in a small community posed complications. These complications double when you have to be leery of common ancestry that may result in web-footed children. Once you've eliminated siblings, and first cousins, your dating pool is relatively slim. The selection becomes even smaller unless you're willing to wade into the shallow end of the gene pool. When you're left with a dozen potential mates, that's when the hilarity of dating in a small Maine begins.

I should start further back; not at dating, but about relationships. While I'm certain this happens in big cities, in a small town your relationship is a community event and we all get to watch the disasters unfold. Before speaking about dating, I should discuss love. It comes in two types, longing and rapid-cycling. The two types are polar ends of the spectrum. To find people in the middle was such a rarity, I believed they existed in the same place as unicorns and Bigfoot.

The first, and most common, is the romantic type you read about in literature and hear on one of the two radio stations that reached my town. It consists of one person being madly in love with another and having it either abused or never returned. It was common for people to develop these crushes in grade school and continue until graduation. They bordered on infatuation, but mostly, they remained loyal despite being rejected. But hold on long enough, and the odds eventually work in your favor.

Crushes never remained secret. In a small town, we peddle in rumors as if they were silver. Eventually the crush would be revealed and a relationship may form for a brief period. The couple would break up, but because of our proximity, and lack of numbers, the split dragged all associates into the fray. I imagine it's a similar experience for the children of divorced parents. We became timeshare friends who suffered through endless custody hearings. Who got us for the 4th of July and heavens forbid if their birthdays were near one another. In true teenage fashion, our relationships are chock-full of over-the-top drama.

The second type is the rapid-cycling relationship. These people partook in serial monogamy at a pace that would leave heads spinning. Relationship statuses could change between classes and you'd have to ask if they were still together for fear of getting their significant other's name wrong. At one moment, you may find one of your friends making out with a girl under a pool table, then find him nuzzling with a new "friend" a day later. These relationships were common, and they were equal opportunity across the sexes. Every school has their "on again off again" relationships, but in a small school it's noticeable.

Reset during summer vacation and the whirlwind would begin anew.

In larger schools, folks might stay within their friend groups, but we didn't have that option. Cliques became incestuous and resulted in reaching beyond the immediate circle of friends. If you drew a map of associations, there would be so many crossovers and doubling up, the maps looked like a freeway accident. It was like maneuvering social landmines during the relationship aftermath. I'm not even sure if there were discussions or rules for when friends dated the same person. It was the Wild West and everybody fended for themselves.

I admit, being gay in small-town America had its perks. I was free from much of the drama unless one of my friends didn't honor one of the unsaid rules of dating. How I loved watching the drama unfold like a soap opera. By the time I left high school, it would be easier for people to say who they hadn't dated. I'm pretty sure it would have been easier and less time consuming if the school just hosted an overnight orgy. Maybe a fundraiser for the next generation?

It becomes even more fascinating when you encounter classmates a decade later as you recount their puppy dog love escapades. I remember a class reunion telling a tale to one classmate about shenanigans occurring on a camping trip in which I drew the short straw and shared a tent with them. She and her boyfriend were cute and in love, mimicking a modern day Romeo & Juliet without the vials of poison. Simply retelling the story made her blush.

Unfortunately, time moves on and these youthful trysts fall away in place for time enduring relationships. As I retold their sharing of a sleeping bag, her ex-boyfriend's new wife listened with a disapproving scowl. For most, these high school relationships died over the summer as people turned their attention toward college. Others remain strong, and it's exciting to hear about children on the way. In small town Maine, we remember every liaison. They become stories we someday tell their kids with good-natured, devilish smiles.

THE ONLY ONE IN THE VILLAGE

I'm gay. While there are many who are die-hard supporters across the globe, Maine tells a different story. Being an isolated town, cut off from the cities, they have a tendency to scoff at differences and often shun those unlike themselves. Even when residents supported these differences, they did so in silence, for fear of being ostracized by their neighbors. For me, being part of such a small minority in rural Maine colored my point-of-view.

 I think I understood something was different about myself when I was thirteen or fourteen (7th and 8th grade). Having worked with kids now, I find it interesting how early they grasp the concept these days. The word "gay," or even "homo" and "fag," weren't in the popular vernacular when I was a kid. I equate the experience to people who grow up colorblind. They are often unaware of their differences because they were never asked, "Is the hue of these two objects different?"

My freshman year in high school, I received my first exposure to the label "homosexual." I was surprised in our health class when it was brought up and discussed. By discussed, I mean our teacher included it in exactly one sentence throughout the entire course. While homosexuality was more of an off-hand topic that wasn't discussed at length, it was at least mentioned.

Introducing a computer into our household opened the door to the world. It gave me the ability to reach out and ask questions without fear of being labelled by my peers. Back then, we considered chat rooms the back alley of the Internet. It only became shadier as I searched chat rooms catering to homosexuals. I was lucky to find a gentleman from Scotland to talk with and discuss growing up in a small town. He had a similar experience when he came out. The Highlands of Scotland might offer spectacular scenery, but it held the same rural values of my home town. The conversation would continue for over a year, a simple exchange of pen-pals talking about life and what it was like growing up in different countries. Ultimately, he convinced me I had to create a support network of my own.

My sophomore year, I did just that. I knew without a doubt, once I uttered those words, even to my closest friends, my secret would be out. Armed with gossip, they'd treat it as currency and by lunch, there would be whispers. I decided it needed to be done. The first person I ever told was Brandy Burns, another student who came into the district from the city. Before school we roamed the halls, and my secret sat in the pit of my stomach until I finally blurted out the words. While I guess I secretly hoped for a pride parade to start and a shower of glitter to fall from the ceiling, she was fairly apathetic. She added it to the many characteristics making me who I am, and we went about our day as if nothing had changed. Years later, I can say I wish everybody was apathetic about it. This strategy continued until a good chunk of my friends knew.

There were roadblocks as the years progressed. The toughest person to tell was

Josh Decker. While he was one of my closest friends, I also believed he shared a similar secret. The idea of outing myself to another gay person was particularly intimidating. Without role models, who knew if this would change the dynamic between us? I thought of it as lying to a close friend for years and having to come clean. Neither of us thought it was a big deal. The worst that came from the conversation was our friends believing we should date for the lack of our options. It never came to be. But I found comfort in knowing this wasn't a hell built for one.

It wasn't all glitter and rainbows. There were several groups of kids who attempted to make my life miserable. Thankfully, when you're the largest kid in school, they keep the insults to whispers. Ironically, it was the quiet discussions that cut deepest. I referred to one group as the "Flannel Fags". Juvenile, I know, but I always found their existence ironic. I hung with the most popular and attractive ladies in the school. They were resigned to looking like a group of hunters, so co-dependent on one another they would never have social lives. Later, one of them approached me about being gay himself, but not able to say it. Had I not been such a clueless bonehead, I think I would have found another kindred spirit. Unfortunately, his secrecy and inability to break free of peer pressure made it impossible for him to start his own healing process.

While I mastered the conversation with my peers, adults proved an entirely different hurdle. I first outed myself to my Current Events teacher. I remember my criteria for picking him as the first teacher to confide in. He, too, was an outsider, only having lived in rural Maine for a year. His youth had been spent traveling the country. He was young enough to not be old, but old enough to not be a twit. I think he gave it the "Whatever floats your boat," speech and that was it. I figured once the adults knew, I could go about living my life. But it was living my life that brought with it a new set of complications.

My senior year French teacher, who also served as my "We have a spare twenty-five minutes in our day and have to pretend we're reading" teacher, was the first adult to approach me out of the blue. Okay, maybe it wasn't out of the blue. Lacey Martin and I may have approached him at some point, to set him up with her brother. He knew my stance on the subject. I remember him asking, "Do you know what the other students are saying about you?" At this point, it was pretty obvious, as it had become the gossip for days. I told him yes, and I didn't care what the small-minded folk of the school had to say. This was later followed by a meeting with the Guidance Counselor who suggested I might be a misguided influence. By this time, I was ready to be obnoxious about it. I could take the heat from peers, adults and even random townspeople. My ability to say, "fuck you," grew exponentially that year.

Random townspeople would tell me stories about a lady on the other side of town who lived with another lady and the sins they committed. I finally asked, "It's a sin to live on the other side of town?" The townspeople eventually stopped trying to save me and resorted to their whispers. It would only be exacerbated when my grandmother, in her misguided attempt to protect me, would have the congregation at church pray for me because HIV caused me to be gay. The prayers worked because I'm HIV free. But the gay thing kind of stuck. My parents were uncomfortable with me around other guys, and the first time they met a boyfriend, they freaked. My father hid in the garage doing "manly" things, and my mother spent the night in tears. I must give them credit, they've grown, and I'm pretty sure my mother would organize a Pride Parade if there were more gays in her town. My father now flies rainbow stickers on his pickup truck. It did, however, take time.

Growing up in a town where everybody has a similar heritage (let's be honest, we were W.A.S.P.s, with the occasional W.A.S.C.) means even subtle changes can create a hostile atmosphere. Being different was met with ignorance; most often from the lack of education but now and then, hatred through fear. I like to think that, over the years, the people in the town have been exposed enough to make strides. But I'm sure many gays, like me, fled to more tolerant places.

I still receive letters from acquaintances I knew back then. Sometimes, I'll get one that has a photo of them with their partner. At the time, I hated the vast majority of the people for letting me take the heat. However, I find joy in understanding they escaped to embrace their authentic selves. Years later, I think it's made me a stronger person. If I had to take the insults so somebody else could be safe while they grew into their own, I would do it again.

I recently found that there's an LGBT youth support group operating in Sebec. I'm saddened they have to operate in secrecy and away from prying eyes. However, it shows a change in the culture and I'm thankful there is a place where young people can express themselves free of the bigotry I endured growing up. I think about how much better my life would have been if somebody had said, "It's okay to be you."

HARK THE ANGELS

I think in most remote frontiers, religion can bind a community together; we could say the same for the Junction. The people in these small towns need the grace of a higher power to justify their many hardships. Along with the hand of God moving them through the world, there is also a sense of community when the congregation stands and joins as one to recite scripture or sing hymns.

Brownville Junction gave you four religious options; Catholic, Baptist, Methodist, and Other. While each of these offered their own theology, in the small towns in the far north, they often blended together, overlapped, and supported one another more than they identified their differences. Religion was somewhat flexible and rarely set in stone. People "converted" depending on the priest or minister with the most charisma. Charisma is synonymous with good looking when you're an elder woman. You might attend a Baptist function early on Sunday and attend a Methodist sermon in the evening. In a land with little activity promoting social interactions, church filled this need.

When I was a young child, my mother served as a Sunday school teacher. I remember the singing. I remember arts and crafts. I remember something about David Monahan and a shark. But what I don't remember is the religion itself. Years later I would ask my mother, while visiting Savannah, Georgia, birthplace of the Methodist religion, "Why was I baptized Methodist?" The reply was a simple one: "Because I'm Methodist." It is one of the elements of our predecessors we inherit.

We might be a church-going folk, but I'm glad to say it bordered somewhere between tolerant and accepting.

Christmas Eve brought out the majority of our town to the great halls of our churches. As I walked in with my mother, they handed us candles like every year. The old floors groaned as we tested their strength. While a normal sermon might only fill half the pews, Christmas Eve meant the pews were filled and even standing room was scarce. My mother would stop to smile, offering a "Merry Christmas," for every person. There was my schoolteacher. My mother's school teacher. And standing in the front pew was the tone-deaf lady, who, on every Sunday, came to church to belt hymns.

Pastor Ron, the man who had baptized me, would begin the service with a blessing, and then music would fill the hall. The church elders would read scripture, focusing on passages that promoted goodwill toward our fellow man. We would continue this cycle of positivity until our candles threatened to extinguish.

I stood there, my candle burning as I sang hymns mixed with Christmas songs. This year would be even more special as we had a bell choir. Pastor Ron introduced this group, whose religious affiliation would be classified as "Other". But it never mattered. Gathered together, under one roof, we identified as human; a connective thread that seemed stronger than any of our differences.

The bell choir was beautiful; something new and exotic. One of my high school friends, Tasha Granger, stood in the back of the room, armed with bells amidst her fellow church mates. The songs were beautiful and, despite the religious differences, not a person cared. We met their efforts with standing ovations. The evening turned out beautifully and at the end of the night, the small children rushed the front of the church to open small gifts provided by the community. We would bid our farewells, Pastor Ron standing at the door, saying a blessing to each of us as we passed him by.

I see in the world, religion has the ability to divide us. A belief system with iron-clad rules that create boundaries between one denomination and another. And yet, in Maine, where we have a tendency to label those unlike us, we never used religion as one of those labels. In such a small town, it allowed us the opportunity to come together and abandon our prejudices, even if for a single night.

Evenings spent singing hymns showed us the best of what Maine is.

STAGE MAGIC

In a small town, our educational institutions become the focal point for the community. With few activities happening locally, our elementary school picked up the slack. Between open houses, band performances, or even line dancing, it offered a few hours of entertainment every few months.

I attended Brownville Junction elementary for first and fifth grade. Shortly before I arrived, the town had pooled its resources and created a brand new school. I have no memory of the building before that or even if there was one. Building a new school might not seem like a tremendous ordeal, but in a town where money is tight, and most of the population has retired, this was a noteworthy endeavor. For our two little towns, having our own elementary school meant not needing to ride the bus for a half hour. It also provided a source of pride for the townsfolk.

From the lobby, there were only two directions to go. If you went left, you'd find the spacious classrooms, a library with a sunken floor, and the copy center. But if you weren't a student, you were most likely moving forward into the gym. During the day it served many roles: the cafeteria, a kickball space, or an assembly area. All of these events had the kids on the floor facing the stage. Behind the presenter, long red velvet drapes hung from the ceiling, holding secrets of what might be.

For the kids of Brownville Elementary, that stage provided magic.

As children, we spent most our days consumed by our imaginations. The jungle gym on the playground might be a castle, or the pillows in the library could make a fort. The stage is a place where that imagination can be harnessed and turned into a spectacle for others to see. It served as the backdrop for school plays and concerts. Everybody remembers those times when you performed a Thanksgiving play. Or the Winter Concert, where you would see how long you could make the "shhhhhh" in "We Wish You a Merry Christmas."

Not only did this give the kids something to look forward to, but it offered a Thursday evening of memories for our neighbors. Teachers would stuff our backpacks with fliers and we'd march home, excited for them to see our school activities. They'd pile into the gym while we eagerly waited in the wings of the stage. Our bleachers would fill and they would lay new rows of folding chairs until only standing room remained. Cameras were held high as grandparents immortalized the event.

In small communities, the children provide mirth to an otherwise sleepy town.

Fifth grade was the first time the school offered a formal music class. Unlike the usual recorders or triangles, this class allowed students to practice with proper instruments. I was jealous of students that could rent their saxophones or trumpets (back then that was a lot of money) so I had watched in envy. Sitting on the stage, they performed "The Star Spangled Banner," while one lucky student, stood and belted out the flute solo. We clapped at their efforts while we dined on tuna sandwiches. This single performance would change a significant part of my life. Once I entered sixth grade, I became one of the band geeks and my love of music would lead to a long list of performances.

While this stage gave me my first glimpse into the world of music, it also fostered my love of theater. They allowed us to spend our recesses working on our student productions. I use this term loosely, since we weren't much more than kids refusing to put on our snowsuits to play in the cold. I can't remember if we even gave our play a name. It had something to do with ninjas attacking while kids watched a movie on their cardboard television. Another ninja showed up to protect them, and that was the depth of the plot. What we lacked in script writing abilities, we made up with gusto in our performance. How or why our teacher ever let this happen remains a mystery. At least we showed a passion for the arts. Unfortunately, we weren't given the opportunity to take our show on the road.

The stage also served as an intimate classroom, used when needing to give more private lessons. In the middle of the year, the boys were rewarded with an additional recess. Meanwhile, the girls were ushered onto the stage, hidden away by the velvet curtains. Many of us were happy to have priority on the swings but we speculated on why the girls were being made to stay inside. This eventually gave way to a conspiracy. For whatever reason, the powers that be felt the boys didn't need to know about puberty, mensuration, and hygiene products. It was only later, on the bus home, that one of the girls divulged what had happened. The girls wouldn't receive their bonus recess, free of the boys, until the sixth grade.

Eventually we grew. We left school and started our own families. The next generation is standing on the same stage, providing musical acts for their parents. Little has changed. The small children continue to belt out of key, dressed as snowflakes and reindeer. I had graduated from the stage to the bleachers, and it was only then that I understood the importance of a single stage in our community.

Surrounded by my elders, the grandparents wearing their finest flannels, we gathered to see the children. The cameras have gotten smaller, but the smiles and standing ovations remain the same. The parents probably knew the program by heart. But for the little tykes, there is something magical contained on that stage and behind those curtains. We got the chance to stand in front of the spotlight and pretend we were stars.

And in a small rural town in Maine, we were.

WRITING OUR OWN STORY(IES)

When we lived in Camp Lejeune, my father would bring home a briefcase with a laptop housed inside. I'm sure it contained missile codes or government secrets about the second shooter, but I would use it to write stories. They were simple, as they should be for a fourth grader, but it introduced me to the world of writing. The stories mimicked the gameplay of the original Mega Man, in which there would be an ice chapter and a fire chapter. To my parents' disbelief, I spent hours working on it. And back then, if it kept me quiet, they fostered my endeavors.

Fast-forward to middle school. The writing had stepped up a notch. English classes allowed for creative writing assignments and my love of comics expanded my story telling capabilities. I teamed up with the only other comic book geek in school, Nick Leonard. He served as the John Byrne to my Chris Claremont. If this analogy escapes you, then you might not be a comic book geek.

Together, we started making superhero teams. With my state-of-the-art Brother Word Processor, I wrote the scripts for our adventures. During school we would trade notes, discussing characters we had created during science and math. After school, on the bus to my house, we'd work on drawings, inking and coming up with storylines featuring our own fantastic characters

The plots were derivative, and bordered on plagiarism, but it provided months of activity. For two boys in the middle of nowhere Maine, we dreamed about moving to New York and working for Marvel. We were a couple dozen issues into the first comic when the stories splintered off, needing more titles. It wasn't long before our universe resulted in half a dozen comics. Of course, the ideas flowed faster than the work. The work went nowhere, but it was a long-term voyage into creative writing that started a landslide that would culminate with my creative writing career later in life.

The Word Processor died and took all the stories with it. Moral of the story: back up your work.

This continued into high school, as Nick would sketch, doodle and come up with new graphic stories. There were stories about not so evil villains, zombie pizza delivery men and more. While he continued his drawings, I did the same with my writing. We rarely collaborated after that, but we remained the dynamic duo and often swapped tales about the ideas we made.

Years later, as I looked for material to use for an upcoming National Novel Writing Month, I found stories I had written as presents; "101 Things About You," "The Slut That Lived Down the Street From Me," "The Basketball Whore." The content of the stories and long-form poems might have been vulgar, but there was something eloquent about the approach and the need to express myself.

For me, my fantasy writing was hours spent muddling through my psyche and exploring a world sometimes similar to Maine. In my younger years, the stories always ended half finished. In hindsight, the plots followed my reading trends so closely I might have been sued for plagiarism. But none-the-less, I continued delving into these unknown worlds, looking for a way to put my thoughts to paper. They offered an escape, and if I couldn't find the stories I wanted to read, I wrote them myself.

Write the stories you needed when you were a kid. This has guided my writing career.

I'm sure during this time the only people who read my stories were my editor and friend, Catie Joyce, a group of girls in my senior English class and those that would listen to my ravings at the lunch table. However, it was a great chance to flex some writing muscle and see what people flocked towards. Of all the things I wrote, "The Slut That Lived Down the Street From Me," a poem set to Dr. Seuss, dedicated to Erica Curtis, is what captivated the masses. I can't say that we were a literary lot.

It took years to break away from the stage of writing that focused on emulation. While it was safe, comfortable and relatively easy, it caused boredom and eventually lead to abandoning projects. My parents always claimed I would be a writer and on the myriad of creative outlets I've taken to, it seemed to be the one I revisit most often. Now, over a decade later, I've written many novels. Each one seems to have a thread of the stories that I told as a kid.

I found the scraps of the superhero adventures in a notebook when my parents moved. While incomplete, I found character descriptions and the misbegotten adventures of my superhero team. Staring at those faded lines of text, the story began anew. Despite having an art degree, drawing had never been my forte, so I relied on the written word. I aged the stories, put them through the lens of an adult, and now have published a half-dozen books in my superhero universe with more on the way.

The dream of a kid has been reignited and there are many more tales to tell.

IT MARKED THE END OF FREEDOM

We spent our summers in blissful freedom. Without the limitations of school or the frozen tundra locking us indoors, we spent our fourteen hours of freedom struggling to entertain ourselves. We'd switch between swimming in the lake, going on long drives to the city, or congregating at somebody's house, never doing much of anything. But as with all good things, summer would end and would always be punctuated with the Piscataquis Valley Fair.

Community or county fairs are fairly common. They litter the landscape of America during the summer months. However, they take on an extraordinary level of importance in *small* communities. Instead of being one of the many activities that might tickle your fancy on a weekend, it is the "go to" affair. It's a spectacle that offers a break from the tedium and allows kids to safely run free with their friends. For only a few short days, the fair, nestled at the fairgrounds in Dover-Foxcroft, marked the end of our summers.

I might talk sadly about many aspects of our town growing up. There is lamenting over the loss of industry and the downward spiral exacerbated by economics, but not when it comes to our community events. I can only talk about the sense of wonder woven into the spirit experienced here. The fair itself wasn't large, only taking up the space of a football field. But there was a something wonderful about seeing our towns come together. Even more so, considering we have always had a rivalry between the towns of Milo and Dover.

I would often play with the Community Band in the evening. People gathered and danced as we performed, basking in the lively tunes. We would pack up and put away our instruments, and for the rest of the evening, we became witnesses to the sounds and lights of the carnival.

During the day we embraced our heritage. In barns at one end of the fair, they awarded prizes to farmers and students in 4H clubs for their outstanding services, best vegetables or care of animals. Some evenings you could even witness cows being milked, or sheep being sheared. While some people might scoff at this, I found it humbling, as these people were the foundation of our community. How can you not respect individuals who live off the land and work with their hands? Some may think this was representative of the elders of our community, but I remember many of my classmates who were members of farm families. To this day, I'm still in awe of the lives they lead. And for a few weekends at the end of summer, we celebrated their skill: growing vegetables and raising livestock.

There was also the sound of thunder in the nearby fields as farmers dueled it out in tractor-pulls. In between bouts, there would be a showing of skill with a lasso or even the occasional pig chase. We packed the bleachers and people cheered for the representative of their hometown.

The fair also consisted of rides, games of chance, and of course, obscene amounts of carnival food. I remember the aroma of the fried dough with a hint of sugar filling the night. We grabbed our food, took a seat and gazed upon the people passing. The people fascinated me the most. For many, this was the event of the year, and you could tell they had taken care in their clothing selection for the evening. Kids ran around with their siblings, cousins and friends, enjoying the excitement the event brought with it.

The magic crept in as the sun set and the sky turned dark.

With the sun was long gone, you could lose yourself. We were essentially in a dark field, and only a few floodlights lit the grounds. However, the flashing lights of the rides, the games and the food stands filled the grounds. I can still see the Zipper, spinning its patrons in the air and the large bulbs flashing between the red, white, and blue. This complimented the sounds of cheers, screams and laughter as people tested their metal against terrifying rides.

As we grew older and could drive ourselves, the fair became a social rite of passage. It wasn't simply a place to go and waste away a day; we arranged dates, allowing the euphoria of summer vacation to reach a climax. While many of the rides were fast, and threatened to empty our stomachs of French fries and cotton candy, they held a bit of romance for us, as well. On the Ferris wheel, as you reached the top, hand in hand with your date, you could see the extravaganza in its entirety. And while summer might come to a close, the romance of that evening promised to stretch on forever.

For me, it was a moment in life where the stars seemed to align. The world moved around you, filling the senses, and you could either stand and watch or take part. While I'm sure there are many things that have change in the place I still call home, I have a feeling this end of the summer gathering of towns will remain a constant.

I miss the flashing of those carnival lights.

WITH THE VILLAGE

I often ponder what it's like for people who grew up in bigger cities? The ability to walk to the store, or see a movie on a whim, were foreign concepts in my youth. Even grocery shopping often required a chunk of the day. Our free time revolved around finding new activities we could do outside. Visiting the mall or congregating at a coffee shop weren't options, so we relied on creativity.

When I think about it, I have mixed feelings about where I grew up. At its core, Brownville Junction had a sense of community I don't think I'd ever trade. If you fell down and scraped your knee while roller-skating, I could find help at the nearest house. They would bandage your cuts without hesitation. Then they would send you on your way, or toss you in the car and drive you home. I believe I've had both happen to me.

During the winter months, you would frequently find a car stuck in the snowbank on the side of the road. More than once, I was the driver of that car. In the middle of the wilderness, you might face walking to the nearest house in sub-zero temperatures. However, the next car would always stop, offering to help however they could. They might offer to tow your car, give you a ride to a phone, or in my case, call your parents and tattle on your bad driving.

It takes a village to raise a child, holds true in these small communities.

I now live in a condo and, have to say, I enjoy the diversity of my neighbors. Next door is a blue-collar electrician, and sharing another wall is a young Indian couple and their child. Upstairs we have a member of the National Guard and a police officer, but out of those individuals, I don't know a single name. Not only do I not know their names, we only talk during emergencies or the infrequent door holding when entering the building. While we live on top of one another, we remain strangers.

In Brownville Junction, there was a vast distance between neighbors. However, the people in the town remained long enough to learn names. To this day, I can name the occupants of every house adjacent to my childhood home. I can also tell you random tidbits about them, maybe when they moved there, where they worked and just because of my age, I could tell you about their kids. I lived in a densely populated area of this rural town; I can mentally traverse the streets and, one by one, name the occupants of the houses. We were many things to one another, but we were never strangers.

Growing up in this environment created the atmosphere of a true village. There were friendly hellos and folks stopped to wave as you passed by. Pleasantries were exchanged while pumping gas, and they revealed local town gossip while waiting in line at the local store. At any moment, a local might stop by for coffee for no other reason than to visit and swap tales. There was always a pot of warm coffee at our house. I often walked downstairs to a neighbor in our kitchen, enjoying a cup of coffee, sometimes chatting with my father or waiting for my grandmother to get ready for shopping. Our doors were seldom locked, and the invitation to come in didn't need words. We set aside afternoon plans, and the world slowed as we partook in one another's company.

Now, when neighbors knock, I assume my television is too loud or they are informing us of an upcoming party. You stand at the door and make sure they don't get the impression there is an invitation to enter. I think this comes to mind as I get to the age when you wish your friends, neighbors or family were close enough you could stop for a chat midday and then be onto your chores. Brief exchanges replaced these moments via virtual rooms and short texts. Beyond the boundaries of these small towns, life moves far too fast for a perpetually brewed coffee.

It's these times I definitely miss the village.

RUSTLE OF THE LEAVES

Fall in New England is a different level of magic. As the leaves begin their winter recession, fading from green to red, to yellow, to brown, the entire state looks like an oil painting. Each morning the air is crisp, threatening snow, but not quite cold enough to invoke a need for winter warriors to begin their routines. Clothes move from the shorts and t-shirts to jeans and sweaters. We lament the waning summer and shortening days as we bolster ourselves for the impending storms.

I've lived away from Maine for more than a decade. Moving to a big city has had its perks, and there are upsides Maine can never offer. I now live in rural Massachusetts, the gateway between city life and the life I miss back home. Outside my window are a plethora of trees and a giant yard I share with sixty other renters.

It's beautiful and the perfect blend of the two spaces. We will watch as the massive trees transition to autumn. The marking of the end of summer will come two weeks later than it should. Unlike Maine, the trees here are slow to let go of long days and warm nights.

I have a yard, but it's not *my* yard. Eventually, the leaves will scatter on the grass, and our landscapers will mow and clean the yard. It'll return to its pristine self. It's the bed of decaying leaves on the ground that helps usher in this sense of magic. Never in my adult life did I think I would miss the hassle.

I want to rake the leaves.

Living in the Junction, we had a decent sized yard. Big enough to play in, but not so big the upkeep required a weekend of backbreaking work. In the summer, I could get away with spending the morning mowing the grass and be free before the sun threatened to turn me into a lobster. In the winter, my father's fondness for snow blowing kept me warm and indoors. But in the fall, with woods all about us and massive oak trees across the street, our yard needed constant cleanup.

I loved the ritual of raking the leaves. While the air held a cool breeze, it hadn't gotten cold enough to require long pants. I'm sure for many in my town it marked the transition from farming to harvesting. Mainers prepared one last push before winter forced us into our homes for the next several months.

In my yard, there would be dozens of piles, looking like collections of multi-colored construction paper. While the leaves themselves have a vibrancy to them, it's the scent of the air that creates the complete effect. The Junction always had a hint of smoke in the air. Many people burned their leaves, and plumes of smoke rose into the air throughout the town. Chimneys would be prepared for the cold months and between the two, there was a perpetual char hanging in the air. And though our houses weren't crammed side by side, it only took one person before it created a cascade and we all joined.

Despite having no trees in our own yard, I worked up a healthy sweat each time

I went out to save our grass from being smothered in the winter. But more than manual labor, it was a chance to connect with the earth. Brownville Junction had many people who worked the land for survival. I wasn't one of them, but I respected them and to some degree envied their symbiotic relationship with Mother Nature. In the fall, you weren't fighting the land by shoveling snow, and you weren't constantly protecting it from the sun's harsh rays. You were simply part of the grander process. The experience was, and still is, humbling.

In all those years, I never truly grew up. With one massive pile sitting just beyond our front porch, it was impossible to resist. As a child, they expected I'd jump in the pile or be buried alive. At some point, it becomes childish, but I never claimed to be mature. In high school, I would spend more time than necessary collecting all the leaves into a single pile, an adult sized pile. I'd jump from the porch into the pile and remember the fun of being a kid. However, as I got older, the pile seemed to shrink. It continued until I got old enough to fear needing a trip to the hospital.

I never thought I would say it, but I wish I had a yard with leaves needing to be raked.

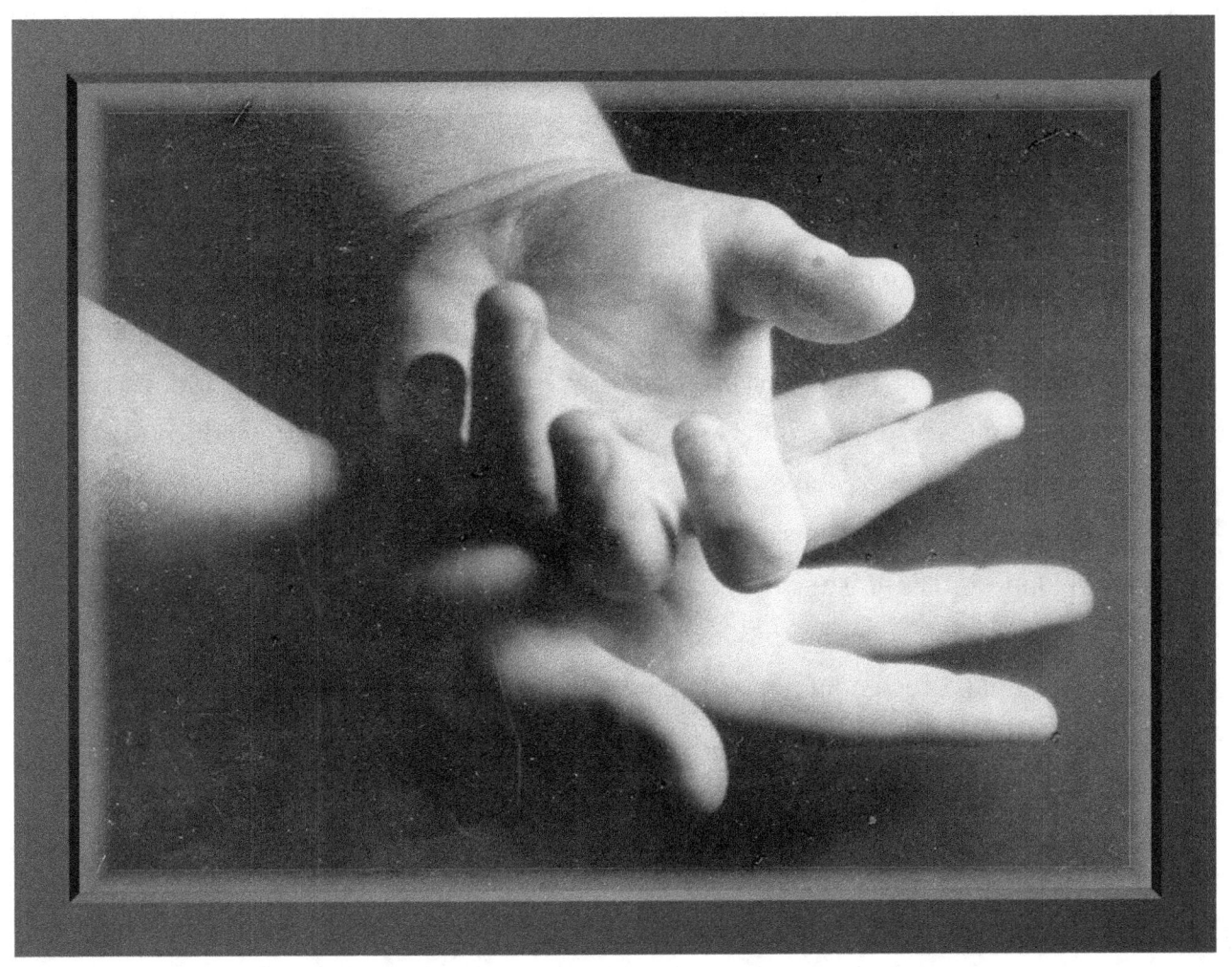

THE MAINE WORK ETHIC

Applying for jobs in education results in a series of tedious interviews. It starts with Human Resources and evolves to the department chair. If you've made it that far, it then results in meeting the principal of the school along with potential colleagues. During my last interview, I sat across from the head of the school and, after a long period of examining my credentials, he stopped and asked, "Did you get time off school for farming?" At first I thought he was a smartass, and I was ready to lash out in a defensive ramble about the awesomeness of Maine. He set the resume down on the table and leaned forward with the follow-up, "What was it like growing up there? It must be a different world."

My soon-to-be boss had grown up in Northern New Hampshire. Not as prestigious as Maine, but we'll consider his tribe the black sheep of our New England family. The conversation stopped posturing on degrees and professional development activities, and proceeded to get personal. The only way to understand the pulse of Maine is by telling stories.

I'm sure there are other states that have seasonal vacations. We had three. I told him that, in September, students might miss a week of school while they helped their family with the potato harvest. Later it would be a week for raking blueberries. During hunting season, we didn't get the entire day off, but we allowed those with permits to leave early to make sure they had plenty of daylight to make their catches.

One of my classmates missed a week of school every year to take part in blueberry raking. Don't mock; it is the hardest day of work I can imagine. I attempted it once and my back didn't last an entire day. Those in the fields, surviving the heat and filling the small green containers, will always have my respect.

I also spoke about it being a small town. He listened intently as I explained we were twelve towns tied together as a single school district. The school I interviewed at had a student population that exceeded the entirety of those twelve towns. And while I told these stories, he listened, only chiming in when he needed more information.

He asked me, "Ever shoot one, a deer I mean?"

Shoot a deer? No. Hit one with my first car and have the folks up the street call the cops and my dad? Then skin it on the side of the road and toss the carcass on a tarp rolled out in the trunk of my car? Then yes, of course. I am a Mainer, after all.

After an hour of discussing the unique attributes of being young in northern Maine, he grabbed my resume and continued the interview. There came the inevitable moment when he asked me about my strengths. I talked about my work ethic and my ability to give one hundred and ten percent of my attention to whatever task I need to complete.

He responded to my comment, "Of course. You're from Maine."

For all the stories I can tell of Maine, there comes an endurance mustered by its people. Whether it be their ability to survive a never-ending winter, or overcoming exhaustion while tending to the land, they push through the hardship. As a kid, I never understood the work ethic of my parents, but in hindsight I can see it was bred, cultivated, and nurtured throughout my youth.

There are moments when I experience an overwhelming sense of pride, and I feel the need to bust out my Black Bears sweatshirt and slip into my "wool socks and sandals." This was one of these moments. Despite what we may think, our Maine heritage can define us.

I received a phone call before I reached my car in the parking lot. They offered me the position.

13 CHANNELS OF MAINE

I frequently refer to the rest of the world as civilized, and I fear I'm giving people the wrong idea about Maine. Yes, it's true we have an overabundance of dirt roads and that some people might still use outdoor plumbing. But it's not like we fend off wild animals with knives, and eat what we kill. Wait, I might have lost my argument.

To outsiders, it may look like we've hunkered down in our state and neglected the world. It's not as if, in 1820, we left the civilization and became a sovereign nation where we blockade foreign communication. But with only three functioning radio stations in my town, I can see where the stigma originated.

Growing up, we had thirteen television stations, eventually.

When I lived on the military base in North Carolina, we had more channels than we had time to watch. However, that changed when I moved to Maine. I remember we had the staples, CBS, NBC, ABC, and PBS, but channels such as the Family Channel and USA also captivated us. The rest of them were fillers.

As a kid, I would run to my bedroom every weekday at 7:00PM. I had pilfered my grandmother's old black and white television and I'd get comfortable knowing I couldn't pull my eyes off the pixilated screen. I adored "Zorro," and the live-action "Batman." The latter might have been in color, but I wouldn't know that for years to come, and truth be told, it didn't matter.

Television was a simple pleasure we had in the evening before starting our bedtime rituals. I'd be allowed to watch "Fresh Prince of Bel Air" and then "Blossom," and then it was time to crawl into bed. To watch them both, I'd have to take a shower before bed. When the credits started at the end of the first show, I'd bolt for the bathroom and be back, smell of shampoo before the next started. I spent most of my childhood outside getting dirty and running around with friends. But in the evenings, television served as a way to wind down.

This would continue through my younger years, but then came the day in high school when our world changed. Out of nowhere, they bumped us to twenty-three stations. Ten extra channels that hosted shows I had only read about in my grandmother's "TV Guide." I hardly knew what to do with myself. What kind of visual wonderland was this?

I remember the day clearly. Brandy Burns came to my house to partake in the awesomeness of our five-hundred-pound, twenty-seven-inch floor television. We ran from the bus, down my street, throwing our backpacks on the floor and heading directly to the living room. What's the first thing we would watch? One would think we hicks would be curious about how the rest of the world carried on so, of course, we would tune into international news to see the perseverance of mankind! No, we were far too immature for this. None of that reality showed up on my television set that day.

Instead, we watched "Mighty Morphin' Power Rangers."

Laugh (it is comical in hindsight) but it was television in a way I had never seen. Despite watching China Beach with my mother or M.A.S.H. with my grandmother, this offered a new and different type of entertainment. Of course, it catered to the lowest common denominator, but it also tickled the imagination.

This horrible monstrosity of television programming fascinated me. It was also back-to-back with "X-Men," which is the real reason we ran home. But, first we had to enjoy the outlandishness of teenagers trying to save the world. You'd think this would be a dark little secret. But after a recent message from my high school best friend, saying he and his wife were watching the series from the start, I couldn't help but recall how I subjected everybody to this bit of television magic. I remember at times the bus would take too long getting us home, and we would miss part of it. Not being able to watch the riveting plot line, outstanding dialog, and the state-of-the-art graphics became a source of anxiety. However, we pieced together the intricate storyline of how the <SPOILER ALERT> evil Green Ranger transformed into the awesomeness of the White Ranger. I think that was the demise of my connection with the outside world. How can a teenager be expected to do anything when the fate of the world rests in the hands of Megazords?

Now, with a thousand channels at our disposal, we spend more time debating what we're going to watch than actually watching it. We no longer skip between channels to avoid commercial breaks. There is a channel catering to every personality. Love Japanese game shows? We've got it. Want to watch crafters make a dress out of items found at the pet store? I think there are two. But as a kid, we were required to watch the few available shows offered. To this day, the sound of Adam West's voice reminds me of hiding in our attic, lying on the floor only inches from the television, sounding out every BAM, WHAM and POW.

No, we are civilized, but we *are* simple. It is just another aspect of what makes us Mainers.

THE SNOWFLAKE WARS

I have found the threat of impending blizzards brings Massachusetts to a standstill. The fear of white powder dusting the ground sends the residents to the store to buy copious amounts of water, milk, eggs and toilet paper. It has affectionately become known as a "French Toast Alert." Milk, eggs, bread, the staple during the apocalypse. Stores become a fight for survival as people wrestle their way to the freezers and try to scavenge the last dozen eggs in the back of the cooler. Every broadcast depicting flurries causes this over-the-top panic. I find it beyond comical, especially considering they are part of the great North and suffer through wintery onslaught every year.

The threat of snow in Maine brings about a very different effect on its natives.

Snowfall has struck as early as October and has been known to last through May. Snow isn't a single, onetime occurrence for the residents of Maine; it's a state of mind that lasts for months. And no matter how much the weather man threatens, we always have natives who will recount the Great Blizzard of '77. That winter, the snow was high enough that people had to climb out of their second-floor windows and be leery of power lines as they drove snowmobiles to aid in rescue efforts. An impending storm from inches to feet hardly receives attention. No, I can't say we fear it; it has become a way of life ingrained in our being.

While we might not fear the snow, we are a people who know when it is time to take action. We prepare before the snow begins to fall. Unlike the rest of New England, the memory of a Mainer spans more than a sports season. We know the snow will come. The residents finish maintaining lawns, pulling the last of the vegetables, and covering any shrubs. We check the machines in the house. Is the oil tank ready for ongoing abuse? Is the backup heater working? When was the last time we checked the cans of fuel in the garage? We check the tires, trees, and skis. Every vehicle has a full tank of gas long before the first flake flutters from the sky.

And while we might be prepared, the real fun doesn't begin until snow arrives. Mainers do not wait out a storm. We are not passive recipients of Mother Nature. Thanks to this frigid upbringing, the residents act much like the white sheets of falling snow: a force of nature. Every hour they can be found outside, shoveling, clearing a path to their doors. It's back breaking work, and during the worst storms, sleep might not be an option. We ensure our pipes work, our furnaces won't die, and that our roofs won't collapse.

Amidst this hustle of activity, the spirit of Maine rises to the surface. There is a sense of, "We're in this together" that happens with every storm. We never shovel just our driveways when you know your neighbor has a slipped disk or an underlying heart condition. There is a sense of civic duty to help your kin. My father served as a prime example of this mentality. In a snowstorm, I could find him within an eight house radius, shoveling, blowing snow and cleaning roofs. Phone calls would come in asking for help and with such a large elderly population, it was expected that every able body pitched in. It wasn't unheard of for it to continue into the night, streetlights illuminating the snow as people worked furiously to clear it away.

Upon surviving the night, we celebrated the next day. Baked goods might be paid forward or stories of the work shared over a pot of coffee. We stood in our yards, eyeing the work. While nature threw down four feet of snow, we repositioned it. Our handiwork could be seen as neighbors waved, shouting their thanks as they took stock of the damage.

But I can't leave it there; every Mainer who works hard plays even harder. This is the moment when you hear snowmobiles clearing the garage and skating along the road towards hidden trails. Snow suits are thrust onto the children as they build forts in the fresh powder. They load ice fishing shacks into pickups and they speed towards the local lake. We are the children of winter, and despite the dwindling hours of daylight, it couldn't crush our spirits.

And for those that didn't care to partake in the winter festivities, we had our gathering locations. After any snowstorm, you'd be hard pressed to find a seat at Mo's or Smith's to have your morning coffee. The tales began with "We lost power for two hours," or "Our pipes froze," or even, "Was out until 3:00AM shoveling." We talk about them like they're wars we've come home from, our scars visible and our bravery proudly displayed for all. We didn't discuss the next impending storm, instead, we focused on the victory.

More than this, we know it may only be an afternoon until we're called back for another tour. With our shovels on our shoulders and jackets pulled tight, this was one of the moments that defined who we are. After all, the next snowstorm was a victory we had yet to claim.

"CLINT EASTWOOD" OF MAINE

Maine is a different world. I almost want to refer to it as the Outlands, a place untouched by civilization's rules and laws. We view the stern glance of justice as a wavering suggestion. With only one police officer for several towns, we have to rely more on our individual ethics than we do the guidelines governing us as a nation. While this can often get us into trouble, and it often does, we uphold a "live and let live" mentality. We might judge you horribly for straying, but rarely does it come to anything more.

Because of our self-reliance, nearly every house contains a firearm. It might be a simple handgun used for protection, but more often than not, there is a cabinet with a range of tools at our disposal. The diversity of our hunting season might require a different rifle for each animal, so we stocked them all. In my household, a rifle sat in the back of our coat closet, loaded and ready to defend the home if necessary.

While many would make a case for removing firearms from the home, I feel that in Maine, we have respect for these tools. Where some may think leaving a loaded gun in a house is dangerous, my parents raised me to understand it wasn't a toy and was only to be used as a means of protection. This knowledge preceded my first experience with a gun, but the knowledge was there none-the-less.

My father later taught me how to use a gun. Instead of a fancy gun range, we found ourselves in one of the many sandpits on the edge of town. I'm sure this story will be familiar with many of the youth in Maine. It not only served as a bonding moment between my father and me, a secret we wouldn't tell mom for years, but it would become necessary as I got older. My father had grown up hunting and was several years younger than me when he started. This is the way of Maine. As we parked, he went through all the information I needed. Having served in the military, he treated it as if I was in basic training. He covered the parts of the gun, how to load and unload, and how to handle the weapon. Unlike basic training, he also discussed the ethics behind holding that tool, when it was safe to use, the situations where I might need it, and at each step, he instilled the fear of what would happen if I treated it in any other manner.

I listened and nodded along. He finally offered me the gun in one hand and put the bullets in the other. I'll admit, I was enamored and thought by the end of the day I was going to be a sharpshooter, recruited by the CIA to run black-ops. Part of me feared the power I held, but somewhere in my head I thought I'd have it mastered in the next fifteen minutes and I'd be combatting spies by lunch.

I don't remember the make or model of the silver revolver. It had a heft to it, heavier than I expected as I clumsily attempted to load rounds into the chamber. My father moved behind me as I prepared my journey to combatting evil. I remember cocking back the hammer and then quickly squeezing the trigger. The world went blank and silent except for the ringing in my ears.

Eventually I could hear the sound of my dog barking from in the truck and my father laughing at me. The shock of the gun firing had sent me backward. As my arms jerked upward, I landed on my ass. In his lengthy training, he had forgotten to mention the term "kick" or "recoil." Apparently, this bit of humor is par for the course when initiating your son into the brotherhood.

"Did I hit it?" I asked about the coffee can fifty feet away from me.

What started as a chuckle turned into roaring laughter. I spent the next half hour taking shots at the coffee can, a foe who proved to be craftier and more skilled than my shooting. I got comfortable with it, or at least I didn't wind up knocking myself over again. The sound of the bang didn't force me to turn my head away, and I learned to hold the gun steady so I wouldn't accidentally smack myself in the forehead.

My father, on the other hand, an expert marksman, defeated his own coffee can before it could execute its villainous plans. I remember being in awe of how fast he moved. It didn't require breathing techniques or staring down the barrel. He raised the gun, squinted with one eye, and fired.

I never defeated my coffee can. But I left there surer of myself. I knew I was learning a skill that would let me be more self-sufficient should the need arise. Despite my lack of grace, the fear about wielding the weapon had faded away. I had been initiated into a specific sect of Mainers, and I always took that membership seriously.

Years later, I would visit a friend who had been a cop in a former life. As I went searching through a drawer for dish towels (because we do hide them in mysterious places) my hand bumped a revolver. I didn't think twice about pulling it out of the drawer, feeling the weight, checking the safety, and snapping open the cylinder to see if it was loaded. Later, we would recount stories about how our fathers taught how to shoot and how the first shot landed us both firmly on our backsides.

We don't all carry a gun like we're preparing for war, but we are taught to respect the tools we experience in our day-to-day lives. This is another instance of the threads that weave together to create the identity of who we are. We prefer to rely on the kindness of our neighbors and fellow Mainers, but let it be known, we also prepare for the worst.

LIVE WITHOUT APOLOGIES

To say I love my grandmother is an understatement. Gloria Jean Cowing served as a second mother for most of my life. Hair white by the time she hit fifty, she had lived a full life, even if she didn't talk about it. Divorced from a bastard husband, she opened her home to us, and thus started our life as a nuclear family.

During my teen years, it was a rarity that we were under the same roof each night. My father worked second shift and my mother would attend the University of Rhode Island and only come home for long weekends. This meant that at the corner of Ryder Avenue and Page Street, it was Mimi and me, taking on the world. She took on the role of my partner in crime, babysitter, stand-in parent, "Wheel of Fortune" buddy, and homework approver. This vibrant, sharp, thick-skinned woman served as the counter-balance for my recklessness. Overnight, things changed.

Mimi developed dementia.

I don't remember it as a slow progression. It's not as if bits of her personality slipped. When I came home from college, she sat on our porch as she always did, but I didn't recognize her. She wore the same clothes, and had the same voice, but the light I cherished had gone dark. The woman who shoved me in the car and chased trains so I could get the conductors to pull the whistle had vanished. Instead, there was a woman who counted down the days until it'd end. Or worst, a woman who was unaware of what was happening.

The moments of lucidity were few. Mistaken for my father, or my deceased brother, she attempted to make sense of her surroundings. Unsure of how to interact with this stranger, I fled the porch. An imposter has ransacked my grandmother's closest and taken up residence in her favorite chair. I didn't want to know this person. The confusion on her face broke my heart. I wanted the woman I idolized as a child, my Mimi.

Once upon a time, we were thick as thieves. We shared tubs of ice cream while watching the roller derby. On Friday nights, we could be found in front of the television watching wrestling matches as if we were active participants. And in the morning, we watched the hummingbirds flutter about the front porch while competing in word searches. In the list of duties required to keep a household running, she watched over the sink, scrubbing dirty dishes as if it were her job.

She had raised three children and should have been done with that chapter in her life. But when she offered us a home, she assumed the burden of parent once more. While she struggled with being a parent to her adult daughter, she didn't hesitate as she became my second mother. It was never easy. She learned to give and take. The amount of eye rolling between her and my mother turned epic as they threw up their hands and stormed off. The truth of it was, she, mom, and I were three identical personalities trying to exist in one house.

Our relationship was never perfect; we fought relentlessly until somebody claimed the other was being unreasonable. As I reached my teen years, she struggled with my constant pushing at boundaries. She wielded guilt like a flaming sword, had no remorse when targeting me and my destructive behavior. Slowly we drifted apart. The dementia had taken hold, and I was too self-involved to see the bits of her personality slipping away. I pushed it out of my head, fearful of the inevitable.

I know little about my grandmother in her youth. There is a dark spot on our family history we simply avoid. But I have photographs, and they tell a tale of a beautiful, hard working woman. Like us, she lived with her mother in the same house. She worked for years at the local convenient store and made sure every customer knew exactly how many shopping days remained before Christmas. The town knew her as a knitter; I had more mittens and slippers than necessary, but she was always knitting me an extra pair.

In those last years, she took to feeling guilty for things she had no control over. She accepted the burdens of the world. A simple comment about a looming storm elicited a, "I'm sorry," as if she dictated the rain. I wanted to shake her and tell her this was not the way to spend her twilight years. I wanted to see the woman who used to cruise behind the steering wheel of her Skylark. But the woman I spent my life admiring never returned. I think she made peace with life.

Gloria Jean Cowing. Mimi. The only real grandmother I had ever known passed away.

Only our late matriarch could bring together this fragmented family, but at the core of her being, she feared she wasn't loved. After decades of abuse and a history of abandonment, I don't think she ever shook these feelings. The obituary went out in the paper and our phone rang morning, noon, and night. Neighbors stopped by, casseroles in hand, eyeing the empty chair on the porch. We proved her so, so very wrong.

Glo was loved. Gloria was loved. Mimi was loved.

The crowd shuffling into Lary's Funeral Home proved her wrong. It wasn't the number of bodies, or the stream of tears that revealed her impact on the community. When asked to share stories, we stood, each ready to recite a tale of the woman we honored. We said our goodbyes as we spoke of the amazing woman she had been and the legacy she left behind. Her children, grandchildren and great grandchildren gathered, paying respect to the head of our family.

Living with a grandparent in a Maine community filled with retirees, you hear them mention a friend or former classmate found in the obituaries. Her passing was no different, a reminder of our dwindling time on this planet. Gloria Jean Cowing was the embodiment of Maine. By sheer determination, she drove that spirit into me. Because of her, I refuse to be sorry for my actions. I refuse to apologize for being who I am. I refuse to live a life with regrets.

She lays buried next to my brother, and I have nothing but fond memories of the silver haired woman. From her demands that there be cranberry sauce at Thanksgiving, to the way she always wore a sweatshirt with flowers or cats, her memory lives on. And when I pass, I'll know that in these pages, Gloria Jean Cowing lives forever.

HAPPY BIRTHDAY FALL

For many, the fall marks the start of the school year. Each September we'd begin our quest for school supplies and new shoes. This period of hustle happens prior to the transition from green to red, marking the start of the new season. The young kids celebrate seeing their friends during the week, and the teens begin the march toward graduation. In September, I have a list of events to celebrate, but the most notable is my birthday.

I am a Virgo. I share my birthday with Grandparents Day. I only had to survive two grueling weeks of school before the big day came about. My birthday started a cascade of similar events. Between myself, my brother, grandmother, and even our dog, there was never a lack of baked goods speckled with candles.

My mother, a skillful homemaker in my youth, insisted on demonstrating her ability to bake. Each year, she'd make a sheet cake in the form of whatever character was popular. Of course, this was only the start of the madness. Each birthday came with a theme, from Simpsons to He-Man. The tablecloth, napkins, hats and noise makers all matched. She was meticulous, and when she finally decided that dealing with a classroom worth of children was too much of a hassle, she'd book the playroom at the local Burger King. I'm quite certain this level of detail was more for her sake than mine.

As a kid, this was a wonderful time to have a birthday. You spent just enough time with your classmates to know who would and would not be invited to your party. Unfortunately, as I reached my teen years, we had left the warmth of the South for the early onset of fall in the north. The temperature went from the low eighties to sixties. My birthday went from a late summer to fall activity.

My parents decided, in an effort to keep me out of trouble, they would install a pool. Above ground, this massive circle of water was big enough to hold twenty people. I spent many days swimming laps, practicing my flips or floating back and forth in an inner tube. This became my sanctuary during the summer, and it was rare you'd find me anywhere else. Once I reached high school, I decided it was time to celebrate my birthday with a good ol' fashioned pool party. I had laser-like focus, and neither heaven nor hell would stop me. We would say farewell to summer as we celebrated the day of my birth.

This plan came with difficulties.

I slipped my friends formal invitations. My parents were away for the day, and knowing my inability to get in trouble, they allowed my party to take over my house. Friends arrived as expected, each wearing a bathing suit with a towel draped over their shoulders. At this point, they were still game to frolic in the water. But when one girl dipped her toes into the water, her yelp announced that swimming might not happen. Even with the thermal blanket on the pool, it had barely made it to sixty-five degrees. While the girls spread their towels in the grass to work on their tans, the boys braved the cold. The hissing and short lived swim session signaled I would label my pool party birthday as a bust.

We would try it again the next year. However, the temperature continued to drop in September. When the attendees arrived, this time they would be wearing shorts and sweatshirts. Only Nick Leonard would brave the water, claiming it was perfectly warm. The goosebumps along his arms told a different story. The rest of us watched as we shivered on the deck.

As an adult, I can understand that my birthday held multiple of layers of significance in our household. Only two weeks before my brother's birthday, it started a countdown. Shortly after that, we'd celebrate my grandmother's birth. The next day of note was my brother's death. The turbulence of celebrating and then mourning is an apt description for how my family functioned. And despite the looming date of Jason's death, my family put everything on hold to make sure I stood front and center on my birthday.

Even with a certain macabre cloud looming over my special day, it remained just that, special. As high school went on, I'd often wake to my mother already on the road to college or my father still at work. Despite the empty house, when I bound down the stairs and turned into the kitchen, there'd be a cupcake with a candle shoved through the frosting.

Though, they still owe me for the year they left a Twinkie with a candle next to it.

APOLOGY ACCEPTED

Like most families, mine had more than its shares of dysfunction. While we spent little time together as a unit, my parents did right by me. In fleeting moments, they developed and fostered my moral compass. Historically, the Flagg clan had less than a noble connotation. But my parents recognized this and emphasized growing beyond a label applied by our surname. I knew at the end of the day, I had a responsibility to be a better man.

During my teen years, a select handful of students at school attempted to make my life hell. It seldom came to the forefront, but in a town steeped in tradition, anything new will eventually become the topic of ridicule. I have always been a large guy with a "don't fuck with me" attitude. It bordered on comical when the group of boys trying to get a rise out of me were tiny, barely breaking one hundred and fifty pounds. While their ringleader attempted to puff out his chest and look threatening, his three companions would step back. If it came to trading blows, even against the four of them, I had little to fear.

Amongst my friends were four of the larger kids in schools; seniors, and by definition, quite popular. It should have been obvious that the confrontation had less to do with me being gay, and more with insecurities, but as a teenager, I didn't have that level of awareness. Standing across from us were four kids with home situations that bordered on abusive. They didn't come from means, and even within the school we knew them as screw-ups. No, them calling me a faggot had little to do with me and everything to do with them.

It continued throughout the school year. There were scuffles, and I broke more than one nose in a fight. But mostly, I rolled my eyes. With each slur they hurled, my skin thickened. I didn't need to reply and give their words power. I had ambition, and it would take me beyond the walls of our small towns. And they'd spend the majority of their adult lives behind bars.

However, despite this harsh reality, there was a deeper story to be had. One day, while driving my father's beater between school and home, I neared Sweat Hill. This rise in the road marked the division of towns and had been aptly named for how the horses struggled to climb it before vehicles appeared. On the side of the road, a bully walked, drenched through from the heat. I drove by without a negative thought in my head. As I reached the hill, I realized how far he had to walk before reaching his house. Turning around, I went back for him.

It might sound like an unsettling thing to do in this day and age. However, our towns had rules for hitchhikers. We offered rides to those who needed them. Most often, we knew the person, and if we didn't, we gambled. With the Appalachian Mountains running adjacent to our homes, it was common to offer a hiker a ride. We did it because it was the right thing to do.

He accepted the ride. We drove in silence other than me confirming his destination. There was an awkwardness and uncomfortable air between us. But without prompting, he started a conversation. I responded in kind, attempting to make a connection. We had nothing in common other than our zip code. Ultimately he spoke, changing the very core of who I was. He looked away from me, staring at the floor and whispered, "I'm sorry."

The apology was out of context for the conversation. He didn't need to elaborate; I knew where it was being directed. I had seen the look on his face during the first fight I had with his ringleader. Those two words were so loaded, it's taken me years to unravel. I had my suspicions about his own sexuality, and I wondered if this was about to lead to his own coming out. It didn't, and understanding our upbringing, I realized that many weren't awarded the luxury of a family who supported them. Now, as an adult, I see his apology as the summary of a monologue; his inability to break a cycle of intolerance.

At the time, I experienced anger at his inability to go against the grain and stand up for me during the many skirmishes I faced over the years. I held a resentment that kept me silent, unable to respond to his apology. Of the few regrets I have from my youth, this holds a spot on the shelf. I wish my seventeen year-old self had replied, "Accepted."

I still believe in paying-it-forward, putting positive energy into the universe for no other reason than the self-satisfaction. My parents taught me to do good without the expectation of it being returned. They taught me that, in the face of adversity, I must hold to my beliefs and act as the bigger man. That day, in a beat-up old truck, the world returned a kindness. Sometimes, it takes a while to realize it's happened.

GOSSIP FROM THE JAIL CELL

I have spent time behind bars.

I should elaborate before my awkward and suggestive comment is taken in the wrong context. For several years, my father worked as a corrections officer in Charleston when we moved to Maine. The jobs for ex-Marines are few and far between in this state. When your resume includes jumping out of airplanes, shooting people and commanding hordes of troops, your job options are limited. Many turned to the police force or other similar civil services. My father was one of many veterans that oversaw a minimum security corrections center.

For my father, a man who loves his rules, guidelines and walking the straight-and-narrow, this position was tailored for ex-military like him. Your gun is replaced with pepper spray, your orders are barked by commanding officers and you oversee people whose crimes include money laundering, tax evasion, and illegal hunting. It might not have been as prestigious as the Marine Corps, and the uniforms might not have been as flashy, but it allowed my father the ability to continue making the world a better place.

I'm sure, given the chance, the officers would have parachuted into work each day.

On base, there was plenty of bragging by saying my father was a Gunnery Master Sergeant. When he issued orders, people listened without question. This doesn't carry over into the world of hardened criminals, or even soft criminals. The guy imprisoned for excessive jaywalking would throw temper tantrums when asked to return to his quarters for lights out. The leader of the crime syndicate of unlicensed sanitation workers (i.e., illegal dumping of trash) would throw down every chance he could. Worse yet, because there wasn't the constant threat of being shot, the officers lacked the fear instilled into soldiers during basic training. Nobody respects a man with pepper spray.

To be fair, this was such a low-security facility I'm surprised they didn't host a "Bring your daughter to work" day. There were prison cells hidden away in the building, but mostly, the facility was like a college campus. Inmates walked between buildings freely, and each day I visited my father, I expected to watch a rousing game of hacky sack in the quad. I would drive up the road greeted by signs reading "Don't pick up Hitchhikers." You would think this common sense for the road leading to a "prison," but of course, I picked up inmate wandering back to the facility. They worked in the woods during the day, unsupervised, and they rushed to return to the facility before curfew. I would drive up and be greeted by random men holding axes or chainsaws all the time. What was there to fear? This was standard protocol in the state of Maine. It took me years before I realized the overly pleasant guy working on painting the gatehouse was an inmate and not an employee. As part of his work detail, he built birdhouses with such care it bordered on an art form, a trait only possessed by cold hard killers. In hindsight, I think the inmates were nicer than the guards.

It wasn't difficult to get in and find my father. Sometimes I would be escorted, but more often than not, they'd say, "He's in Building Five." Either my wretched sense of direction or inability to read signs resulted in me being escorted by an inmate.

While the corrections facility was a rehabbed military outpost, there came a time when the state expanded on their juvenile detention facilities. This resulted in a state-of-the-art prison (and I mean *prison*) being built on the premise. The college feel I had grown accustomed to, was replaced by this massive brick building with fencing, and a recreation area surrounded by layers of barbed wire. Unlike the prisoners my father oversaw, The Mountain View Youth Development Center would be a medium security unit. It was like every episode of *Oz* or *Prison Break* you could imagine.

While my father never worked there, he would frequently go in while they were constructing the interior. I found the high-tech security to be fascinating. Pressure sealed doors, security cameras, automated door locks, the magnitude and scope of work made my geeky heart sing. We'll ignore that it was being used to house youth whom society had failed.

On one visit, they were working on the automation locks for some of the solitary cells. My father offered me up as the sacrifice. A light shove forced me into the cell. The door locks worked. And that's when my father decided this was a suitable substitute for babysitting. He had co-workers to jab with or exchange war stories about the good ol' days. Meanwhile, I sat in a ten by ten cell that didn't even have the bed or toilet installed. The lovely shade of robin's egg blue was the only thing to note. It could have been an hour or a month. After the first six minutes, I was concocting a plan of escape, a way to breach the gate, climb the fence, and run to freedom. By the eleventh minute, I had started my own gang and come up with a secret handshake.

My father would later claim it built character. I always joke that if I had superpowers, I'd be a super villain. Now the truth is out there: this is where my evil persona first emerged. The sight of robin blue walls still makes me contemplate moderately evil victimless crimes.

Yes, folks, let's discuss child abuse. My father left me in lockdown in a prison as he went to talk to his co-workers. How I left that day without prison tats and a toothbrush sharpened into a shank, I'll never know. It might not have been a lengthy incarceration, but perhaps it's been what has kept me out of jail all these years? We'll never know, and never in a million years will I give my father that satisfaction.

I am proof that even the good ones have a history. I'm as dangerous as the jaywalkers and tax evaders.

A SMALL TOWN HALLOWEEN

In small towns, every holiday is celebrated, and despite our differences, it becomes a town-wide affair. With little to do in our community, we managed to take these insignificant events and blow them up. They became a celebration that spread from house to house in a manner that makes you proud to be from these quiet towns. Halloween is no different. For us, it started with placing expertly carved pumpkins on front porches and as the big day approached, we would hang cobwebs, erect tombstones, and blare spooky soundtracks from the windows. But before I can delve into the events sponsored by our town, I have to talk about the extra love and care that went into the costumes.

I don't recall every costume mother created for Halloween, but there are definitely those that stand out and need to be noted. My mother's sewing machine never ceased as the spookiest of holidays approached. The first came in the form of a family costume, Raggedy Anne and Raggedy Andy. It was a hand-me-down from when my brother had been alive, but I begrudgingly assumed the mantle. People stopped to take our photos. My mother's handiwork propelled us to the top of the Halloween social circle. We were like gods amongst the costumed.

This, however, was only a warmup. My mother is a bit of a genius with a needle and thread. She presented two sewing patterns as if it were the biggest decision of my life, and for a kid barely to tie his shoelaces, it was. Would I be a giant pumpkin or a ferocious spider? Of course, I went with the spider. Not only did I have this cool black costume and fangs, but when I raised my arms, the cobwebs attached to my wrist would extend my other arms. It wasn't only a costume; it was a show piece. Yes, I was jam-packed with awesome.

Later, as I grew, the costumes shifted between lazy or simple. There were only so many times you could go out as a vampire before they figured out you were recycling your cape from the previous year. Eventually, as I became more engrossed with my fantasy novels, I went as a wizard. Mom got to work again, and in no time, I had a full-length cloak with a hood. Being from Maine, it was also one of the most practical costumes. Made from corduroy, I was the only one of my friends warding away hypothermia the year we walked through the foot of snow to garner our confectionary treats. Fashion can also be functional, even as a costume!

Unlike Christmas or Easter, Halloween rarely turned into a homebound day. It didn't matter the age, there were events for all. We understood and even embraced our lack of options, and we made the best of our resources. We divided it between day and night, school and town.

For the youngest of us, Halloween always started with a parade. Our teachers wore their literary inspired garb while we moved from one classroom to the next, showing off our parents' ability to craft a costume at the last minute and on a shoestring budget. Later, as the sun set, we'd march down Main Street so the elderly could see the toddlers bobbing about in all their cuteness. We were like a 4th of July parade, except no floats, no flowers, no music, and it only consisted of one hundred and fifty kids. We were fricken' adorable. Before the end of the night, our little legs cleared four or five miles and we'd still only have a small bag worth of candy. I think they were determined to wear us out before we binged on sugar.

For the pre-teen kids, we had the haunted house hosted by our American Legion. How they dragged so many bales of hay to the second story and then had a dozen people hiding amongst the sheets and straw, I'll never really know. The veterans must have found a disturbing amount of satisfaction in the screams of children as masked goblins and serial killers chased us. I knew it was lame. It wasn't nearly as scary as the haunted house in Camp Lejeune where I was chased screaming out emergency doors by a guy with a chainsaw. No, it was nothing like that. They created it with the best of intentions. The adults understood the shortcomings of a small town, and they banded together to give us an experience. Despite the cheesiness, you enjoyed every moment.

Then we grew up.

In a town that doesn't offer parties or locations to gather and be social, Halloween lost its sheen by the time we reached high school. For us, there were rarely parties in which we dressed up. We were often sent to be the caretakers of younger siblings or guard the bowl of candy on the front porch. For several years, I played the dead guy on the front lawn. I have to admit, watching small children run screaming as they abandoned their bags of candy made me understand the joy the veterans experienced in the haunted house.

Most people think of Halloween as a holiday where the teens go out and cause trouble. Armed with toilet paper and eggs, they delve into the darker side of tricking and less the treats, but thankfully candy was provided regardless of age. I can't say we were those daring teens. In a small town, parents know your every movement and should we be caught buying eggs during the month of October, the store clerk would call our parents. More often than not, we roamed around to the houses where the owners had eyesight so bad we passed for kids and still received king-sized candy bars. We'd eat it on the spot and move onto the next location. When even that got boring, we'd play hide and seek using the town borders as our boundaries, chasing each other on bikes. Nobody was ever found, and we quickly gave us to stand in a circle and talk about nothing.

Looking back, I'd be one of those people sitting on their porch to gawk at the young ankle biters as they wobbled down the sidewalk. It'd be adorable to see them sporting their Ninja Turtle costumes or wearing household sheets with holes cut out. I never claimed we were the most creative of towns.

Despite the limitations of a small town, we managed. We pooled our resources and did our best to make sure that kids of every age were given an opportunity to partake in the festivities. Whether it was escorting your younger brother to the houses with the best candy, or acting as a corpse ready to terrifying children, we managed. Then, for the next week, we'd speculate on which of us stayed out late and toilet papered the mean woman's house on the corner while everybody fell victim to their sugar induced comas.

Answer: it was me.

CHRISTMAS TRADITIONS

By Christmas, the snow has fallen and the landscape of Maine has transformed into a winter wonderland. The trees are barren except for the peppering of the state's persevering pines. In the morning, there is a stillness, while the fresh powder goes untouched. The air is crisp and holds a sharp bite before the sun can push it away. Through the stillness comes the ability to hear snow sliding from roofs or the street plows miles away.

If we lived further out in the country, I'm quite certain the morning would include a herd of deer standing at the tree line trying to decide if hunting season was truly over. The only thing the scene was missing was a jolly fat man in a red suit, loading his sleigh with a bag full of gifts. But to be fair, I'm pretty sure Santa is from the northern part of Maine we call, "The County." Things like that are probably common place up there.

In a town that consists of multi-generational homes, we often inherit the traditions of our elders. At one time, four generations occupied the same home. There weren't many required traditions amongst my family, at least not pertaining to Christmas. My family had never been particularly religious, and as I grew older, we rarely attended the late night Christmas mass. Instead, our traditions were contained within our household, insignificant things that have stayed with me even as I left Maine behind. For me, these seasonal habits are reminders of the wonderful family I have been blessed with and the place I still call home.

The most important tradition I can recall is the spaghetti sauce. I hear people talk about the intricate cuisine they create for the holidays. From hams to freshly baked bread, in my house, it always revolved around a pot of spaghetti. For a while, my uncle lived with us and he'd bake bread with every meal, but left to our own devices, it was the long simmer of a red sauce that made our mouths water. It started a day earlier; the ingredients chopped, sautéed and finally mixed with jarred sauce. We're not fancy. We're not culinary masters. But for us, we'd find every opportunity to excuse ourselves to the kitchen to have a taste. Eventually, we'd sit down and eat dinner in the early afternoon on Christmas and then again that night. We'd repeat this ritual until the sauce vanished days later.

On Christmas Eve we'd spend the night in front of the television, the perfect picture of a nuclear family. The tree would be decorated and the lights shining brightly (never flickering) and the floor would be littered with presents. Each year my mother would declare, "It's time for your gift," and I'd have the opportunity to open a single present. As a kid, I'd always try to pick the largest object under the tree, and mom would redirect me to something a bit more mundane. It was most often a simple gift, new socks or a t-shirt. I was always disappointed that it wasn't the wish list item I'd requested from Santa. But there was a method to my mother's madness.

Later, it would become comical as we seldom included name tags on our presents. Some had sat there for weeks and we could hardly remember what we wrapped. More often than not, I'd open a present to find that it was thermal underwear meant for my father, or a new nightgown for my grandmother. While I wouldn't have minded the comfortable garments, I always sought out the rectangular small presents that resulted in a new novel to read that night. My grandmother and I would retire to our rooms and my mother and father would stay up late playing the part of Santa's elves, wrapping all of the last minute gifts. I always found it humorous that, the next morning, even the gifts meant for the dog would be wrapped. Yes, our dog unwrapped his own gifts.

Probably the most memorable tradition came the morning of Christmas. I'm sure it started as a young child. Bustling with excitement to see what Santa had left under the tree, I'd wake with the sun and begin knocking at my mother's door. To buy herself additional time in bed, she would set a stocking stuffed to the brim with small gifts against my door. Eventually I'd be bustling with excitement to see what Santa had left under the tree, and I'd begin knocking at my mother's door. While this might not sound much different from many households, the stocking grew to have requirements.

1. There must be a small set of Legos. It never mattered what they were, but it was something to keep my idle hands busy. Even as I grew outside the recommended age, they still appeared. I'm nearing forty and I still expect a stocking with the tiny stepping hazards.
2. There must be a large Hershey's kiss. I'm not sure if it's because we visited Hershey park frequently growing up, or because my parents knew the fastest way to slow me down was through chocolate, but it was there. Even in my zeal, I couldn't finish it, but I put forth a strong effort.
3. There must be an accompanying food item. As a kid this took the form of candy, but as I matured, so did the gift. There is a local brand of beef jerky I ask for every year, and without a doubt, they will cram it into the toe of my stalking. I will admit, there is something about beef

jerky for breakfast that I will always associate with Christmas.
4. The rest varied from year to year, but one last rule must always reign supreme. No gift in the stocking can have a practical purpose. It must have a certain bit of frivolous to it. Whether it be candles or my name on a grain of sand, or a guardian angel for my car, there should be no amount of practicality. To this day, this remains a constant.

In a busy household that was constantly moving between work, school or visiting with friends, Christmas served as the rare time when we slowed down. It's a piece of the magic of growing up in a remote town, far away from the bustle of the city. To some degree, we were isolated, relying on those within arm's reach. For me, it was my parents and grandmother. Now that I've left home and live several states away, our visits have evolved into phone calls where we start sentences with, "Remember when…" and we take a heart-warming stroll down memory lane.

BEYOND THE THUNDERDOME

The towns in northern Maine are small clusters of houses connected by long and winding roads. The scenery is beautiful, with trees lining the road, and as you reach the crest of a hill, you might get a glimpse into the mountains that surround our valley. Farms filled in these spaces, dairy on one side while the other contained corn or potatoes. Frequently, you'd have to slow down as a tractor crossed the road, or now and then, a herd of cows. While it might be majestic for the visitor, for residents, it meant that every trip to a neighboring town was a hike. A simple, "I'm going to the store" might result in an hour-long excursion.

The driver's license in Maine isn't only a rite of passage for teenagers. Our parents were more excited than us to reach that magical age of sixteen. No longer did they have to spend an hour in the car driving to and from school. There were no more late-night pickups from sports or band practice. Even the dreaded "I'm going to get milk" now fell on our shoulders. Needless to say, our parents surrendered the keys to distribute the burden.

We took Driver's Education at fifteen. Driver's Ed was held in my school, the same room and chair I sat in two years earlier when I had to take our mandatory health class. The attendees were the same friends I had in school, each one of us reaching that magical age when we'd take to the roads like it was the end of times. It'd start with watching instructional videos and learning why it's bad to hit pedestrians. Eventually, we would get behind the wheel and get first-hand experience on how to swerve to miss deer, drive on roads without pavement, and repair flat tires after striking a massive pothole. I think it says something when the opening statement from our instructor was, "If I hear about or see you written up in the police logs, driving a vehicle before the end of my course, you will be removed."

Funny story.

I'm certain there is a law stating that a non-licensed driver is not allowed to drive on paved roads. It makes sense, requiring each person to take a basic competency test. This should be easy. However, this becomes dicey in Maine as we have a very loose definition of what is a road. Many of them aren't paved, have no street names, and often are on private property. Growing up, we would say you're only lost when there's no pavement or power lines. You'd be surprised, but this remains a problem to this day. Thankfully for many kids like myself, this benefits us as we learn to drive at a young age.

As soon as I could touch the pedals, my father let me drive the car. It was one of those things dads do with their kid, attempting to score cool points. We would take back roads, often dirt, and so far from civilization there wouldn't be a chance of our lone police officer catching me, straining to see over the wheel. In these wild parts of Maine, we were more concerned with the sudden appearance of a game warden. They never spotted us. It wasn't as if we were drag racing, at least not all the time.

In my father's defense, he *was* teaching me how to handle the car, often yelling for me to use the breaks, and as we reached the end of the road, forcing me to make a three-point turn.

My father insisted I learn to drive as he had, outside the rules and regulations thrust upon us by the Department of Motor Vehicles. To my father, he was imparting the same wisdom. He'd laugh as I struggled to figure out how the clutch worked when we'd take his pickup truck. While he showed me early how to *drive*, it wouldn't be until much later when my mom parked on a steep hill and said, "Your turn" that I would master the third pedal.

It was harmless, but for a child, it was beyond amazing. The windows rolled down, wind catching my hair as we soared down the road. The radio blaring one of the two country stations we received. In no time, I was popping the emergency brake, spinning the car around and preparing for my life as a stunt driver. Okay, perhaps I'm cherry picking my memories. Despite breaking the law, my father refused to turn on the radio. The rest is true, I swear.

We spent hours driving around the baseball field or in the sandpits at a neck-breaking ten miles per hour. Half a decade later, when I would take driver's education, I was amazed at how much I already knew. The knowing looks from each of my classmates made it abundantly clear that they too had been driving for years. We endured the formality, but for most of us, this was not our first cruise through the Thunderdome.

But now, I knew to keep my lips sealed. The problem with teaching a ten year-old how to drive is their utter lack of discretion. At the first opportunity, I would tell my mom about my father's teachings and it would only be a matter of seconds before her face turned pink as her blood boiled. However, this lack of common sense was an ongoing theme in my youth. One day, while my parents were in Bangor, I wanted something from the store, which was nearly a mile away. Whether it be comic books or a soda, I decided that a mile might as well have been the other side of the planet. Looking out the window, I saw our other car sitting in the driveway. I knew the keys were sitting in the ignition (yes, we do that in Maine). I couldn't help but think how easy it would be to get to the store.

Mad Max wouldn't have hesitated.

I hopped in the car, turned the key and with a bit of gas, it roared to life. Seconds later, I was backing out of the driveway. Cruising at a respectable fifteen miles per hour, I tried not to arouse suspicion. Too fast and I'd be pulled over, too slow and I'd have been better off walking. I reached the stop sign and eased the break with the grace of a falling tree. Waiting a minute, I ensured no vehicles would magically appear and run me down. I proceeded through the intersections and around the bend to the store. For a moment, I believed my rule-breaking ways would have no consequences. I was living the adult life, and after I had made my purchase, I probably had more pep in my step than required, but I was a man now. Then came the trip home. I drove proudly, abiding by more laws than the typical hillbilly. Then I rounded the corner underneath the train trestle and it all came crashing down. My parents were heading to the same store I was leaving.

I had been caught.

The quarter mile back to the house was the longest drive I ever suffered. I remember getting home and putting the keys on the table. Like the grown man I was, I booked it to my bedroom to hide. When they returned, my mother let loose like I had never seen. She was never one to swear, but she'd bring out the parental "tone" and I knew I'd be spending quality time grounded. Thankfully for me, my father, the brave soul, tried to pacify his screaming bride. Not even he could withstand the anger. In hindsight, I bet he got grounded too.

So when my driving instruction uttered those words "If I hear about…," nothing after that mattered. I would survive his teachings, get a passing grade, and get my license without worry. However, if he thought his tone of voice kept me from getting behind the wheel without supervision, it didn't hold a candle to the tongue-lashing I received from my mother.

I passed with flying colors.

I was then promptly grounded, again.

WHERE TRADITION MEETS MODERN

I do not handle transition well. Many venture to the state of Maine in pursuit of rocky beaches, outstanding seafood or communing with nature. For a young kid who spent his time in a densely populated town where all the adults worked at the same job, Maine was less thrilling. More than that, it was like a prison. And once I had received my sentence, I found I would need to adjust to survive.

While moving along the eastern seaboard might not sound worldly, for Maine, it is a bigger world that many never see. In a land where people live their entire lives within a six square mile town, the land beyond those borders can be intimidating.

The most important lesson learned: keep my worldview to myself.

Many of my fine country men were knowledgeable and understood that geography kept them in isolation. However, there were many who viewed anything beyond our borders as *them*. I do not hold this against them. In some ways, it's charming how they clutch to their way of life and fear change. Like I said earlier, I don't handle change easily myself. While I do not hold it against the people of Brownville Junction, I learned that when I spoke of life outside Maine, I painted a target on myself. Having views outside that of a die-hard, born and bred Mainer, created issues. To anyone other than the veterans, whom I grew to love, being exposed to the world beyond our borders placed me in an ill-favored minority.

In hindsight, there were many of us who came from outside the boundaries of Maine. In my circle of friends, we had girls born in Saudi Arabia, Boston, and Philadelphia. But much like me, we didn't speak of the "before times." It was clear in our mannerisms that we were part of a small group and we'd discovered that glazing over our pasts allowed us to fit in.

For those of us with ambitions of "getting out," the school offered rare opportunities to travel beyond the state line. My sophomore year I attended the annual school science fair field trip to Boston's Quincy Market and Museum of Science. For me, it was a chance to get back to a world I once knew as a kid. I longed for a place that wasn't a sea of white people, and fine cuisine that didn't revolve around pizza from the local market. I wasn't the only one. For those of us born elsewhere, there was a gleam of excitement. We hoped it would rub off on our classmates, but even if it didn't, we would bask in the diversity.

When we finally reached Boston, it wasn't what I expected. Quincy Market is a historic area of Boston, blending eras between the Revolutionary War and the Modern. It's hard to put into words exactly what I experienced the moment we left the bus. There was a sense of wonder as we saw the buildings far taller than anything I had seen since moving to Maine. While it maintained the quaint appearance of a century gone by, it held a noticeable pulse. I saw more people in passing that day than the total population of the many towns in our school district.

It felt alive.

Most of my time was spent alone, wandering, absorbing the culture of this historic place. I watched people hurrying to their destinations, their eyes pointing toward the brick walkways. A local woman sold flowers to passers-by. I knew at the time she was homeless (or it was a scam) but I was amazed to see a world so utterly different than our own only a few hours away. The building at the center of Quincy Market is relatively long and slender. Inside, there were people gathering during their lunch break, shouting orders for street food. Even the veranda housed people reading the newspaper or scarfing down their food. In Brownville Junction, nothing like this existed. We come from a town that has no community epicenter. I was amazed.

It was through this dining area I found the double doors that lead to a bookstore. You would think that once you've seen one bookstore, you've seen them all. Shelves lined with classic tails and new releases. But unlike the small bookstore a half-hour drive from my house, this one offered something new and unique. It was the first time I had ever seen a "gay" section in a bookstore, and for a questioning teen, it offered answers. Here, nobody knew me, and I didn't need to conform to the ideals of my hometown. I was terrified about the reaction from the cashier when I placed the book on the checkout counter. Would I receive dirty looks? She hardly batted an eye or raised her pierced eyebrow as she rang up my purchase. For me, this was a turning point that made me promise that while I loved Maine, I'd find my place in the world, even if it was hours away.

This excursion in the flatlands of the South was the first time I realized that it wasn't the rest of the world straying from a sense of normalcy. It was Maine. They were the culprits, the ones who were different. They were the ones who guarded their towns and shunned the outside world. Thankfully, there were those who found it important to make sure we didn't lead sheltered lives. As somebody who grew up inherently different, I appreciated these glimpses into what might be.

It's ironic that this happened when I was fifteen, and years later, I call Boston my second home. Bostonians accept the melting pot of America, and with their less than mainstream ways, I fit in without issue. However, I fled the hustle and bustle of the city and now live in a small working-class town west of Boston that, under a microscope, has more in common with my hometown than I believed. I wanted change, but like I will keep reiterating, change is not something I adjust to. Leave it to me to find the one town in all of Massachusetts that reminds me of small-town Maine.

FACES LONG FORGOTTEN

For a while I worked as a photographer, inheriting my mother's love for capturing moments. At the request of a childhood friend that I reconnected with as an adult, I travelled north for an engagement shoot with her and her soon-to-be husband. With so many options at our disposal, I knew I wanted to return to the lake and get photos of them sitting on the dock with their feet in the water. Of course, this required me swimming with an expensive camera, but to the capture a magical moment with two wonderful people, I did just that.

However, as we were packing up, preparing to leave Lakeview Plantation, a young man was putting his boat into the water. There were sideways glances you grow accustomed to (even when you're not emerging from a lake with a camera) and it spoke of "recognition." This gentleman was attempting to put my foreign face to a name. He asked, "Are you from up here?" I answered yes. The light went on and his eyes grew wide as he said my name. I had to raise my eyebrow as he didn't look like anybody I knew from school. Then I realized: twelve years ago, we each looked different.

When he told me his name and I couldn't quite recall it, we started the dance. We'd spend the next few minutes tossing facts back and forth, trying to jog my memory. He told me his name, and I couldn't place it. "Class of '98." That's how we identify one another in such a small town. I shook my head. "What about my younger brother?" I had to shake my head again. I realized at that moment, not only did I not know who he was now, but I'm not sure I knew him then. But how could I possibly have forgotten one of the four hundred students at school? In small town Maine, we're all connected, but even then, our memories still fail us.

It made me think about the people I had forgotten since moving nearly three hundred miles south. More so, not simply the people I've forgotten, but the many people in this small town who will be forgotten as time marches forward. The saying, "They live forever in our memories," comes to mind. I can't help but think, these people too, as our memories grow hazy and first-hand accounts become second, will someday fade from existence. Often, I scour our family tree, hoping I can bring long-forgotten ghosts to life, to keep them from being nothing more than a mysterious name etched into a gravestone. So many people will fade from the world and will be forgotten if they haven't already.

This sentiment was echoed by two small children I had the pleasure of meeting while I returned to the Junction to stroll down memory lane. They recognized my father's dog and came over to talk while I took photographs for this book. Once they established my lineage (and by lineage my relationship to the dog's owner) and my right to be in the Junction, they were quick to bring me up to speed on the latest gossip heard by children.

They asked why I was photographing empty buildings. When my parents grew up in the town, it had a booming industry. As I came into my own in the same home that raised my mother, I watched the town decline. Now, for these small boys, even the memory of what it once was had vanished. I told them I enjoyed photographing things that people forget and as I prepared to capture the old country store, their next statement shook me.

The owner, a gentleman named Chuck, had passed away a month ago.

Despite their playing with the dog and previously dashing down their Slip 'n' Slide, a sadness came over both children. They revealed his struggle with cancer and by the time the community learned about his battle, he passed. It was obvious in their tone that much like me, they knew him as the local Shopkeeper. In a small town, this is a person you see every couple of days. This is the person who knows your favorite beverage and how thin you like your ham cut. They're an extended part of the family.

BJ's Market is part of my story.

Before Chuck bought the store and moved his family up from New York, my grandmother had been an employee. Throughout the year she maintained a note on the cash register, counting down the shopping days until Christmas. When it snowed outside, the owner let her sell homemade mittens near the front counter. Later my mom would work there, filling in for my grandmother as she neared retirement. More than having family be employees, it is where I went every Tuesday to purchase comic books. I'd sit down in front of the magazine rack and flip through the pages, deciding what to buy. Later, Chuck would keep them off the shelf until I could arrive after school, giving me first pick of the bunch.

I had never been particularly close to Chuck or his family, but like all residents in a small town, we were friendly and exchanged small talk whenever we bumped into one another. I realized he will someday become another name fading away with time. This weighed down on my heart as much today as it did then. But then the kids reminded me why I'm proud to be from a small town nestled in the heart of Maine. They told me about how the town raised money to donate to cancer research. I'm not sure if that is the truth or if the town rallied to help pay for his funeral. Regardless of the truth, the sound of pride in the kid's voice left tears in my eyes.

While I'm sitting here, detailing the highs and lows of a community separated from the world, I have to take a moment and make sure a man is not forgotten. Not because I knew him well, or because he was even a great man. I have to speak of him because if I do not, I'm unsure of who will. There will come the time when a generation from now, they remember when the store closed, but not the dying man who kept it alive.

Despite not knowing him well, I need to take a moment and say, "Chuck, thank you." He had no reason to come to our community. He was treated as an outsider for years and despite the uphill battle he fought with the community, he worked to keep us as just that: a community. There were many times when he could have thrown in the gloves and said to hell with it, but he endured. He stayed until cancer forced him to step down. While he might not have been one of us in the beginning, I'm proud to say, he was one of us when he passed.

When our memories fade, we will not forget his name.

Charles R. Pribus.

THE REASONS FOR GOODBYE

I was recently asked, "Why did you leave Maine?"

The question was simple and direct. I thought the answer would be equally simple and direct. But as I started to reply, I realized I couldn't find a way to summarize an answer that fit into a small and easily defined phrase. It's not as simple as saying, "I left for work," or "I needed a change." They would be superficial statements without meaning. I could discuss the missing opportunities or my parents moving from my childhood home. They all had a hand in deciding to depart. But there is a singular reason I moved away.

The truth is, Maine itself made me leave.

Social Life - At this point, it's become fairly obvious that I am gay. While many people believe this is the source of my exodus, I think they misread the statement. In my youth, I had my fair share of scuffles due to my sexual orientation, but I imagine it would have been similar to any other place in the mid-90s. I do not see Maine as a place of bigots or a land of unrighteous hate. I have experienced more bigotry in a state claiming to be progressive and gay-friendly than in the conservative countryside of Maine. This will sound comical, but the reason for leaving was because it was impossible to date in Maine. When I attended University of Maine Farmington, it was the first opportunity to meet other men and begin dating. However, because of geography, our visits were reduced to weekends and required a full tank of gas. When that fizzled out, the search radius grew until it turned laughable. It was time to go.

Opportunities - Maine is not without opportunities. But in my collection of twelve towns, the largest employer is the school district. That means unless a job opened within the school system, I would be a cashier or, if I learned a trade, a mechanic or long-haul trucker. I am a creative person by default and even if I worked in a book store or a museum, it'd be an hour commute each way and just enough money to pay for the gas. I'm greedy. There needs to be options and I want the ability to explore them without having to uproot my life and move each time I find a new passion. Unfortunately, with the size of Maine, that is a way of life for many people.

Progress vs. Recess - I think Mainers are progressive. I think they take much longer at it because they don't push forward with social trends. They take time to digest and adapt progress to their traditions. While this is one thing that makes Mainers such hearty folk, it is also a detriment. I do not believe in change for the sake of change, but some change is essential for survival. Mainers can struggle with this. Change needs to happen within a generation, and we can't continue to pass it off to those who follow us. I admire their fortitude and determination to honor their history, but this is part of what gives them a reputation as being backward. For the peace of mind with my existence, I needed to be in a place that at least adapted to the modern decade.

Holier Than Thou - I think this comes with any small town, but in Maine, it was a level I found not only uncomfortable but also downright absurd. I can think of several individuals from my youth looking down on those around them. My hometown has an extremely high poverty rating. Because this levels the playing field for most inhabitants, people must create an artificial caste system in which they can place themselves above others. Community members would stand on their pedestals and preach their superiority to any who would listen. It makes me think of the phrase "People bully because they hurt." I grew up rallying for the underdog and wanting to see them overcome hurdles and emerge victorious. To my dismay, in small town Maine, people leave the status quo alone because it is all they know. Instead of playing by their rules, I left to make my own.

Familiarity - There is something beautiful about being in a community where you know the history of the town and its inhabitants. It's great to know your mother was best friends with the neighbor's daughter or that your dad played basketball with your friend's father. But this invisible thread connecting its townspeople also has a dark side. We carried the burden of the generations before us. There are plenty in my family tree who have baggage. While we forgive much of it, I didn't want to be known as "that guy from high school." I didn't want my legacy to be reduced to a period. I wanted to be seen as an individual and not because of blood ties or a friendship that faded twenty years ago. Leaving gave me the opportunity to begin a new chapter of my life. I feared that staying in Maine would have let one chapter grow too long.

Self-Sabotage - This happens on several levels. On the individual level, people who self-sabotage want something to bitch about. There is an innate need to keep themselves at rock bottom because of the attention they receive. Instead of wiping themselves off and moving forward, they start a downward spiral to cry out at the injustice. Sometimes, the spiral is easy to stop. But how would they define themselves if they weren't complaining? I think they only exacerbate this at the community level where people have rooted themselves in the "Why me?" mentality. In a small town, even with our big cities over an hour away, we are the victim of the general population. Outnumbered during voting and the whims of our politicians, we feel neglected and the victim of ignorance. While this creates a robust character and allows us to rally as a community, I feel it's depressing to see the light at the end of the tunnel grow dimmer and dimmer each day. I commend those who stay and fight. I respect their determination, stubbornness and inability to let their light dim. For me, however, it was a battle I wasn't ready to fight.

Many of these reasons are the same reason Maine holds a special place in my heart. They represent the flip side of the coin and after many tosses, I had to leave. It boils down to these six reasons and while it will always be a part of my being, for now at least, it can't be my home. Until I return, alive or dead, I'll continue introducing myself as a Mainer.

YOU CAN'T GO HOME ANYMORE

My parents live two hundred and fifty-six miles north of me. The four-hour trip will put me just south of Bangor and in a position to travel and visit all points in Maine. In a few hours, I could cross the border or stand on the shores of Bar Harbor. Growing up in the middle of "nowhere" has always meant a long commute, something you grow accustomed to by the time you receive your license. Even in the center of activity, there is another leg of the trip.

It's another forty-five miles, North by Northwest to return home.

Every once in a while I return to Brownville and the Junction to photograph the changes. At this point, I've been documenting my childhood home for twenty years. Thanks to my grandmother and mother, I have photos spanning generations and it's easy to see the rise and fall of this small town, both in the buildings and in the people. My parents sold my childhood home a few years ago and from there, I noticed the significant changes in the Junction. But more than that, I noticed the changes in myself, my connection to this community fraying until it snapped.

Again, I became an outsider.

The neighbor kids recognize my father's dog more than they do me. From the front porch, I might hear somebody ask, "Are you Gloria's grandson?" As time passes, even those moments of recognition have dwindled. To some degree, it stings to realize that in a community where everybody knows the name of its residents, you are no longer part of that network. However, the most painful thing is the moment you return to your childhood house.

My folks said they had boarded our house, and the buyers had moved out. We've made jokes hoping the place went to hell, but there was something real as I stood across the street and saw the abandoned property notice. I had to take a breath. My home, the home of my parents, grandmother and great grandmother was left in shambles. I was mad. I was angry. Most of all, I felt lost. The foundation of who I am was physically swept out from under me. This icon of my identity was on its way to being condemned.

I had left my car at the gas station while I photographed the house. The emotions raged. Part of me felt guilty for learning, allowing this bastion of my childhood to fall into disrepair. There were tears as that thread snapped and I became disconnected from a previous version of myself.

As I returned to the gas station, an attendant said, "It's becoming a sad town." I did not know who he was, and I doubt he was aware of my own origin story. Either my emotions were clearly written on my face, or he this was a conversation he had frequently. As he pumped gas, I asked, "Why don't you leave?" He didn't even look at me as he replied, "Where would I go?"

I nearly sobbed at the sound of defeat in his voice.

I wanted to argue. I wanted to shake him and say there is something beyond these borders. I wanted to yell that there are places where communities thrive. But like many of the town, I'm sure this is home. He was most likely born here, grew up in these houses and raised his own family. Like many in Brownville Junction, I assumed it bound him to the location and he couldn't fathom resting his feet elsewhere.

I asked him about the people living in my former home, 11 Ryder Ave. "Never made a payment, took them this long to be kicked out." I don't know if it was the truth. In a small town you learn to dissect gossip from reality, but I can't help but wonder. I'm wounded knowing they set foot in a place that had created memories, birthed generations and became a home to my clan, with no intent of treating it better than a hovel. And as I stood there looking at the shell of my home, I realized it's not home anymore. It's a building, one I choose not to remember.

The town is dying.

I've gone back and photographed it numerous times, each snap of the shutter depicting a fading glory. Each excursion I hope to see new life, a source of vibrancy cut through the sense of sadness. But I leave with a sense of sadness and heartbreak. All I can think of is that gas station attendant. I want to think the best of its inhabitants, but I also know I want to see a better life than what the Junction offers.

But this was the last time I'd visit, the end of my hope. As I drove by my former house one final time, I realized my story is over. The small sliver that once kept me connected to the dying town had been severed. If only for a moment, I was homeless and to the Junction, I was an outsider.

INTO THE FIRES WE STARE

As I write this, I frequently wonder how much information I should provide about myself. While these stories are told through my perspective, they're not always about me. In a way, I am the product of a small town in Maine. Despite how I arrived in the town or having left it in my twenties, I still maintain that at my core, I am a Mainer. Because of this, I often find myself opening complicated scars created by this place I call home. As an adult, when my world crumbles, I find that the parts refusing to relent are those created by Maine.

My relationship with my partner, ten years of building a life together, came screeching to a halt when he said, "I'm leaving." Overnight, I went from being part of a dynamic duo to staring at the vacant space on the couch where he'd sit while we watched movies. My identity for years had revolved around being part of a couple and suddenly and without warning, it ceased to be. Meanwhile, I found myself suddenly financially dependent on receiving tenure at my job. Things weren't all bad, but they were unstable. I cannot say it enough, but I do not handle involuntary change well.

Between the packing of boxes, finding a new home and trying to keep life amicable with the ex, I decided I needed a new tradition. Once the year begins at work, there isn't a lot to look forward to in the fall. To remedy this, I decided I wanted to return to a childhood favorite and go camping. Since it had been more than a decade since my last excursion in the woods overnight, it was only fitting that I convince a friend to journey into the mountains of New Hampshire. Where a sleeping bag and a box of matches would have sufficed in my teen years, my gear now includes pillows, blankets, air mattresses and an uncanny amount of beer. If we could have hired a four-star chef to cook for us over an open fire, it would have happened.

We arrived at the camp site just as the rain came down. In the summer, it would have been a delightful break from the heat, but in late October, we were already questioning our decisions. We quickly erected our tent, and slid in the air mattresses and blankets. There was a moment standing there, our clothes absorbing every bit of moisture, we came to a startling revelation. We were too old for this shit. The kid who grew up surrounded by forest, and the ex-army man, found that roughing it might be a tad too rough.

The logistics of this trip had taken a miserable turn. Somehow that magic of packing up the car and driving out into the woods had been squeezed out of us like a rain-soaked flannel. We stacked the logs for the fire and after a few misbegotten attempts, we had achieved warmth. The moment we created fire, it pushed aside our sour attitudes. It might have also been the copious amounts of beer. At this point, beer was the only thing keeping us from checking into a hotel.

The mood changed when the rain stopped and I turned my eyes upward.

In the cold, crisp air, my jacket wrapped around me, and my hood pulled tight, I stumbled down the bank to the edge of the lake. Looking across the water, I could see the stars. With the camp at my back, the only light pollution came from the speckled fires as others partook in the same experience. Living in the suburbs, I have a beautiful view of the sky, but it's not the same as when you see it under the overwhelming intensity of the night.

The sky isn't the dark cloud that people often paint. It's shades of blue and purple, illuminated by the twinkling of stars. The trees lining the opposite bank created a dark black line that cut through the horizon. Without the moon, the stars themselves had a life. Pulsing with light, they gave a choreographed dance for any who looked to the sky. Here, in the middle of nowhere, I bathed in the light of a pantheon of celestial bodies. The smell of moist ground, a gentle breeze, and a symphony of nature nurtured my soul as I stared into infinity. I remembered that impervious kid that started my story.

For a moment, I ceased to be. I became inconsequential, and I felt as if I was part of the infinite. I felt thankful for being brought up to appreciate the splendor of the natural world. It wasn't a quick endeavor. My problems, the things causing me anxiety, they washed away bit by bit. The sense of dread lifted as I became unburdened by my other self. Minutes dragged on until my friend climbed down the banks and joined me.

He stared into space, fixated, mirroring my expression from an hour earlier. We shared similar life experiences, bringing a certain amount of appreciation for natural wonders. While his small town experience occurred in the wilderness of Alaska, the tundra of nature shaped us.

Our cathartic experience carried on as we returned to the fire. Whether it be the dark of night, the dancing flames or the sound of rustling trees, camping has a way of lowering one's guard. We talked about life, the good and the bad. Sitting there, speaking into the night, my stress washed away. I felt cleansed as I confessed to the darkness. Eventually the topic of music arose, and we put on the radio, sharing the songs that shaped our youths. As the conversation continued, the core of me shone. My *world* hadn't crumbled, just the exterior. Underneath a shattered veneer I found a solid foundation. I took it in, embracing the things that forged my outlook on life as a kid.

There is always a bit of melancholy as I follow the strand of thread that connects me to nature. Of the many attributes Maine instilled in me, this is the one comes with a side of sadness. How could somebody go through life without understanding these moments? While my thrill of sleeping on the ground away from my overly expensive mattress might not be as immense as it once was, there is a part of me that will always long for these simple moments.

Childhood memories pour in, much like the rain had earlier. Building forts in the woods. Finding streams to cool us off in the summer. The survival skills needed to endure being lost in a blizzard. Learning to hunt and respecting the land that provided. The imagination that transformed a river island into a magical kingdom. Each occurrence ended in me emerging from the tree line like a vagrant to return home in pursuit of a hot meal. These are the building blocks of who I am, ones created by a small town in the North. I remembered. My world hadn't crumbled; it had cracked enough to show me the man Maine made.

I went camping, not knowing I'd visit my childhood. Drawing upon that tether, it eased my burdens, aches, and pains. I wrapped myself in the title of Mainer and wondered how could anybody live life without experiencing the wonders and awe the universe provides to those willing to look upward and listen?

It had been ages, but I finally felt right. I long for the therapy of a star filled sky and roaring fire.

LE LANGAGE DE L'AMOUR

While walking down memory lane, there are tales that rise to the surface. They are those poignant moments that help define who we are. They arise from a familiar sound or smell. Then, there are others that require more coaxing. They're faint and stand just outside what did or did not happen. But every once in a while, there are those that only surface because of a conflict between two people as they attempt to recount fact from fiction. Mine version can sometimes steer away from fact, but when they do, they're far more fun.

Being from Maine, we have a love/hate relationship with our Canadian brethren.

We have more in common than we like to admit. Try as we might, we admit that our French-speaking cousins are as far removed from us as those big city dwellers. But this isn't a story about how our ancestry intertwines. This is not a story about experiencing diverse cultures that create the bedrock of our villages. No, this is the tale of how a field trip to Quebec City almost turned international incident.

In Maine, we dream big.

While in Canada, my class experienced an alien world. While we immersed ourselves in French culture in class, the reality couldn't be taught through textbooks. In the span of three years we had learned Persian French, French Cameroon, and more than our fair share of Quebecois. By the time we reached Quebec City, it was near impossible to blend with the locals. But we did have one student in particular who dove headfirst into all that Canada offered.

Wandering the streets of Old Quebec City, a gentleman suitor named Jasmine courted her. More than a decade her senior, he dazzled her with his foreign ways and delectable accent. Jasmine promised a fast-paced romance, surely leaving her with a Canadian baby. He wooed my classmate, to her protest I'm sure. Ultimately, he kept her out far longer than our Den Mother permitted.

Curfew came and went, and we wrote her off as a casualty. We only hoped that our French was fluent enough to make out the missing person's notice in the paper the next morning. As we prepared for bed, a familiar flashing blue and red light shone through our third-story window. It shocked us to see an American police officer getting out of his squad car. Reality sank in as we identified it as a car from our hometown. Somehow, we had caused enough trouble that an officer had driven six hours to make an arrest. It surprised none of us. The Chief of Police might not have arrived if it were me, but Jasmine had courted his step-daughter.

He whisked away our classmate to Maine with such ferocity, it didn't even provide her time to retrieve her belongings. This left her suitor and potential "Canadian Baby Daddy" bewildered. It might sound like speculation, but it was obvious his confusion turned to anguish as he stood outside our third-story window, yelling up in his most dashing French. Below, he waved about a bouquet like a true gentleman. He cared not that his love violated American law, and his passion could have landed him in jail for statutory rape. No, he cared not for these things. But alas, we stood at the window, cooing with admiration for a love that transcended legal boundaries. He may have also been standing next to a Vespa, but I admit, my memory may have added that for the sake of amusing optics.

These hardly seem worthy of warranting a disagreement about the facts from decades ago. To be fair, in the numerous things categorized as weird from our youth, this hardly deserves a mention. No, their love, while tragic in multiple languages, was not the source of the war over facts, just the prelude.

Our lovely Den Mother, an ebony Princess of Africa (she really was a princess) had immigrated from Cameroon years prior. This meant that every border crossing required a more thorough inspection than if we were only Mainers. Our chariot stopped as we attempted to enter the luscious state of Maine. We had experienced a similar "stop and question," on our entry to Canada. Searching for terrorists and undocumented entrants, we were never sure, but the officer stood at the front, exchanging words with our chaperone.

While she dealt with the border patrol, we sat at the back of the bus, transporting the forgotten belongings of our classmate. Her roommate switched seats, gripping my arm in a panic. With the level of guilt scribbled across her face, I momentarily thought she was a terrorist and undocumented entrant. Trying not to be obvious, but in the same way a toddler claims to have not eaten a cookie while covered in crumbs, she nodded toward a duffle bag.

Inside, tucked underneath a hairbrush and gently nestled beside the deodorant, rested a small plastic bag. In this bag was the sweetest herb (okay, maybe not sweet, but suspend disbelief) and we gasped in horror as the border patrol announced they would search the bus. It wasn't customary, not for a field trip. We believed the man possessed a sixth sense, an uncanny ability to detect teenagers smuggling drugs from country to the next. While this might have been a risk our classmate might take, we were merely good Samaritans attempted to return her forgotten possessions. In that moment, we understood why she hadn't taken the bag with her in the cop car.

Just as the man started poking at a suitcase in the first seat, our Den Mother, perhaps wise to the mischief occurring under nose, whispered to the man. His eyes quickly widened and for a moment, I feared she threatened murder. The smile that spread from ear to ear didn't appear to be the result of his life being in jeopardy. Loudly he shouted, "Really? I'm originally from Brownville."

Even then, we understood our shared geography meant salvation.

Yes, our village saved us from bringing down the wrath of the Queen. They bantered for a few minutes, him asking how she liked our hometown. The inspection ended as he gave our bus driver a pat on the shoulder, signaling that we could return to our country of origin.

Days later, at school, we finally returned our classmate's duffle bag. We neglected to mention the absence of a little plastic bag. The debate that started this story came from speculation on what happened to our classmate's stash. To this day, we're not entirely sure what came of it, just that our classmate never talked to us again.

Sidebar: ninety-nine percent of this story is true. I'm not sure which ninety-nine, but I assure you, it's accurate.

THE SACRIFICE OF $.65

Gathering spots in small towns are sacred places. In Brownville Junction, there were few places you could congregate and talk with your neighbors. Moe's served this purpose for us. The small convenience store had a few shelves of necessities, and a car garage attached to the side that hadn't seen service in years. But in the back, past the check-out counter, there was a ten by ten room with four wobbly tables and chairs that had seen better days. While the kitchen had a limited menu, the only thing that mattered was the perpetual pots of coffee.

Our veterans came together over their morning cups, sharing war stories, sipping for hours. They were our fathers, mothers, our grandparents and served as our historians, teachers of the world beyond the boundaries of our village. These individuals were the staple of our community, giving us a perspective of the bigger world. Having spent many mornings with my father listening to their tales, it's obvious they were the lifeblood of our small town, the heart that keeps the community from dying.

They wore their hearts, proudly displaying their division. Upon arrival, there'd be handshakes, small talk about the weather or hunting season. There was always light ribbing, Jarheads, Grunts, Flyboys, and Squids. But then the coffee would be poured, and their stares became distant as they talked about "the life." They rarely talked specifics, never mentioning a war or the atrocities they saw, but the wounds remained on display. The prosthetics, canes, aching muscles and trailing words made it clear; admittance to this fraternity came with a steep cost.

My parents raised me to understand the price heroes paid.

In my household there was my mother, father, and grandmother. But as a young kid, living on the military base, my extended family included entire platoons. I have more aunts and uncles named Sarge or Doc than I can count. Having stood on the home front during a time of war, the stories told over coffee touched close to home. While they might not carry shields or wear armor made of steel, I have always associated soldiers with knights. Protectors.

Military service defined my life. While my father, Bud, is known for his service in the Marine Corps, my mother is also a veteran. She didn't serve seventeen years like my father, but her decision to join the Navy for a year aligned her future with my father. Once she returned, my father graduated high school and shortly thereafter, they became Mr. and Mrs. Phillip Flagg.

But long before my conception, the military had a role in my existence.

My father served proudly in the Corps, and shortly after my brother passed and I was born, the military shipped him overseas. I often ponder my lack of resentment towards my father for abandoning his family at a time of upheaval. But try as I might, I believe there is a higher calling, similar to priests summoned to the Church. They say when you marry a Marine you marry the Corps. We were a military family, and this was our sacrifice. I have to remind myself that my father missed having a baby and returned home to an infant. My mother sacrificed having a partner, widowed for a short period by the Corps. My father's sacrifice occurred when he returned, a stranger to his own child.

This trend continued, and I remember living in Philadelphia, where my father worked in the Motor Pool. I enjoyed the lifestyle. There were always kids to play with, and my father was a big deal. I remember teaching myself to wake up so I could watch him leave. There were days when I'd scream, begging him to stay. Every day my father drove away, I worried he wouldn't return.

We were living in Camp Lejeune, where my mother worked two jobs, when my father was shipped to Iraq. By this point, it had become normal, and I didn't miss my father's "stints" away from home. Mom stayed busy with work and with the wives' association. I remember the numerous events where we would sit and create yellow ribbons. For the longest time, I assumed it was a social activity for the wives to gather and gossip. I was too young to comprehend that it served as an opportunity for them to pool their knowledge and cope with the news received from overseas. The underlying fear at these events was, "When will I get the phone call?"

My family had been through hell, and I have to remind myself that this story isn't unique. It's so common that, to see another serviceman or woman, there is an instant bond. There is the weathered look on their face or the distant stare in their eyes, and you know, without a doubt, they are reflecting on the many decisions that lead to so many sacrifices. Beneath the sense of sorrow, I can't help but respect these individuals. This is not a nameless mass. Whether they served out of patriotism or out of necessity, they offered a part of themselves I never could.

There was always an argument when it came time to put the sixty-five cents on the table. The youngest man in the room, often my father, offered a simple gift for their service. For less than a dollar, I received my lesson in history, economics, and foreign affairs.

Coming from a small town, there is an undercurrent of military aspects to our culture. I never dissected the reasoning behind this, but once I dwell on it, I find my version of the truth. Our small towns offer no future for many of its inhabitants.

They look for a path that would allow them to escape; a career, a trade, a chance to experience the world beyond the valley. They serve proudly, travel the world, and fight battles we have never heard of. During this time, they fall in love, get married, and start families. As with my father, they serve twenty years and the day they're discharged, they're lost, adrift as they had been when they first entered the recruitment office. There is no comfort in losing a tie to the life you've led for twenty years.

They return to where their stories started.

The retired gather around a table for coffee, and recount war stories. There is talk about their travels and what they did while they were in the service. These veterans hover in our post offices, grocery stores, and gas stations, searching for the telltale signs of their extended family. There is a need to be seen, heard, and comforted by those who share a similar past. They become the backbone of our small towns. Shortly after, the story begins with a new generation.

With sixty-five cents, the price of a single cup of coffee, you discover the soul of our small town. It not in the buildings, nor the railroad, but in the shared experience of its people. With a tip of my father's hat, a round of "Semper-Fi," we would exit more connected to our community than when we arrived.

THE MAINE TUNDRA

Memory lane can be a smooth ride, rehashing fond memories that make us smile. However, there are detours along the way. We visit moments in our upbringing that give pause. They're not always fond, and some leave us questioning the choices we made. Nostalgia can be painful and leave us asking, "What if I had done this differently?"

There are regrets.

I wish I'd spent more time with my father. Trained as a mechanic, he frequently asked me to join him in the garage to repair whatever heap needed fixing. I remember his hands, blackened from the grease. He'd clean them on a dirty rag, just further smudging the stains. It was an absentee father's attempt to connect with his child, but I resisted. He'd point to a tool and wait patiently as I failed time after time. Not educated by textbooks, he attempted to impart his knowledge on an unappreciative youth. Explaining how to calculate foot-pounds for the torque wrench, I listened, unaware of how this would affect my life. Twenty years later, as I took an engineering test for work, there was a question about torque. I teared up as I did the math, recounting a missed opportunity in my childhood.

While he tried to form a bond, I was too busy reveling in my geekery to be bothered. Thankfully, the military infused a sense of determination in him. He formed a new plan and convinced me to go ice fishing. The combination of cold, sitting idle, and touching fish should have made this an instant no for me. Yet somehow, he sold me on the idea of adventure. I don't remember bribery, but it must have been part of the equation for me to put down comic books for an afternoon. We loaded the truck with our traps, the snowmobile, and toboggan. The drive took hours as we ventured even further north, into forbidden territory.

The lakes were vast, reaching to the horizon in a glare of white. It appeared as if choppy waves had been flash frozen. We'd dig out the holes, bait the hooks, and set the traps. Ice fishing is a game of patience, a trait I did not possess as a child. While my father sat calmly on his upside down bucket, I taxed our snowmobile's throttle. In hindsight, I think I completely missed an opportunity. I zoomed about the lake like a frozen Mad Max, while my father waited for the land to provide.

As I process a myriad of dodged attempts, I try to justify it. I was young. I was estranged from my father. There are lessons that can only become clear with distance and a sense of maturity. Despite my efforts to remain firmly outside his world, he persisted. I should have known any man willing to sit in sub-zero temperatures waiting for fish to bite is tenacious. In hindsight, he proved himself my father on those ice fishing trips.

While zipping across the ice, I found myself stuck in the snow. Barely a tween, I couldn't pull the vehicle free and with the sun setting, I could either continue shoveling or start the two-mile trek across the lake. Even with four layers of insulation, as the sun vanished, it reached a dangerous temperature.

Panic set in. Having taken snow survival skills as a kid, I knew there was a ticking clock and eventually I'd be in trouble. Barely out of view of the snowmobile, my fingers had already grown numb and my feet were heavy. It might not sound terrifying, but growing up in Maine, we frequently read stories of frozen bodies found. I prepared myself to be another statistic.

Half a dozen lights shone nearby as a group of nighttime riders appeared. They changed direction once they saw me, aware of a fellow rider in distress. They were quick to offer hand warmers for my gloves and take me back to my abandoned vehicle. Tying on ropes, they pulled me free and accompanied me across the lake. There were no judgements, no questions, just fellow Mainers ensuring one of their own wasn't claimed by the cold.

I feared my father's wrath. For hours, I had left him to his traps. I didn't know if he'd still be perched on his bucket, or if he'd packed up and returned to the truck. Taking it slow, I tried to fathom the many ways he might scold me. I suspected I'd be grounded and this would be my last trip on the ice.

Instead, he hugged me. Holding me tightly, he thanked my escorts before they returned to their adventures. Instead of scolding me, he went through the list of emotions, the worry, the fear, and ultimately the relief. He had just finished loading the truck and was preparing to drive across the ice to find me (a dangerous tactic used by foolish Mainers). But as I sat in the passenger seat with the heat cranked to the max, he repeated his thanks that I returned in one piece.

Memories come with a bittersweet tangent. There is laughter and plenty of eye rolling at the foolishness of our youth. But there are also moments where you wish you could tell your younger self to stop being a petulant child. Each decision helped create the man I am today, but I wonder how much better I would be if I had stopped resisting and accepted the olive branches my father offered.

Thankfully, I still have the opportunity to stare these regrets in the face and rectify them. New memories can still be made.

DRIPPING WITH INK

I believe the body is a tapestry. As the bags under my eyes darken, they tell a story of late nights, working. When the laugh lines deepen, they remind me I am laughing. But of course, as an artist, I want tales printed on my skin like words in a novel. These serve as a reminder of where I am going and who I was at a specific point in my life.

I branded my skin again, prepared to tell a new story.

Like many teenagers, I believed musicians performed for a party of one. They spoke to me and gave voice to ideas I had yet to formulate. Of all of them, Counting

Crows had spoken to me in a way that helped push me through a tough childhood. As I thought of the next marking I would etch on my body, I wanted something that spoke to my need to believe in myself.

Adam Duritz had put it more eloquently than I could hope to do for myself. In "Mr. Jones," he talks about his need to believe in something beyond himself, and in turn, believe in himself. As somebody who has doubted his existence for the better part of their life, it serves as a reminder. Wrapping the lyrics around my left leg, it's out in the open for all to see. It speaks of my doubts about myself and how I want to believe in anything, to believe in myself. It isn't a sad depiction, but a reminder to myself about a journey I'm still taking. But it's not the first time I branded myself with a reminder of my beliefs.

Long ago, in a distant land called Skowhegan, my tattooing adventures were about to take root.

I have no memory of why we were there. Skowhegan was a town Catie and I visited on my way to the University of Maine Farmington. I would like to think we were doing something unique and interesting, but we could have just been visiting this little pit stop to look at the used bookstore. If you sneezed, you'd pass through without noticing. Our adventures were random and I remember thinking, "Today, something amazing is going to happen." Yes, we frequently boasted our positive affirmations.

I had dropped out of school. In this uncertain limbo, I was lost. I had no direction and honestly, I fought a battle with depression, struggling to make it from one day to the next. My faith in life dwindled, and these outings were a chance to silence the voice of self-doubt. Every outing with Catie brought a bit of magic, and her perspective offered hope during a trying period in my life. Before we ventured into the bookstore, we had to make a brief detour: a shady tattoo parlor. A very, very shady tattoo parlor.

We journeyed up the stairs like we were ninjas preparing an assault. We entered like giddy school girls, blowing our clandestine operation. The man behind the counter looked as if recently released from prison. Ironically, he had. While we wanted to be flies on the wall and remain focused on our mission to infiltrate this parlor, he was determined to strike up a conversation. Not with me, mind you, but with my lovely sidekick. I could have screamed, "You're under arrest!" and even that wouldn't have stopped his failing attempts at flirting.

We flipped through the copious amounts of flash art on the walls. I pointed at the various tribal designs I liked, while she gravitated to a panel of dolphins. We were daring enough to enter the parlor, but try as we might, neither of us could muster the courage to take the plunge. Our idea of danger was taking a business card and promising to return.

Ultimately, we came to our destination, a small bookstore tucked away on the main street. The store lacked the same thrill, containing old books never opened before. The lack of science fiction left me bored as I politely looked around. I pulled a lackluster tome from its place on the shelf, green with black text along the spine. While the smell might have been intoxicating, I suspected it'd be another tale of politics. With a gap on the shelf, its neighbor caught my eye. Embossed on the cover was a swirling Celtic design I'd later learn was called a snaidhm Cheilteach.

It may have been the design or the words now escaping me, but it made me think of a cross I had worn years ago. An aspiring seminary student had gifted my mother with two cross necklaces. It wasn't the crosses themselves or the religion attached to the small pieces of metal that provided the sentimental value. The kindness infused in the goodwill gesture had stuck with me. At the time, I wasn't sure what these unconnected threads might mean, but somehow, those crosses and our adventure had crossed paths.

The first cross I gave to a young lady who, without knowing, had shifted my views on life. Even at a young age her bright, innocent and even at times naïve personality made me jealous. Her perspective on the world reminded me, somewhere out there, people were still inherently good. I gave her the necklace as a gift, paying it forward. When I thought of the one I wore, I'd have a reminder to find the good in mankind. Offering this gift, I wanted to say, "You hold a unique place in my life, and I value you." To this day, I don't think I ever explained it to her.

I would fish out the second cross and wear the talisman a while longer. After dropping out of college, I found myself unable to keep my head above water. On a night when I believe I had reached rock bottom, I reached out to a friend for support. He came. He didn't ask me questions and didn't ask what was wrong. It was the first time I relied on him to be the rock in my life. He stayed the night to watch over me. I couldn't think of any grander gesture than giving him my second cross. I no longer had a physical connection to these reminders.

While looking at the cross on that book, I found that, despite a difficult year, I had persevered. The adventure not only had yet to end, it was just beginning. It didn't offer me solutions, nor a direction for my life, but it cemented a belief that had all but evaporated. Surviving wasn't enough; I had a life that needed living.

Indeed, something amazing happened.

A year later, with my father in tow, we revisited that shady tattoo parlor, determined to spend my first paycheck on a symbolic milestone. On my left forearm, the artist branded me, a high cross identical to the two I had received and passed along. It is a horrific tattoo, an embarrassing piece of artwork that would make any talented artist cringe. When asked if I want to cover it, I can't help but think of that book, that adventure. An object on a shelf set in motion a series of events that I can clearly trace, that forced me to move forward living my life.

In a little bookstore nestled away in Skowhegan, Maine, life took an unexpected turn...

... for the better.

INSIDE SECRET ROOMS

The first time I lived in Maine, I had just turned five. We lived in my ancestral home; me being the fourth generation to take up occupancy. With only two true bedrooms, my grandmother occupied one while my mother and I shared the spare. We were a different kind of nuclear family. With my father serving overseas, it was up to the three of us to hold down the fort. While the second floor held two bedrooms and a bathroom, there was a third story. Often blocked off by insulated blanks to keep the winter cold at bay, it did little to deter a curious child. It was in the attic where I would spend my afternoons, and when we returned, it became my home.

This wasn't the wardrobe from Narnia; more like a b-rate, low-budget alternative that offered the same magic.

During my mother's youth, she had lived in the attic, a level with no actual doors. It was split into two rooms by a narrow archway and she had the back room. Her brothers would share the front room until each of them left the homestead. Cobwebs and long-forgotten boxes of Christmas decorations occupied the space once the children moved away. On my first stint in Maine, it served as my playroom away from the watchful eyes of my mother and grandmother.

The attic had become frozen in time, reflecting the era when the home had first been erected. While other parts of the house received paint and remodeling, the attic had seen no sprucing since its construction. The two windows at opposite ends were single pane, dirty, and cracked. When the curtain, a thick wool blanket, drew back, the air sparkled as dust flittered about the room. It never smelled of must or mildew, but it did smell of old. The vinyl flooring curled at the corners, pulling free from the floorboards. For a small child, it served as a majestic fort, a place perfect for epic battles with Ninja Turtles and Transformers.

When toys bored me, there were other adventures to captivate my attention. Even at a young age, I understood that this had once been the home of somebody else; I just didn't understand that it was my mother and uncles. There was nothing before "me," but the artifacts squirreled away suggested otherwise. Crawling into the cubby's wings, I'd paw through boxes. Photos colored by time held faces I had never seen, but found awfully familiar. A garment bag held a white dress with dried flowers. A box was brimming to the top with homemade stuffed animals. Each treasure gave insight into the occupants who once lived there. Later, I learned those faces were of my mother's Grampy, her wedding dress and stuffed animals her mother had made for her new baby.

But even from old things came new memories.

I discovered a black and white TV with bunny ears. It seemed a relic, as it was only able to pick up four stations using its tuning dial (and fine tuner). Every evening I would lay sprawled on a bed of old pillows and watch the original Zorro jump from rooftops atop Tornado. With each crack of the whip, I'd jump, enthralled by this southwestern hero. It'd break for commercials and as the credits passed along the screen, the theme song to Batman began and I'd hardly blink while they smarted their way out of disaster. Watching on a black and white television for some might have removed the magic, but having grown up watching colorless shows with my father, it added to the adventure. It wasn't until years later that I learned one show was, indeed, in color.

But the history of the room wasn't only in the items stored away; it existed in the structure itself. While remodeling, we decided to paint the walls and pull up the breaking vinyl flooring. Beneath the floral patterned plastic, the builders had used newspaper to line the floors. They had preserved hundreds of pages, recounting a time decades earlier. We spent hours on our hands and knees, looking for local news. But of course, we had a job to do, and that required removing this treasure trove of history.

Even with a fresh coat of paint and reinforced floors, it maintained its magic.

One weekend, I ventured home from college. I suspect it was out of necessity to do laundry or beg my parents for pizza money. Much to my surprise, my childhood bedroom had a new owner. For some unknown reason, my best friend from high school had made arrangements with my parents, giving him claim to the spare bed in my room. After the many years spent lounging there reading comics and listening to cassette tapes, I couldn't think of a better roommate. There were no questions about the how and why, just a discussion about who controlled the remote to the television.

Separated by a stair case, the room remained frozen in time. It shifted from the era it had first been built to the horrible paint choices of the nineties. When I ultimately moved out, I felt it only appropriate to hide away a bit of nostalgia hoping another would-be adventurer might find it. In a small compartment next to the stairs, I tucked away an old cigar box. Inside were a dozen photos featuring friends who had, at one time or another, had shared in my home. I included a marble that once belonged to my grade school mother. But on top of it all, an article preserved from the floor. I offered no context for this time capsule, just threads sparking the imagination of a new generation.

Who knows if the new owners discovered this hidden gem?

Defining moments of my youth occurred in that room. I grew up on the third floor of 11 Ryder Avenue. Thinking back to that kid, hiding in a pillow fort while Batman and Zorro stopping evildoers, I can recall the mint green walls and layers of dust on every surface. But despite its disuse, that attic is where I learned to imagine.

THE SCRUTINY OF A FANTASY

There is a fantasy that comes to mind living in Maine. Across the globe, there is an image of vast forests filled with moose. We are thought of as a "simple folk," who work the land. We're part of this idea of a time long since passed. Mostly, it is true, and with our quaint small towns, we adequately represent this ideal. It also helps that we boast the most successful horror author in the world. With millions reading the work of Stephen King, there is an image to maintain. Please remember, it's Bang-ore, not Bang-er.

A friend came to the northern wilds of Maine later in life. At the beck of her father, in his pursuit to raising chickens, she too left behind the world she knew for the adventures of Maine. While I might have been bitter about first moving there, I have aged to the point where I consider returning. The fantasy of buying a small plot of land and building a cabin away from the hustle of the world is alluring. Waking up each day and standing on my porch to see nothing but the wilderness is part of the fantasy, and I find it drawing me in. I am brought back to my senses when I consider the lack of fiber optic internet. Reality crushes the fantasy rather quickly.

I assume this is a feeling that many experience; the need to return to the happy memories of their youth. We brush aside negative sentiments and embrace the idealistic world that raised us. Unfortunately, each time I journey down memory lane, I find myself confronted by a reality that slams shut the possibility of returning. While I might have packed my bags, wanting to return, I never closed my suitcase. A small town offers a lot to its occupants, but there are too many aspects to it I could live without.

We rise and fall with the sun. While we're not all farmers, there is something about a farmer's ethics burning in every fiber of our being. For much of the year, rising with the sun is early, but manageable. However, the same goes for when it gets dark. As the sun draws near, we slow, and over time, this becomes daunting. As the days grow shorter, we hunker down in our home, determined to survive until the planet ventures closer to the sun. During the winters, we spend more time in the dark than we do in sunlight, and, for many of us, this results in the horrors of seasonal depression. I question sometimes how we maintain our redneck status when there's only a few hours of sunlight each day. Contrary to popular belief, not everybody in Maine takes to the winter months with reckless abandon. There are plenty who refuse to icefish, snow mobile or take to the slopes. For many, it's a time to catch up on reading and make sure roofs don't collapse.

The copious nightlife. I know that the mere thought of this is chuckle-worthy. It's true. In our town, we were fortunate to have a store staying open till 8:00PM several nights a week. Our gas stations close at five, and if you forgot to gas up your car, you'd have to drive twenty minutes to the next station. We had no restaurants. We didn't have a single place to gather unless you were determined to take part in

Bingo on Tuesday nights. If you wanted more than a pizza (which we could only get made two nights a week) you'd be required to drive at least forty-five minutes. This required us to make plans and spend the majority of our time sitting in vehicles defeating the concept of an "effortless dinner."

Small towns breed familiarity. This makes a small town magical. I can say growing up, I knew the entire town had an eye on me. Playing outside, no matter where I might find myself, I could expect a neighbor to wave with a friendly smile. There would be small talk, and a general, "You behave yourself." Because of extended family trees, the only strangers in the town were newcomers, and even that passed quickly. However, the concept of familiarity has a dark side. There were several occurrences when a family emergency transformed into town gossip. I would have townspeople asking me, "So I heard..." to which they were only attempting to ferret out details. In such close knit quarters, there is little in the way of privacy. Folks sit next to police scanners, hoping for excitement and a chance to be the frontrunner in a game of "Did you know…" It meant that there was little in the way of independence if neighbors had their eyes on you. So I spent most of my youth hidden away in the forest, away from prying eyes.

Fun is what you make it. This should be the anthem of my childhood. While my imagination kept me company in my younger years, once I became a teenager, the town offered little. For the sake of our sanity, we became adept at making our own fun. It turned into a steady rotation of commandeering a friend's house. Gathering made it easier to conjure games to keep us out of trouble. We became card sharks, movie critics, campers, and swimmers. I'm pretty sure we even put on a pretty spectacular supper show. My town had no options for teenagers. Once I got my license, these adventures took place on the road as we explored the vastness of Maine. Unfortunately for many, this boredom turned to addiction. By the time I graduated, there were more than a few teenagers suffering from alcoholism. The drug use in my school ran rampant, and with such a small population, it consumed classmates. I suspect as the town continued to decay, these statistics will be less shocking and become the norm.

Grown Local is a lost possibility. Now that I have simple luxuries at my door, a grocery store, a mechanic, a fast-food joint, I am not sure I could return to the middle of nowhere. Having sneakers with a hole in them could require a two-hour drive, only to find out the one store in the "big city" doesn't have your brand. Looking for food that isn't good ole fashioned meat and potatoes? Expect to drive far even further. If time was money, I can't imagine how much money I wasted hoofing it back and forth for everyday items. It would be better if each of us could grow food, chop wood, and raise our own livestock, but we're not quite that rustic. Sometimes you would kill for a milkshake in the middle of the night.

We dream of being self-sufficient. Along with the romance of being a Mainer is this idea that we are self-sufficient. Because of our isolation, this is often true, but it comes at a price. The reality is that we are not an entirely self-sufficient town and because of that, we have to earn living wages. Unfortunately, living on the fringes of society comes with a financial burden. The biggest is the lack of employers. When the largest employer of a town is its school district, there is something revealing about the destiny of the town. I think about going home, but I would have to take a sixty percent pay cut even if I could find a job. Many jobs are seasonal, and for those in "high demand" fields, there is little demand for them in the furthest reaches of the North. Because of this, I couldn't afford my cabin with high speed internet. My dream is crushed before it began.

I love the idea, the fantasy, of going back and living out my best years in a tight-knit community. However, I find the stark reality screaming "unlivable." I respect those who return or those that never left. They are hearty folk that persevere despite the growing list of challenges. I'll continue to remember the best of what my small town offered, but I've grown up and expect a town to offer much more.

It's unfortunate; the reality is at the cost of all the things I once loved.

A SECOND SET OF FOOTPRINTS

Maine provided the clay to shape who I am as an adult. It built my form and gave me the durability to face the weather a harsh world would use to test me. Despite the haphazard materials composing my form, I have moments in which I can appear as a polished figure. I give Maine much of the credit for sculpting me. However, it only created a husk of a human. Like Pinocchio, I was lifeless and merely a vessel. There were many Geppetto's breathing life into this golem, but it was a single woman who gifted me a soul.

The men of Maine are made by its women. My mother is a Mainer to her core. I share a similar story. Neither of us was born within the boundaries of Maine, but we hold a mantle passed down from our parents. Birthed to a "true" Mainer, she would move to the state in her youth and spend her formative years in the same house, the same school, as I would a generation later.

She fights against her inherited title, but she has become the definition of Mainehood. My father has always been my idol, worshiped in the ways a young boy does his father. He never worked for his admiration, but my mother fought tooth and nail to be the most important person in my life. While my father fought for our country abroad, she assumed the role of both parents. As the disciplinarian, she fought daily battles with an angry child, some of which were lost causes from the start. It would be later that I see life thrust her into the role of caretaker, villain, heroine, teacher, confidant and many more. With each role, she adapted, building herself into a new definition of remarkable.

If my mother gave me a soul, Maine is my maternal grandfather.

My birth took place amidst a tragedy. Three weeks after I was born, my brother, at eight years of age, passed away. My mother's first born, a child who, partly because of her love and partly because of his unique needs, had been my mother's entire world. I will never be capable of fathoming the experience of holding one child while another dies. Knowing how I would react, I would have given her permission to neglect her second born while she picked up the pieces. With her husband departing for parts unknown, she set aside her pain. She did the unthinkable: continued being a mom. The strength she wielded in the decision to continue astonishes. Over the years, her armor has shown signs of fatigue, chipped and cracked, but when called upon, she stood ready.

My story starts in North Carolina. We moved as my father's station changed. From North Carolina to Pennsylvania, to Maine, to North Carolina again and then settling on Maine for retirement. My father was overseas fighting a war, leaving my mother to fight a war waged within her house. It wasn't enough of a challenge to be a single parent; she joined the workforce, as well. At first, my mother found work as a barista and later, employment alongside family friends at a clothing store. She tells people she worked as a cashier in a "sports apparel store," but the humor comes from the owner's *second* store. I never miss an opportunity to mention that my mother worked in a "porn store." Don't get me wrong; it wasn't seedy as one would think, though I leave that out of the conversation. Mostly, they sold intimate apparel, a few pairs of fuzzy handcuffs and chocolate penises.

My father returned from the war, and whether because he was tired of fighting battles or his family needed him, he prepared for retirement. For our family, this meant returning to our ancestral home in Brownville Junction. For me, it was difficult. My family had been the Corps, a vast network of men and women in fatigues that served as aunts and uncles. My home had been wherever my father received marching orders. I was raised a nomad and for the first time, the prospect of establishing roots terrified me.

With the addition of my grandmother, we were a family again. It seems ideal, but nothing prepared us for this new sense of normalcy. When our routine involved a key member being gone for years, replaced by the spouses of a platoon, there is a lengthy adjustment period. My father was and will always be, a good man. He is the ideal of which I hope all fathers aspire. Despite this, I can say my father was not a parent. My mother was blessed with the singular role of raising me, even amidst the company of my father. She would lay down the law and struggle with a child who had grown beyond his years. My father would now have to wrestle for the mantle of "man of the house" from his would-be usurper, a role he never quite obtained.

We had a home. While this would be a blessing, for my mother, it was a struggle. Her mother assumed the mantle of the second parent and three generations coexisted peacefully. The house in which we settled was the same house my mother grew into her own, and while she worked at creating new memories, a haunted past dogged her at every step. She would come back to a town having experienced the world. This broad view, this understanding of our place in the world might otherwise enlighten, but here, it served as a detriment. She adjusted to the "Maine Way," and took a position as a cashier at the local market place, a title also held by my grandmother.

It was at this point in my youth I became aware of my brother. While he has always impacted my life, it wasn't until one night sitting in bed with my mother we talked about the pictures of the "other" boy in our home. Being the adventurous youth, I had already gone through her hope chest and was very aware of the items hidden inside. I realized she attempted to put aside the past to live in the present. Surrounded by a home she grew up in, albums of a child long since gone and a hope chest filled with painful memories, my mother was hurting. If ever there is a hard lesson to learn, it is how to console your elder. But as my mother stopped me on my way to bed, she read me "The Neverending Story." As she read the same few pages repeatedly, where Bastian dares to cast aside his doubts and free the Childlike Empress, I drew parallels. I listened to her read over and again well into my teens. To this day, the passage read aloud gives me goosebumps.

While I noticed hints of an unhappy mother, she did well to continue her own journey of growth. After a hard-fought battle, we stood side-by-side in our caps and gowns to celebrate my high school and her college graduation. My mother, the first college graduate in our family, served as a role model of what determination and perseverance could accomplish. The photograph still sits on her shelf. I can't help but think that was the moment things changed for us. My anger and the constant lashing out tempered and she stepped back, loosening the reins. It would still take years until we reached a peaceful existent, but this served as a milestone. While I was determined to forge my own path in life, my mother had laid the groundwork. The road less travelled might have more bumps and bruises, but I followed in her tracks as she took the brunt of the abuse.

During my high school years, my mother and I were at each other's throats. She was the sole disciplinarian and the focal point of my unruly rage. Even gently delving into the source of so much yelling, swearing, and empty threats, I'm astounded to see how clear the problems were. My mother raised me to be independent, know right from wrong, and how to make mindful decisions. She did her job well, too well, and I think I learned them quickly. While she was still attempting to impart minor lessons, she had already taught me the most important lesson of my life: be good. Be good to yourself, to others, and expect nothing in return for your goodness. Accept that doing good is its own reward. While that applied outside our home, inside, it was one screaming match after another. Being a large teenager, you'd think I'd have won more than a few, but even my rage couldn't overcome the guilt by doing wrong by her.

As I uncover these lessons, subtlety implanted into my psyche in a way only a deviously smart person can manage, I have to stop and think, "What an amazing mother." I feel this sentiment so strongly all at once, I'm filled with pride and sorrow. As her child, I'm proud, knowing that someday I'll be asked, "Where did it all start?" I'll be able to reply "With my mother." Part of my heart is also heavy with sadness as I think about how long it took me to understand this.

While I try to wrap this up in a way explaining the reverie and awe I feel when I think of my past with her, I realize there is no way to adequately thank her. She has stood at the edge of the abyss, and by sheer will, founded in an unconditional love, she never relented. I think for all the sacrifices she has made, I can never pay her back. However, I will pay her back in the manner in which she taught me. I will continue to do good things, be good to the people I encounter, and do it all because, simply put, "That's how my mother raised me."

FINDING A NEW HOME

My life had a sudden shift. I went from a ten year relationship to being single. At the same time, I started a new position as a design teacher at a large urban high school. Life continued to throw me a series of curve balls, and while I tried desperately to knock them out of the park, I took the biggest plunge of my life. Staring at a "For Sale" sign, it was time that I went from being a renter to a homeowner.

It wasn't the brightest idea in terms of stress or finances, but it was time to take on a new adventure. However, let's be clear; the adventure was less than twenty feet from my current rental. I only needed to move across the hall to begin. Having grown up in a military family, we never owned the homes we lived in. Once we reached Maine, I understood what it meant to put down roots. It might not have been the smartest move but I craved stability.

Until this point, the most adult thing I had experienced was standing as the best man at a friend's wedding. The transition from college student to adult in the "real" world happened without warning. There was no parental supervision, nobody guiding our hands as I watched two of my closest friends tie the knot. It was the first time I found myself firmly rooted in the future my younger self longed for.

Buying my first home redefined adulthood.

This new reality didn't quite hit me when I put in the offer. The inspection, meeting with realtors, lawyers and signing the closing papers happened so quickly, I barely wrapped my head around the process. But none of that struck a chord. It was administrative busy work. The smack in the face happened as I opened a can of paint, preparing to change the blank white canvas. I didn't need permission from my landlord. I didn't need to consult my parents. I didn't need anything. When I rolled the light gray onto the wall, it sank in; this is mine. I had achieved the proverbial American dream.

While I underwent this step into adulthood, my parents were going through a similar process. They had boxed away their lives as they made repairs on my ancestral home with the goal of moving from the small town. The isolation and small-town feel had turned sour for them, and they sought the conveniences of living near the city. They had sorted my childhood into donations, keepsakes, and trash.

While they underwent this process, found myself with a plethora of mixed emotions. A house that four generations called home, Wright, Cowing, Flagg, was about to be passed along to new occupants. Much to my mother's dismay, when she asked me to come help, I refused. Even from a distance, I found myself angry at the prospect of losing the home, and overjoyed that they were moving away from the crumbling town. But as I've said before, I find it difficult to cope with severing ties to memories of who I once was.

While I often talk about Brownville Junction passing from grandeur to struggling town, you can't help but root for it like the underdog. There is always this underlying idea that maybe, just maybe, things will get better. You want the best for the community that made you, but the flicker of hope dwindles until there's nothing left. In my head, my parents selling our home felt like a betrayal, that they gave up that last bit of fight. It would be years before I understood it wasn't a death, but an evolution. We had grown beyond what a small town could offer.

Of course, during the process we compared notes. Having moved in with my grandmother, my parents had also never purchased a house. The process is daunting and often required commiserating how difficult the experience had become. Despite purchasing their first house, they found it nearly impossible to sell our home. In a town with a decreasing population and no economy, large purchases are rare.

I can see the glaring differences in a comparing homes separated by three-hundred miles. Stripping away the sentimental value, removing the idea of a home, and returning it to a house with four walls, you can only categorize it by the stats found on a realtor's website. When compared side-by-side, it is evident that my parents were escaping more than moving. In a few years, the numbers that increase throughout the rest of the country continued on a downward slope.

Anybody who has purchased or sold a home will tell you "Prepare for a ride" and it's true. It is filled with emotions, many of which you'd never expect to surface while making financial transactions. Ultimately, there is a point when you must face the severing of ties. What I learned, as I started making memories in my new home, they do not exist because of a place or thing. While the visual cues and familiarity might no longer be there to act as a trigger, the memories exist regardless.

While I stood at a wedding, I thought I had reached adulthood. When the realtor put the keys to my first house in my hand, I knew this must be the moment that propels me into that mythical land of adulting. While they started a new chapter in life, the first time I felt I finished the epilogue of one story and began the prologue of another, came when I said farewell to an object, but not the sense of home it once provided. I am saddened that I no longer have ties to the environment in which my childhood took place, but the memories remain as vivid as the day I created them.

Adulting is knowing that home isn't a place, but a state of mind.

FROZEN IN FRAME

As we age, do our spouses continue to find us attractive? I asked myself this as a child. Living with my parents and grandmother, I had questions I didn't dare voice. But for a kid, it baffled my mind that you could still find somebody attractive decades after meeting them. I always thought they must somehow be able to overlook their spouse's appearance and rely on personality. It was one of those thoughts plaguing the mind of a child. When somebody asked me about my passion for photography, the thought returned and I had to laugh.

Each time we crack open a forgotten album of photographs, there is an overwhelming sense of nostalgia. While they slowly lose their color, tinted by time, they serve as a trigger, sending us tumbling into a world of memories. Even the photographs taken long before my birth leave me asking questions. They serve as conversation starters, a moment of reflection. Most photographs taken are to commemorate happiness, and they leave my heart overwhelmed with joy. But do they offer insight into a child's quandary?

Tucked away in my father's wallet, there is a black-and-white photograph of my mom. She is wearing her Navy dress uniform, a formal shot required by all new service people. It has survived multiple migrations, and countless rounds in the washing machine. The edges have frayed, folded to where the image is peeling, and the top right corner was torn off decades ago. He asked me to restore the photo so he could have a new copy for his wallet. Even after reviving the image to its original splendor, he keeps the frayed image on top of the new version. I asked him, "Why? Of all the photographs, why this one?"

His answer was simple. "That's how your mum will always look to me."

My father is not an overly sentimental man. He falls on the side of practicality. But underneath the steely gaze, he can be emotional, even if he doesn't voice it often. Once in a great while, he'll take his heart out to play and speak in such a poignant manner you wonder if you've met his doppelgänger. As he pulled apart the folds of his wallet, confirming the photograph was safely tucked away, it was one of these rare exchanges. With a single phrase, he changed my perception of the world. He answered a childish question and offered me a new way to view surrounding people.

Upon close inspection, my parents appear as my grandparents did. Their hair has turned to more salt than pepper, and the lines on their faces have grown deeper. The artist in me observes these aesthetic changes, but it is a struggle to notice these signs of aging. When I look at my parents, I can't properly explain it, but they remain the young parents who gave birth to me in their late twenties. Despite their years, there is an overlay, this ideal image of who they are. With every smile or glare, it's hard to see them as anything other than the parents from my youth.

For my mother, she remains this bohemian woman wearing sunglasses. She is a beautiful young mother laughing beside my brother. She hams it up for the camera, experiencing life for the first time with a zest I admire. My father, on the other hand, is a rigid Marine in dress blues, white gloves and white hat obscuring his eyes. The image of him oozes with pride and a sense of duty. They have both grown, and added layer upon layer of who they are, but the image of them always remains the same. While the years march onward, the image of who they are remains frozen in time, captured by photographs in albums tucked away under beds.

This sentiment isn't only for people; it can go for places as well. Filling shoeboxes are photographs of Brownville Junction during its peak. There are photographs of deceased family members hammering spikes into the railroad, or passenger-filled cars carrying Canadians into the town. High school photos show a winning basketball team and cheerleaders rallying a school that has since been torn down. Each of these capture of spirit that has steadily faded, and much like the people in the photos, we see them and remember a fonder time. Then, as we look to our dying town, we overlay the reality with these memories of what once was.

My passion for photography comes from its ability to remind of us a simpler time and allow us to dwell in the bliss while ignoring the eventual. There is a sense of relief seeing the smiling faces, with their entire life ahead of them and not a care in the world. As I stare at the photos in the shoebox, I see my parents madly in love, living an adventure, life having yet to thrust a burden down upon their shoulders. This is why I snap pictures of my own, marking my journey and wanting to remind myself when life gets difficult, there are reasons to look forward and smile.

I reconsider that childhood question, and I can't help but chuckle. We all age, and eventually time will leave its mark on our bodies. But in photographs, there is a thread that ties us to a world of hopes and dreams.

POORLY CONCEIVED SHENANIGANS

There are a number of rites that define the teenage experience. These can range from a first job to passing the driver's test. It can be the first time wearing a tux for prom or even the moment the school principal hands over the diploma. These triumphs are universal, periods in our teenage journey that transcend geography or even differences in generations. But of course, this can't be about one of *those* occasions.

From time to time, I need to remind my students that like them; I am indeed human. I sit at my desk staring at a stack of papers while they believe they're being subtle in their loud whispers. Eventually, I bite and ask them about their discussion. Once they realize I'm asking out of curiosity instead of guilt, they decide to humor me. They've been discussing the annual senior skip day. Two upperclassmen approach my desk, confused expressions scribbled across their faces. "You probably didn't have one…" The other elbows her friend and adds, "Senior Skip Day…it's when seniors…." I have told stories of growing up in Maine often, and yet they believe that this foreign land to the North has an alien culture. While hard to believe, I need to remind them I, too, was a teenager.

The year was 1999, and it was expected to end - this year, decade, century and millennia - with a bang. There was no way we were going to let any rites of passage go by the wayside. Our class was known for being tame, and rightfully so. When the student body includes the daughters of our superintendent and two school principals, we could be rebellious, but only within reason. Even with the limitations roping in our ambition, we started plotting.

For us, the tame and cautious class of '99, we refused to miss our Senior Skip Day. Today, people communicate through social media or via texting. Information can travel at an alarming rate, and within a few minutes, we can alert several hundred people to dastardly plans. Back then, we had to rely on notes passed in the hall, slipped between hands as if we were dealing drugs. With only minutes between classes, we relayed our intentions. For a class of fifty-seven people, it didn't take long, but the debate started; what would we do?

On a chilly April day, we went to the beach.

In landlocked Brownville Junction, the term "beach" is used rather haphazardly. Any place where the water touched land and offered a spot to congregate was referred to as a "beach". Because of the two-hour drive, our definition never included an actual ocean. Instead, these were lakes and rivers with rocky inlets where we could unroll our towels and bathe in the sun. The most common beach for my neck of the woods was Peaks Kenny, a state park in Dover-Foxcroft. Not only did our plan include the beach, but also offered a layer of rebellion as we'd be invading our rival town.

The plan was genius… until you factored in Mother Nature.

The night prior, we activated the phone tree. We spread plans throughout my class as we conjured reasons to be out of school. While some played sick, and others claimed doctor's appointments, my parents looked the other way. Growing up as a responsible kid with good decision-making skills had its perks. While I thought I was walking along the fine line between being a good and living a life of crime, my parents let me take a walk on the wild side. In hindsight, their willingness to cover for me should have been a sign that this idea might not be as daring as we thought.

We met in a parking on the far side of town where students often spent their evenings blaring music and smoking cigarettes we stole from our parents. Piling into cars, we started our adventure, free from school and destined for greatness. In the middle of the week during the school day, Peaks Kenny was deserted, a godsend for a bunch of teenagers on the run. Parking, I remember thinking, "We did it," like we had successfully pulled off a bank heist.

Stepping out of the car in my shorts and tank top, something was amiss. As we crossed the parking lot, kicking off our sandals to bury our feet in the sand, the scene lacked its usual warmth. We had made a grave error. Despite it being a beautiful, sunny, and windless day, the fact remained: April in Maine. While we are a hearty folk, this pushed our limits. Determined to make the most of our slightly aloof scheme, we headed for the water.

Most of my classmates spread their towels, deciding to make the most of the sun. They rotated, soaking in the rays, completely unaware of their skin turning shades of pink. Being a frigid day, it was impossible to determine when our bodies had enough. Instead, we absorbed what warmth we could find.

I didn't care about the temperature, one way or another, I was getting in that water. Leaving behind my classmates, I bravely marched to the edge of the lake. I was a Mainer, and one thing we don't fear is the cold. Charging in, it did not differ from any other time we swam. Living in a region where every river and lake are fed by mountain snow, we understand it will be cold even in the middle of summer. I'm not sure if it was adrenaline or the instant numbing sensation, but I continued. It wasn't until the water hit my waist that I understood I had made a mistake. My plan to dive headfirst into the water and celebrate our victory wasn't the only thing that shrank.

There were brave (we'll go with brave) people who ignored my shrieks. Plunging into the water, we feared the shock would set in and we'd have to send out a rescue party. Their rallying cries turned into cries for mercy as they spun about and ran out of the water faster than they entered. Needless to say, we didn't last long.

Sixty degrees does not make for a day at the beach.

Teeth chattered. Skin blistered. We were threatened with not being able to walk during graduation. But dammit, we did it, another item on our farewell tour through the high school.

While we crowded the main office the next morning, supplying forged notes from our parents and doctors, the secretary was less than thrilled. It might not have been a problem to let us proceed without a lecture. But as we stood there, each of us blistering red, smelling of aloe, it was obvious that a call from our parents couldn't hide our deed. We had taken the risk, and we were ready for the consequences. But as I said before, there are perks to having the daughters of school officials in our class. The secretary accepted our notes and excuses with a knowing glare.

My students laugh as I tell the story. Suddenly, we have poor decision-making skills in common. Correcting papers go out the window as they sit down at my desk, asking for suggestions for their skip day. Their ideas are as poorly conceived as mine had been. Ultimately, I make the only suggestion that seems fitting while the goosebumps on my skin recall the frigid water.

Senior Skip Day, a decade later, takes place at the beach.

OASIS AT THE END OF THE TRACKS

Measuring six by six miles, and fewer than two thousand people, it's hard to imagine that the town is divided by its residents. Even in rural America, where we are seen as woodland creatures, there is a hierarchy that comes with where you live. Try as we might to be "one people," we are, in fact, like any other city. There are good parts of town, and parts you avoid, if given the chance. For me, I grew up outside of the town center.

The marker dividing Brownville Junction from Brownville had long since vanished. The folks in the Junction didn't dislike Brownville Village, yet there remained an uneasy truce between the two towns. But in our world, an invisible line crossed Route 11 as you passed the rest stop. There is plenty of green space in the town, but the first things of note are the giant mounds of sand and gravel, lined from chunkiest to finest. For many, the pits were a way of life, providing sand to the state to maintain the roads during the winter. As they reached your rearview mirror, you entered the first signs of civilization and, as the houses grew more dense, you reached burbs of Junction.

The primary division in Brownville Junction came with the black trestle bridge. This divider of black steel lattice work crossed over two lanes of roads and stretched across the Pleasant River. While it offered no genuine change in population density, number of houses or even booming industry, we referred to this metropolis as "uptown." I assume because when you look at a map, it is technically "up" geographically, otherwise I always thought it was just one of those weird things Mainers do. The tracks themselves weaved across streets throughout the town, peppering roads, all leading to the station that sat in the middle of the Junction.

There was an unspoken law that anything relating to the trains was strictly off limits. The train yard, the tracks, and even the bridge were "out of bounds." My parents never had to explain this, but it didn't diminish the importance of the rule. Needless to say, when the trains littered our entire town, inevitably, we would step over the line.

Thirty feet above the Pleasant River, we darted across the underside of the train trestle. A series of giant Xs composed the support for the train tracks above. Below, in the lazy river, pillars of wood remained visible just beneath the surface of the water, a support structure that helped build the original bridge. We held our arms out, balancing on the beams, stealing glances to the pylons that would impale us should we fall. For some reason it always reminded me of the creek in "Bridge to Terabithia" and I was Jess crossing over into a magical world.

Much to my surprise, there was indeed magic.

In a landlocked community, we have a fondness for the water. There are countless brooks, streams, rivers, and lakes scattered across central Maine. Wherever possible, we've turned them into gathering spots where we escape the heat and try to shake off the mosquitos. An older friend introduced me to the "beach" hidden on the other side of the tracks.

It wasn't like our coastline, a lengthy expanse covered in more pebbles than sand. This was a beach capable of holding a dozen stretched towels. The bend in the Pleasant River created a bank of sand, barely worth mentioning. But here, the water carved out a crook deep enough to go swimming, and with a current keeping the water moving, we were safe from the dangers of leeches. While it required a hike, a little rock climbing, and beating through the bush, it served as a private area where we could escape. In no time, word spread. Friends of friends mentioned this oasis in our otherwise dull town. Quickly, it went from an undiscovered beauty to being littered with classmates.

I spent my afternoons hiding from the civilized world. There would be swimming and with the speed of the water, it proved a good workout pushing against the current. But more than that, I spent my time sitting on the rocks drawing in my journal. It didn't take long to find myself emerged in that wonderful part of Maine. The beavers gnawed at wood, falling trees for their home while their young splashed nearby. Eagles would fly overhead, swooping down to snatch fish from the water and return to their nest. Even the deer stepped out of hiding to wade into the water to avoid the persistence of blood-sucking insects.

Our hidden gem had another secret. After weeks of vanishing after school, my parents finally asked where I was going. Used to saying, "the ditch" that housed an enormous expanse of forest behind my house, I admitted to this new location uptown. While I thought I was offering this new, amazing insight into the town, my father coughs up, "Oh yeah, you mean the old swimming hole?" Just like that, my father reminded me that in a small town, there are no secrets. Then came the history lesson.

A generation before me, there had been a different swimming hole, only a short distance from my beach. I had climbed around it each time and hadn't stopped to think it had been the go-to destination decades before. Before the river changed its course, my parents had spent their teen years splashing in the river. It seemed innocent fun until my father explained they used to climb onto the bridge and jump into the water. Yes, folks, those pylons in the river that could have easily impaled a man? They treated them as inconvenient obstacles to avoid while jumping three stories into a river not nearly deep enough for the feat. As usual, my parents proved that, out of my household, I was the timid and cautious one. While they were cheating death, I was admiring beavers making a home.

To this day, I'm surprised they didn't kill themselves.

After hearing stories about kids jumping into the murky waters, I had to see it for myself. Once more, standing on the black trestle bridge, balancing against powerful gusts of winds, I found the spot my father had mentioned. In a narrow space in the water, you could see there was little margin for error or it'd be an ambulance trip to the hospital. Climbing across the bridge no longer felt as "out of bounds" as it had before. These unspoken rules might have been in place, but they were relatively new creations, as my parents proved. I felt as if I should lecture them on their dangerous behavior.

Thirty years have passed, and yet again, I discover that, in Brownville Junction, little had changed about the people. While they had more gathering spaces as youths, we still found a way to overlap. Within the six-by-six mile square, there were no new adventures to be had, just old ones discovered by the next generation.

As the summer rolled on, this location offered a different bit of magic that is only apparent after years of distance. Our town didn't quite have a "good" and "bad" side of the tracks, but there was definitely a rift between the two sides. But for a while, in the oppressing heat, we found common ground at the *end* of the tracks. It didn't matter who you were, or which side of the town you called home, the beach became neutral territory. Unfortunately, as with many activities in the summer, there is a short shelf life before the leaves change and the water turns icy.

Years later, I returned. I wanted to revisit the spots where I spent my childhood. Swatting at black flies, I climbed through the woods and found the rocks where I sat for hours at a time. Unfortunately, because of the rising temperatures, the beach had been washed away, leaving little evidence it ever existed, a reoccurring theme in Brownville Junction. But as I trekked back to my car, I found a new path recently carved out in the underbrush. Following my curiosity, it lead to another spot only a few hundred feet further up the river. Just out of sight, I could hear the splashing of kids in the water. Like me, like my parents and their parents before them, they discovered their own version of a classic.

A new generation, a new beach.

TO THE BREAKING POINT

There are events in life that are burned into our memories. These flashbulb moments for my parents include the Challenger explosion and the assassination of President Kennedy. They are etched in place, making the most obscure detail crystal clear, as if it happened earlier that morning. These events, while often tragic, can unite a people under a common sentiment. We abandon our sense of self and look to our communities for stability.

During my high school years, our flashbulb moment would be the Ice Storm of 1998.

It is true that small communities in Maine show their spirit as the snow falls. Neighbors near and far become a well-armed militia of shovels and plows. We fall in line like an army, prepared to do battle with nature itself. While the town has a single plow working tirelessly to keep the streets clear, those with trucks join the march, working on driveways and side streets. It is a well-rehearsed performance; we had endured it every year. Despite our readiness, nothing prepared us for the snow that fell in January of 1998.

For two weeks the snow tested the spirit of every Mainer.

We grew up hearing our elders recount the great snowstorm of '78. Listening to them talk about the event, you couldn't help but wonder if they were exaggerating for the sake of drama. It isn't until they dig out the photos (because every person has photographic evidence) that you understand their stories have tamed with time. The snow had reached the roof, burying them in frosty coffins. When the people of Maine display fear of snow, there is rarely an understatement in their confession.

Sometimes even a Mainer has to admit we are at the mercy of the land. Our troops stood in doorways, triggered by a memory of the last great snow storm, frozen as their usual strategies seemed like feeble attempts. When the snow dances between rain and snow, there is a different level of worry. It's possible to put on enough layers to ward away the cold, but rain finds the chips in our flannel armor. But like true Mainers, we refused defeat.

We shoveled. We plowed. We scraped. But before we could finish our first round of clean up, our tracks were filled, and the snow returned. Our determination faltered as we quickly realized we were losing the battle. The conversations shifted, no longer about safety, but about survival. It might sound dramatic, as if we were attempting to give our lives a bit of excitement, but our people die in these storms. With only one grocery store, one gas station, and bridges on either side of the town, we become an island. Our worries are not only founded, but they came to the forefront the next night.

The power lines gave out and three hundred and twenty-five thousand Mainers found themselves without heat.

One-third of Maine found themselves without electricity. In the denser cities, this isn't as alarming. They have heat alternatives or communal gathering areas where they can go for warmth. The cities become the priority. For those smaller towns, and sparsely populated villages, our battle against nature became a fight for survival.

Portable radios turned silent and the few signals reaching the North were no longer broadcasting music; they were broadcasting survival tactics. Broadcasters offered weather reports, predicting that the worst was yet to come. They suggested preparing kerosene heaters, shutting off parts of the house too difficult to heat. Water was stored as we prepared for our pipes to freeze and we inventoried food as we relied on a single gas stove. Those few homes with generators, that were able to receive communication from the outside world, walked house to house, making sure we had up-to-date information.

The limitations of civilization trapped us. Our cars and trucks were frozen to the ground, and those that could get free couldn't navigate the several inches of ice on the roads. Plows became scarce as the night pushed on. The first night without power isn't worrisome, as it happened several times throughout the year. But even we knew we wouldn't be waking to the sound of the heater kicking on. Families relied on backup batteries for medical equipment and generators for heat, while crank-powered radios offered a bleak glimpse into the coming days.

The first night Maine dug in its heels and showed the world we could survive. But it was the next day we showed the world what it truly meant to be a Mainer. It wasn't enough we as individuals survived; we acted as one. It was our responsibility as Mainers to make sure our brothers and sisters, our family by geography, survived.

The reports were coming in throughout the state. The power wouldn't be on for days, and the snow had no end in sight. We woke to cold homes, buried under blankets and wearing layers of sweatshirts to bed. At my house, it was common to be awakened by the sound of my father snow blowing, but even that was silent as he had moved onto combatting snow at the homes of elderly neighbors.

We didn't stand in our chilled homes and wait for the plows to clear our roads or the power companies to restore our electricity. We didn't wait for the hospitals and ambulances to check on our elderly. All these things are in the job description of a Mainer. We began shoveling walkways, backs ready to break under the sheer volume. Neighbors emerged, working together to scrape the ice from roofs to prevent collapsing. Doors were knocked on, and blankets were exchanged as we made sure our brethren were ready for more of the unyielding storm. Snowmobiles transported goods from the store to needy families. Shelters began to open in our community buildings, making sure we survived the cold.

School had been cancelled as bridges were flooded. We were in the midst of the snowpocalypse. I only saw my father when he returned to fetch more gas for the blower. He stopped in the house, drinking his coffee, warming his hands on the mug. After swapping out his pants and socks for new sets of dry clothing, he spoke of the snow like a combatant in the military. It was relentless and no matter how fast he worked; he was outgunned. Even my mother would take to the roof, making sure the snow was pushed off, ensuring it wouldn't find its way into the house.

We were under attack, and backup wasn't coming.

The snow didn't stop for almost two weeks. Newspapers weren't printed, and the college even pushed back the opening its spring semester for two weeks. The people of northern Maine were without power for weeks. While this seems frivolous in the time of disaster, it was the small towns that were truly on their own. Unlike the cities, we had been running drills for our entire lives to prepare for this moment. Every winter leading to that January had been a boot camp, and now we had been deployed to face our foe.

Despite the relentless beating of the storm, you could wake up in the middle of the night to the sound of a snow blower going or a neighbor scraping the ice from the roof. Those with trucks braved the roads and filled their gas tanks, delivering fuel to the homes with generators. Lights returned for a select few, and instead of hoarding their comforts, they opened their homes to those in need. Meals were prepared, covered in tinfoil while they offered showers and a warm respite from nature.

I believe by the second week, we had been humbled. I always think of Mainers being "of the land" and co-existing with the world we live in. It was a tough lesson to learn, but I came to understand that while we respected the land, we could still be victimized by its ferocity. But we continued for fourteen days. The people of Maine were still enduring like they had on that frightful first night.

Not everybody survived. There were deaths, those who suffered from heart attacks shoveling, and those unable to reach their medicine. We would gather at the post office, the grocery store, and the gas station, and we would commiserate with others, sharing the worst of the endeavor. But it ended with a handshake, a thank you, and a good job. In January 1998, I thought we discovered our limitations. What I found, a spirit flowing through our veins that refuses to break while our hearts beat.

OUR HIP DATE NIGHT SPOT

In a small town, dating is problematic. The first and most obvious barrier is finding somebody to date. Out of the few thousand people in our collection of towns, only about two hundred are within the same age bracket. Then you have to filter out family, which for many leaves only a handful of options. Then you divide that in half between the boys and girls, and suddenly the fish in the sea are starting to look more like goldfish in a tank.

But love finds a way, even when the statistics make it look unlikely. So now that there is a person to pursue, and, let's say, they return the sentiment, there is a question of, "Now, what?" The Junction was not exactly filled to the brim with date destinations. Our movie theater was an hour away, and even a rousing game of bowling required forty-five minutes. Depending on the scenario, that is an awfully long time to sit in a car with another person, especially for a first venture into the world of dating.

When we returned to Maine, much to my parents' horror, I started dating. There was a string of girlfriends in my youth. I recall my mother frequently asking, "Where are you going on dates to?" She didn't understand that dating simply meant you were involved with somebody. My mother couldn't possibly understand. She had never been ten and in love.

Our collection of towns covered a large geographic area in Maine. My school district consisted of twelve towns, villages, and territories. But despite the physical size of the space, there wasn't much in the way of communal gathering places. Of course, there were always the churches and their socials, but that hardly seemed like the place for a first date.

Being in middle school, we were too young to take the car Looping, though I'm sure plenty of kids my age were in their siblings' backseats as they racked up the miles. We were too old to be entertained by the playground found at the elementary school. Our pre-teen love was destined to be shunned by the community as we giggled at the prospect of holding hands. Thankfully there was one clandestine destination where we could wave our love like a banner and not have parents ogling us the entire time.

We had the roller rink.

The exterior of the building looked fairly decrepit, the gravel parking lot only adding to its abandoned visage. The building had been repurposed multiple times throughout the years, and the newest iteration was a godsend for the younger kids in our town. From the outside, you might think it was one of the many buildings waiting for nature to strike and cave in the roof or knock down the walls. But in small town Maine, our interiors rarely align with our gruff exterior.

The double doors were industrial, thick, and capable of stopping a battering-ram. Other than the lit sign next to the street, it appeared as if a giant Lego brick had been plopped down at one end of our infamous Loop. But on a Saturday, you'd hear the music before you exited your parent's car. Upon entering, there was a narrow hallway with coat hooks and cubbies, all leading to a wooden counter. Sliding a few dollars across the table and uttering your shoe size, you'd be greeted by a pair of roller skates. The weekend ritual.

Our parents rarely stayed. It could have been the loud music, or lack of comfortable seating, but you never saw anybody beyond their teen years. In hindsight, the reasoning is obvious. The idea of being in a tightly packed space with scores of children would be enough to drive a person mad. Now, add speed to the equation and you have tiny banshees on wheels zipping about the room like bullets. No, parents were wise to leave us to our own devices. The benefit of a small community was that my grandmother knew the owners. My parents went to school with their children and their grandson was my classmate. Despite our hormones raging, my parents trusted the supervision they provided.

With skates in hand, you entered the seating area of the roller rink. In true Maine throw-back fashion, there was an overwhelming amount of orange carpeting, once famous in the 70's. In an attempt to provide safety for the disasters on wheels, the counter, slots, tables, benches, even the front of the food counter fell victim to the great orange beast. While many consider flannel our pride flag, it would always be the neon orange; evidence that we are slow to transition to the modern era. The roller rink itself was a disco wonderland, sans the disco.

The seating area had the food counter, bathrooms and a small collection of arcade and pinball games, but we didn't come to the rink for video games. Through a large archway next to the DJ booth, you entered the rink. An oval measuring about one hundred feet in length was the real purpose of these pre-teen dates.

We skated in oblong circles.

Why might this be such a hot date spot? Roller skating is only romantic if you have a penchant for sharing shoes with hundreds of other people. So it all came down to the DJ booth. The owner would drop in cassette after cassette, filling the rink with music that included a pretty steady rotation of modern hits. I'm sure at least once a day, an 80's power ballad was played and, if they were feeling gracious, you could request songs. With enough kids requesting, we'd finally get our moment to shine. The lights would dim, and those magical words would echo from the speakers: couples only.

The three couples in attendance sought out one another, entwining their fingers as they sailed into the rink to perform victory laps. It acted as a status symbol. Today we use the phrase, "Is it Facebook official?" In that rink, this was the premiere method of announcing to the world that you were indeed a couple. It forced onlookers to bask in our undying love. It was the first moment of forever, a tale we'd tell our children and our children's children.

Of course, it also dispelled rumors. From week to week, you'd notice the same handful of people switching partners. Had their forever love not survived the week? Had they moved on to another happily ever after? It couldn't be; nobody would treat the roller rink with a lack of reverie.

We zipped about in circles. So. Many. Circles.

There were never many couples in attendance. At most, five sets of two worked around the rink, sweaty fingers locked in a death grip, while sneaking glances at the jealous onlookers. It was a cruel snubbing, showing the world our love was strong, that we could skate in synchronicity. Meanwhile, blaring from the speakers were big hair bands singing about how we would make it against all odds. Nothing could rival this romantic affair.

Even when single, we spent our weekends there throughout middle school. It served as a geographic central point for many of us. For parents needing to drive us all over the vast emptiness of Maine, it was an easy negotiation. There would be times we would go to talk and listen to music, while never putting the skates on our feet. Much to my surprise, like the eternal love I shared with my ten-year-old sweetheart, we outgrew it.

But, much like the kids who once spent their weekends there, the building moved on and reinvented itself. The couple who ran the rink continued for many years, but with a dwindling population, it is difficult to maintain a business without customers. For years, it remained empty, a foreboding sign of the state of our towns. Thankfully, it has been given a second life, selling parts for snow mobiles or some such. While any business in our towns is a good thing, I can't help but hear Bell Biv DeVoe's "Poison" when driving by. And though it isn't the premiere date spot for the neighboring youth, it will always hold a special place in our hearts. This was where we dreamed about forever, before we learned that some things in life, much like our date spot, are temporary.

THE FORKS: A WHITE WATERY DEATH

During middle school, I joined Project Reach, a program put in place by my school to help ensure at-risk students graduated. There was little chance I would drop out, but I wanted to spend the days with my friends, and apparently they weren't so sure about the future. Along with helping us with our schoolwork, during the summer months, we partook in outdoor activities meant to build morale, promote position interactions, and take us beyond the confines of the classroom.

In the span of two months, we had hiked ten different mountain ranges surrounding our community. It wasn't enough for us to work together and learn about survival skills; it served as community service. Armed with cans of paint, we marked the trails to keep hikers from getting lost. Along the 100-Mile Trail, we helped ensure future travelers wouldn't appear on the evening news as another missing persons case. For a bunch of would-be-degenerates, it was a way to give back while keeping us out of trouble.

In late July, one of our adult supervisors thought it would be fun to take a rag-tag group of youths white water rafting. If you have ever seen an episode of Jerry Springer's "Scare Kids Straight," series, you'll quickly be able to understand the thought process behind this excursion. Instead of a scary drill sergeant screaming at us, whipping us into shape, we had two unsuspecting adults prepared to hurl us into dangerous waters. I would like to believe they didn't get permission slips signed, leaving my parents innocent in this outlandish and diabolical plot.

Dragged from our beds before the sun crossed the horizon, we piled into a van pointed toward The Forks. I don't remember how long it took, just that most of us fell asleep. The next memory is being handed a life vest. That didn't surprise me, but when a helmet was plunked onto my head, something seemed off. There was a brief crash course on dry land. Our guide, a villain for sure, showed us how to brace ourselves, remain upright, and what to do if we were thrown from the boat. I expected it to be a leisurely stroll, similar to being in an inner tube and being splashed now and then.

My typical inner tube experience did *not* come with drowning procedures.

Piling into another van, we headed to the top of the river. The would-be rafters carried our vessel down a path, and the roar of the river grew louder. My lazy river seemed to have gotten a little active. It became obvious as we trekked downward, that the dam to our right was holding back an uncanny amount of water. I stared at the rubber boat, wondering why seatbelts weren't included with the price of admission. Only then does our guide casually add, "The dam is emptying out today so the rapids will be higher than we've ever seen them before."

At that moment, I promised that if I survived, I'd start doing my homework. False promises, I know.

Fear and age have blocked the full list of crew along for this adventure. We had the daredevil, a kid who would be voted most likely to jump out of a plane without a parachute. The person sitting next to him, I'm convinced, screamed at the river, believing they could bully into submission. My seat-mate was more terrified than me. I quickly suspected they'd jump at the first sign of turbulence. The newspapers would read, "Town not surprised Kid Drowns." I didn't have a good feeling we'd survive, let alone make it to the end of the river unscathed.

We could still see our launch site when we first hit white water. Half of the crew on my boat was thrown. To "save" you from spending the next six miles splashing for dear life, there were little bags with rope in them the guide threw in your general direction. As the boat dipped downward and then rocked straight up, I said farewell to my crew. They might have tried to rescue me, but only the guide remained in the boat. Little bags of rope were being thrown in all directions.

As I finished my trip through the air, I struck water and the extensive prep we had undergone kicked in. Don't take off your helmet, okay. I remembered that as my head smacked off rocks. Try to get your legs up; not doing so well there as gravel scraped across my shins. Don't let Maine piranha eat you alive, I thought I mastered that one until I realized I made it up. Somewhere in the swirl of chaos, I was expected to reach out of the water and find this tiny bag and drag myself back to the boat. Sure, easy enough, right after I remember I couldn't breathe underwater. Of all the superheroes I could be, never had I wanted to be Aquaman. The fates laughed at me.

Like an expert marksman, our guide hurled the bag, striking me between my eyes. I grabbed on. They tell you to position your body so you're floating on your back to prevent gashing yourself along the rocks. However, holding your toes high results in your head frequently dipping below the surface of the water. In the chaos, with the water whirling around you, you believe your face is clear of the water. You take a much-needed breath. Then you find out you're below water when you choke.

Yup, I barely paid attention during pre-algebra and they thought this was a smart idea?

The current took me through the rapids, launched me into the air and again, buried me under the river's surface. I spun myself around, bobbing on my back long enough to finally make out our vessel. Other than a drenched classmate screaming for mercy, the boat was empty. Our guide had either suffered the same fate as us, or he abandoned his ship full of hopeless kids. Either way, I hope he suffered!

However, much to my dismay, I spotted this wild man clutching the side of the boat. As if it required no effort, he hurled one of my mates into the boat, then a second. With far too much grace, he sprung out of the water, standing at the helm of our craft. I swear this is where he ripped off his life vest, roared loudly, and forced nature to bend to his will. He had a paddle in one hand, taming the river, while he used the other to reach out to drifters, who he then lifted and dropped into the boat. If I wasn't mistaken, he might have paddled upstream to prove he could. This imagery may have resulted from oxygen deprivation; not from being underwater, simply from screaming like a toddler with a scraped knee.

At some point, he started pulling at the ropes, dragging me into the boat. It felt like a lifetime, but was most likely only a few minutes of near-death experiences. The adventure continued. As we ventured further down the river of doom, we stopped along the shore to pick up abandoned students before heading into another stretch of rapids. After that first bout, we were timid, and the moment the boat shook, we dove to the middle, praying that we wouldn't be thrown again.

Once we cleared the rapids, it turned into a more leisurely trip, like the one I thought we'd experience from the beginning. The guide suggested people jump out and float down the river. Needless to say, after our battle scars, most of us were more than content to sit in the boat and dip our feet. For those who jumped back into the water, I feared they had contacted Maine Jungle Fever and they were lost causes.

Once we finished reliving the scene from Indiana Jones, where they jump out of a plane in a raft, skid down a mountain, and go over a waterfall, we were again on dry land. I'm not saying students fell to their knees and kissed the dirt, but we all considered it. We proved that, despite our copious amounts of survival training, our teachers had skimped on our aquatic skills. The rest of the afternoon was spent sitting in a hot tub at the compound where we received our earlier instruction. Each of us recounted the numerous ways we almost died and as a group, we vowed to never go white water rafting again. It might be my dodgy memory, but I'm pretty sure several students sat in the hot tub, gripping their knees, and rocking back and forth from the sheer terror of the day.

In all honesty, I've always wanted to go back for another round. It's hard to remember if the horrors I keep locked away are justified. Alas, every person I ask to go with me can see the tentative look of fear on my face. They ask, "And kill myself?"

From then on, each time a supervisor asked if I did my homework, I could hear the undercurrent of their threat. What they meant was, "Do your homework, or I'll take you back to the rapids."

My grades improved slightly.

FROM ONE GENERATION TO THE NEXT

As I grow older, the face in the mirror has looks more like my parents when they were younger. From the raised eyebrow to the pursed lips, bit by bit, I am transforming. For some, this can be a terrifying experience as they cling to the remains of their youth, slowing transforming into a person they said they would never be. For others, it is the graceful carrying of a mantle from one generation to the next.

If I stare at the reflection long enough, I see my mother's eyes staring back at me and my father's ears stretched from the side of my head. It isn't only our appearance that changes; the habits of the previous generation seep in. It could be how I roll my eyes just like my mother, straight up followed by a glance to the left. The transformation starts with the innocent comment, "You remind me of your father," and just like that, I have become the thing I swore I'd never be. Not only am I an amalgamation of genetics, but I've inherited their personalities, as well.

While most people will see mannerisms from their parents emerge over time, I grew up with an extended nuclear family. There are moments when I can see my mother, father, and a maternal grandmother staring back at me. I think I've dodged the bullet with some of their more annoying habits. But upon closer inspection, on the patchwork quilt of who I am, there are large swatches of fabric stolen straight from my parents. I fought kicking and screaming against their teachings, but I'm finally old enough to appreciate the world they filtered and the good they passed along.

Strangers are friends whose names you don't know.

My father is a curious creature. He didn't outwardly lecture me with adages and lessons to be absorbed like a student in school. Instead, he allowed his actions to speak for him. My father is the stereotype of the Mainer: a coffee in one hand, sitting in a dive breakfast diner discussing the weather, politics or his gardening with anyone that might listen. While this may sound off-putting to some, in Maine, it's a way of life. Conversation will eventually flow, and, surprisingly, these companions become nameless comrades. My father, while still incapable of asking for directions when lost, has no problem walking into any social situation with the expectation he is about to discover a new best friend for life.

As a child, his clumsy and awkward approaches were horribly embarrassing, just shy of him whipping out baby photos. He is a likable guy, with just enough "rough around the edges" charm that people let down their guard. He wields his bumbling lack of social graces like a honed blade. If the conversation is out of his wheelhouse, he had no problem spinning the conversation, making light of his lack of knowledge. It's captivating to watch, and as he's aged, he might look more like a crotchety old man. But he still has that toothy grin that somehow cuts the tension and starts the conversation.

I attribute most of this talent to his time with the military. When left to his own devices, which happened with regularity, I would come back to find him in a discussion with a complete stranger. They'd be speaking about their time in the Gulf and discussing their least favorite assignments. From there, it might delve into physical ailments and places to get treatment. I couldn't figure it out. I had only left him alone for five minutes; if I'd allowed him another five minutes, he could have very well had a new roommate.

This trait has been passed on. I might not take to social situations as readily as him, but when necessary, I know how to flip on the switch. Whether it's casual, formal, work related or friendly, I thrive. I can thank much of my employment history to this trait. It's a lesson that has served me well.

He never taught this, but like any child, I learned to imitate my father.

You need to play "The Game".

Once we returned to Maine, my academics took a downward turn. I had gone from a vibrant and diverse community to something far more stagnant. The pacing of school was slower, and quickly I grew bored. I did enough to keep my parents off my back and advance to the next grade, but I never attempted to apply myself. The rare times I did, it was met with disapproving marks. I counted down the days until I left school.

My mother, not thrilled with my less than average grades, did her best to motivate. There was always talk about "potential" and how I wasn't living up to it. I didn't see the point in working harder for less and found myself comfortable in the middle of the pack. As I discussed an English paper with her, and how much I disagreed with the teacher's point of view, my mother offered her greatest piece of advice.

Let's be honest, life is nothing but a game for which there are no solid rules. We spend a lifetime searching for the playbook, only to find that it's every man for himself. But with that tidbit of advice, something in my head clicked. I went from the victim to the perpetrator. My teachers were no longer the masters of the classroom as I learned to harness the game. They thought they had me under control, and to a degree they did, but I was using them as a means to an end. It might sound vindictive, or vicious, but it was about getting what I needed to move on in life. I did what I must.

I played their games.

During my senior year of high school, I had a particularly vicious English teacher. My mom had been classmates with her, an arch-rival from decades ago. While I disliked her, my mother loathed her existence and thus urged me to play the game. The game was underway; the goal was graduation, and I would get there on the honor role to prove a point. For every assignment, I spent more time dissecting my teacher's wants and what boring requirement was needed to earn high marks. The execution was less important, it only served a means to an end. After three years of being a degenerate, I watched as the grades came in, nothing short of perfect. I played the game, and I played to win.

This mentality rarely translated at home. My family are upstarts. We see right and wrong, and we follow our moral compass with unmovable conviction. More often than not, this lands us in hot water. But beyond the confines of our house, we have learned to spot the cues, sort out the needs, and gamify our response. My mother continues to use this phrase when my I attempt to stand up to injustices. She reminds me to pick and choose my battles and when necessary, play the game.

Between these two lessons, I have learned to become a social ninja. And while it might seem like a trite and insignificant trait to inherit, it serves me every day. From being at a party where I know nobody to coping with the struggles of work, I have learned to charm my way in, learn the rules, and play the game.

For many, there is a moment when you look in the mirror and the only thing visible is the memory of our parents when they were young. But in my case, it's not just a visual that reminds me I have grown into my mother and father. No, for some of us, our parents live in our actions, proof that with each passing day, we are turning into the best of who they are.

BASKETBALL: PEP BAND EDITION

Each high school is known for one or two key things. This might be a particular sport, an academic achievement, or even school spirit. While large portions of America have their "Friday Night Lights," we never managed to form a football team. At Penquis Valley High School, we were known for basketball. Our varsity teams reached the tournaments each year, and on Friday nights, we filled our gym with fans cheering for these athletes. For a few short months, the townspeople gathered, and it became the liveliest of locations.

During my high school years, I was not an athlete. In truth, I was probably as far from an athlete as conceivably possible. At the best of times, I'd call myself a klutz. At worst, I'd be rushed to the hospital with broken bones. Thankfully, Penquis had methods of allowing us to be involved in the spectacle, that sidestepped physical ability.

For the awkward, we had pep-band.

If you were to believe Hollywood, a school is divided by stereotypes. The jocks sit on one side of the cafeteria while the band geeks occupied the other. But our band was a mix of cliques from the school. We had the disenfranchised, jocks, nerds and deadbeats amongst our ranks. Band was one of those places with little discrimination. It was a break from the tedium of our academics and allowed us a chance to take part in a communal art.

I think for many of us, this neutral territory was, in part, because the performance space was far removed from the rest of the school, but also because we arrived to do a job. For most of the year, we performed concert pieces, preparing for our seasonal shows or state competition. The purpose of band changed as we transitioned into the winter sports season. Weeks before basketball season began, our stands were littered in small six inch by three inch sheets of paper. We replaced the usual elegant and melodic music for something more upbeat.

The energy turned electric. It was time for pep band.

We rehearsed hard and fast, making the most of our first period each day. By my senior year, I had memorized most of the songs in my flip book. For a short time, the quality of our music didn't matter as much as the intensity in which we played. The roster of songs was mostly classics from the previous generation, fuel to help rile the crowd into roars. To be honest, we weren't spectacular, and I'm sure we made plenty of people cringe. But pep band wasn't about hitting every note with perfection; it was about forcing the crowd to their feet. We practiced until we were ready to be the half-time show.

It finally came time for the first home game. As you walked through one of our four front doors, you entered the lobby. Another set of four doors led into the gym. Along each side of the court, there were wooden bleachers, pulled from their resting place. But at the far end, just past the basket, that was *our* domain. Four feet above the court, behind the red velvet curtains, rested the stage - our turf. While the junior varsity team played, we ducked behind the curtain to begin our warmups for the big game.

We were a ragtag bunch of performers, but employed by the brass in our hands; we prepared to explode. The curtains drew back, and we stood, ready to begin the evening's festivities. While performing the national anthem, we subdued our energy, causing the crowd to remove their hats and place hands over their hearts. With the first round of applause, we finished the formalities. As the players prepared to take to the court, we started playing one song after another, faster than necessary, but we were determined to fill the gymnasium with as many songs as feasible. Every once in a while we'd pause, allowing the cheerleaders a chance to steal the spotlight.

We weren't glory hounds. Mostly.

The funny thing about sitting on the sidelines for years is that you become an excellent observer of the sport. When you're required to perform during every time out, you look for the signs. You learn to read the court as if you were a player. I was never interested in watching sports on television, but here, it became a necessity. With a word from our conductor, we'd spring to our feet and have thirty-seconds to hit the chorus of one song or another.

Having become accustomed to the sport, it wasn't surprising that my senior year I tried out for the team. I finally became an athlete. After describing my coordination, it might be hard to believe. Yes, after a thorough vetting process, I became a proud member of Varsity Girls' Basketball. I joined as one of the managers of a notoriously fierce group of women. I thought it would entail sitting on the sidelines holding a clipboard or handing off water bottles, and during games it was. But during practices, it felt like I served as a professional tackle dummy for these women. It would be the closest I ever came to lettering in a sport.

In a small school, many of us served multiple roles.

I couldn't rush the stage fast enough for timeouts, but during half-time, without the ability to go in the girls' locker room, I still had pep band. I'd pull off my team windbreaker and proudly reveal my band uniform. Sax in hand, I'd quickly join in the burst of music meant to keep the crowd moving. And move we did. You can't be a true band geek until you've started creating dances for your own music.

With a tight-knit group of students, we could collaborate. What's better than a band blaring music? Having the cheerleaders dance the Hustle as we played. In turn, when the cheer captain signaled to her team, we joined in. It became a competition, pushing one another to be louder. Now and then, I would receive dirty looks as I hijacked the cheerleaders, goading them into a cheer against their will. It was all done in good fun and each time one of us stole the spotlight from the sporting event, the crowd joined in. I was often more pep than I was band.

Our seasonal performances might have a few hundred attendees. Our basketball games could reach capacity. But it wasn't until one of our teams entered the tournament that we felt the pressure to perform. Not only were we competing on the court, but it would be the only time our tiny school would have to share the spotlight with the opposing team's band. It also didn't help that the games and performances were televised, something that rarely happened in our little school. We might not be basketball fans, but we were the Penquis Valley Patriots and we wouldn't let our size diminish our pride.

The auditorium was tenfold larger than our school gym. We would prepare in the depths of the auditorium and set up just before the teams showed themselves. The energy from the bus ride, coupled with team colors, face painting and general trash talking had us ready. Much like the basketball team, the pep band was going toe to toe with the other team. We outnumbered their band despite having half the population, proving that at our school, music is one of the things that unified our community. Win or lose, our spirit never wavered.

It might be hard to believe, but somewhere between our bouts of pep, there was a basketball game.

FOR THE SUPERMEN

There are a thousand stories to tell about my father. Phillip James Flagg is a quirky guy who, without realizing it, has passed on his best and worst traits. I wouldn't openly admit it to him, but I am blessed for both. Being born in our small town, and raised by a Mainer himself, my father is the definition of the men in our town. There is a certain ruggedness that blends with a work ethic that borders on a superpower. If you peel away his gruff exterior, you find that, like many of our people, he defies the stereotype.

During my youth, the relationship with my father was a struggle, strained to the point of breaking. For the first year of my life, I was fatherless, as he was fighting a war. When he returned, even as an infant, I perceived him as a stranger. This became a recurring theme as the military took him away from his family. Just as we were finding our groove, he'd receive the call and it would be another stint on the other side of the world. My mother and I became inseparable. My role models rose from the platoon wives who made up our extended family.

One of my earliest and most defining memories is when he returned from Desert Storm in 1992. He had vanished for a year; one of the first called to war. My mother did a fantastic job of making him part of our family despite his absence and he would send trinkets from the Middle East that served as birthday and Christmas presents. But for nearly a year, he physically didn't exist. It's not a new tale, nor is it an unfamiliar one. I along with many of the kids on my street were being raised by a single parent while their spouse carried out their duties.

But the big day came: the return of our brave men and women. We counted down the days, waiting for these mysterious family members to return. I expected us to arrive at the hangar, and there would be slow motion running. I expected to see him in his fatigues, duffle bag over his shoulder as he lifted my mother and ruffled my hair. There were a lot of things going through my head, even as a kid. But like much of the military, the fantasy falls short of the reality.

We waited.

Inside a building located somewhere on base, the crowd of spouses and military children grew. Inside, everybody speculated, gossiped, but mostly they anxiously waited. Each time the radio roared to life, the room grew quiet as we listened for words like, "touchdown," "delivery," "en route." They had served for a year overseas, writing letters and making the rare phone call home. Despite being in a war zone, it seemed as if their return was less of a promise and a dream everybody hoped to be true.

I remember being told by every adult to go play outside. While I'm sure a room full of children, not fully aware of what was happening, only added to the anxiety, one benefit of being on a military base is the plethora of large vehicles that serve as makeshift jungle gyms and forts. We wasted away the night hiding underneath giant convoy trucks. I don't remember the frantic embracing or the overwhelming amount of tears. When the convoy showed up near midnight, women began crying as they tightly gripped their husbands. News crews frantically tried to capture images of our embraces: my mother in her giant glasses, perm and turtleneck while she gripped my father and me while she cried, my father dressed in fatigues, rucksack, helmet and goggles; a modern-day Superman.

My father and I didn't get along through most of my teen years. It's a common story. He wanted me to partake in his interests, for which I had no desire. I resented him for not being able to reach me on my level, and all the while, being an ass and forcing a growing rift between us. During those years, I viewed my father as an outsider, a visitor in the sitcom of our lives. My mother and grandmother were my family and he was what I imagine a stepfather is for the kids of divorced parents. He was the outsider attempting to be my dad. We occupied the same space, but rarely interacted.

My father worked the second shift. We could not talk for days on end. On weekends, my father invited me into the garage. Having been a mechanic in the military for many years, he wanted to impart his knowledge to his son. Part of me looked down at this grease monkey, not wanting to grow into *him*. He would spend countless hours in our garage, cursing at machines. He'd only come inside in the evenings, his hands grungy and clothes covered in black streaks.

Acting as our moderator, my mother would convince me to go out and give him a hand. He wasn't the best teacher, or perhaps I was a petulant student, but he tried. His demonstrations were hands on and he expected me to get dirty. I was small enough to climb under the hood and sit next to the engine while he reached over the grill. He put the wrench in place and had me crank it from side to side while he explained how to calculate torque. I had no interest in learning, but in rare moments of not being a condescending teen, I absorbed his practical skills. Being more of a book learner, I started asking questions, and though he didn't always have answers, he did his best. I can't tell if I was more of a help or a hindrance, but he always seemed willing to slow his pace for me.

My father is not an educated man. He completed high school and from there, his learning went from text books to skills based. While he might not be educated in an academic sense, he is far from dumb. For his generation, having a diploma of any sort elevated him beyond many of his peers. I wouldn't call him simple, but he approaches life in a common sense, practical manner.

No, stupid is not a word I would associate with my father. He understands survival, mechanics, and how to learn. My father would make an excellent farmer, mechanic, or lumberjack, each a respectable and necessary occupation. He taught me the value of working with my hands and the importance of using my brain to go *beyond* working with my hands. He is incredibly self-aware and would often tell me to stick with my studies. He never said it, but he set into motion the means for me to surpass the caste I was born into. Despite asking me if I had finished my homework or how I was "getting on at school," my father would never be the one to help with my calculus work, play an instrument, or correct my English. Academics taught my mother; life taught my father.

I came home after school one day to discover a sheet of paper on the kitchen table. On it was a poem about my brother. With my mother being an English major, I assumed it had been her doing. The sentiment moved me, and by the heartfelt voice used to express my brother's brief life. It was only later that evening my father confessed to writing it. I was convinced he was lying. To think my father had indulged himself in an art form, any art form, was preposterous. He later wrote one for each of us. He puts his thoughts to paper, fueled by an observation that changed my perceptions of him. On the outside, he looks as if wolves raised him, but somewhere in his head, there is an elegance.

He continues to dabble now and then as the mood strikes him. It took me years to realize this had been one of those moments we connected. When I stopped writing to pursue other arts, he frequently asked if I still worked on my stories. I never understood why or where his conviction for this support originated, but he continued to tell me in college, "You should go into writing." My mother was the hammer of our family, and to push the metaphor even further, she tempered me. She honed my skills and pushed me to be my best. But then there was my father, the one with no actual skill at creative endeavors. He attempted what struck him in the moment.

Between the two of them, I can account for much of my life to temperament and passion.

My father and I took a rocky road to get where we are today. It didn't matter the subject, the goal, or the request, I fought him every step. When I finally came out of the closet, the act labeled me the "gay son." This was the final straw, and it shattered any hope that he was going to get the ideal child discussed in parenting books. We had our issues during this discovery phase, and we quickly learned to avoid topics that would lead us to a confrontation. At some point, without informing me about his change in perspective, it stopped being an issue. While visiting me in Massachusetts at my first apartment, he sat down at my computer. It had a screen open and a photo of a guy I was chatting with. I feared this would lead to another slew of arguments with no real basis. Instead, he asked me a slew of questions and eventually added, "He's attractive enough." Thus began his descent.

My father's overly massive truck now boasts a rainbow sticker, and he ponders why older men give him odd glances. He hasn't figured out that everybody in the state thinks he's gay, and from time to time, his casual conversation is mistaken for flirting. He doesn't care. At some point, he had a dialogue with himself that allowed him to move beyond the hang-ups often found in the men of small town Maine. He blindly supports me and has no problem being part of an inside joke.

My father is many things. He's an ass. He's stubborn. He's angry. He's cock-sure, and often you want to deck him. He is prideful. He is driven. He's compassionate. He's confidant. He's loyal. He's forgiving. He's the one man you want to have your back. I'll paraphrase an eloquent statement made by a friend: "To many, our fathers are Clark Kent; to us, they are Superman."

Phillip James Flagg is my Superman.

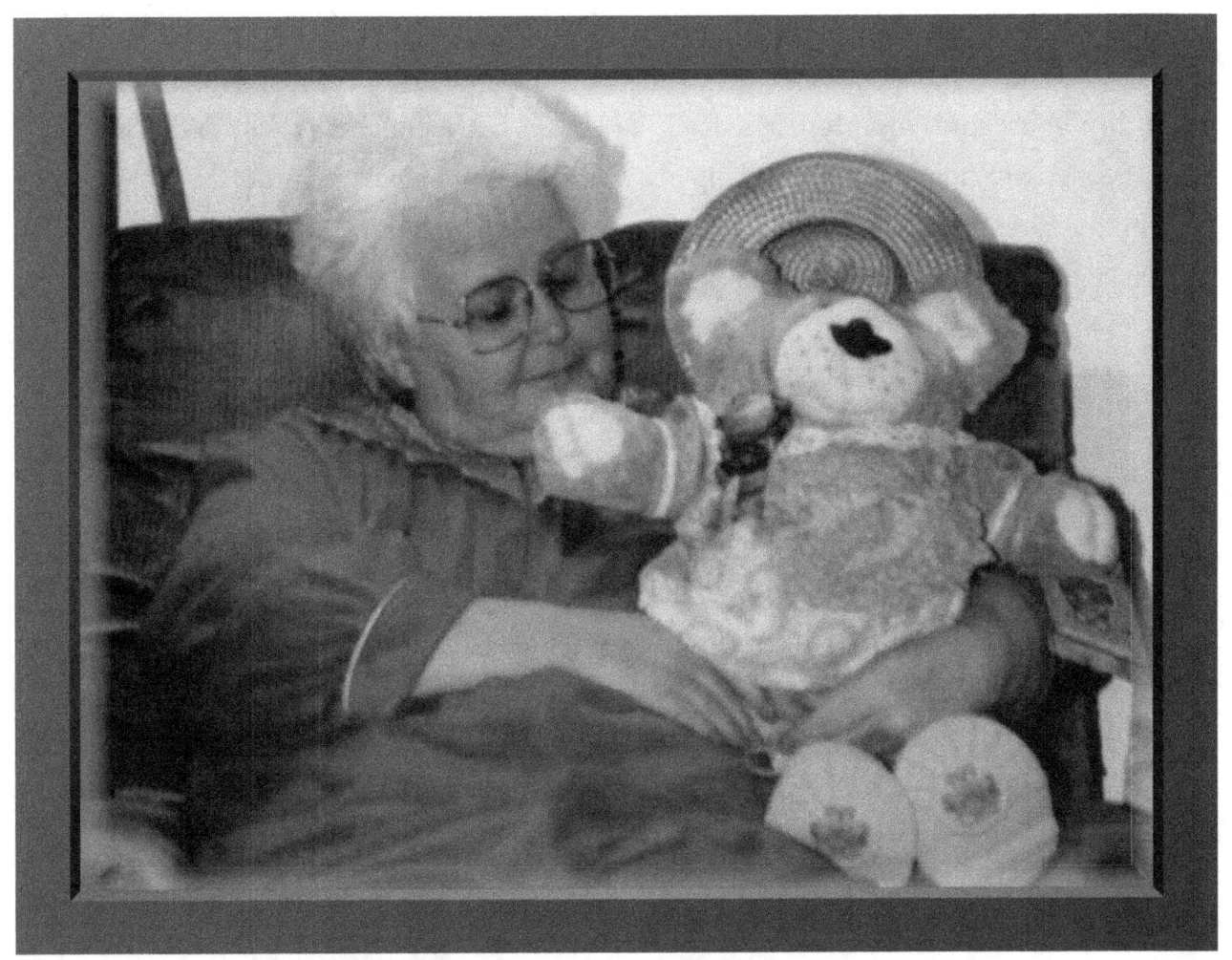

IT'S IN HOW WE GRIEVE

Scrolling through Facebook on my lunch break, I discovered a dear friend passed unexpectedly from a heart attack. After searching for him the previous night, they found his car had gone off the road. Only a few years older than me, he was taken years too early. While we had comfortably fallen into the role of friends, our relationship once been more complicated. At one point, this was the man I was willing to spend my life with. When distance and circumstances interrupted our romance, we settled on a less romantic partnership. With few exceptions, he was the person knew me the longest and remained a permanent fixture in my life.

To be fair, I haven't lost many people in my life. Of those, they were ghosts long before I came into the picture, or they lived a long life before departing. Living in a town filled to the brim with senior citizens, death is part of our culture. In my household, my brother's death had been a monumental event defining my existence. Because of it, I can't help but celebrate him and even his death. When my grandmother passed, she had lived a long a vibrant life on this Earth. Death offers a pause, a moment of reflection for us to self-evaluate.

I believe we are meant to die.

This perspective didn't come from my family. With my parents in a lifelong battle with mourning, I believe my matter-of-fact approach arose from the need to overcome this dreary mindset. Having lost a sibling, I spent many days dwelling on this, attempting to align my belief structure. Standing on Charleston Hill and surveying the miles of forest and fields, I often questioned my faith. Surrounded by this all-consuming beauty provided by nature, it's easy to think someday, it would honor me to join the land that made us. While I am determined to live my life without regrets, it's often because of having death as a bedfellow my entire life.

The first "new" death I had to face was in high school. One of my classmates passed away unexpectedly. To this day, I'm unsure of the circumstances of his death. For a small town, losing one of our own brings out the insecurities of our mortality. With a small population, this absence of one leaves a gap and we experience it as a community.

I didn't know him very well despite being in my class; likable, I guess, what little I knew about him. But when the news of his death reached us, it was obvious he had a lasting impact on my classmates. By midweek a service had been arranged, scheduled in the middle of the school day. They warned us that skipping school would have consequences, but we didn't care. One of our own had fallen, and we each felt obligated to bear witness. On the day of his service, the vast majority of the high school walked the mile down Main Street to town hall where his service was held. We marched not because he was a friend, but because he was a peer, a member of our school, and a member of our community. In a town with so few people, our ties to one another run strong.

One by one we climbed the stairs, entering the old basketball court. Chairs were set up, though not nearly enough for the masses that followed. More were brought out, and when there were no more, we stood. If his family was unaware of their son's legacy, we made sure to remind them. Words were said, memories shared, and tears flowed. The words themselves didn't move me as much as sheer numbers. Looking around at the sea of black, like most things in Maine, we were in this together.

We are brethren related by geography.

Every Sunday morning my grandmother and father would flip through the paper, and it was without doubt one of them would yell to somebody in the house, "Did you know Mister X passed away?" I never knew their names. My grandmother would go through a family tree and eventually say, "They lived in the house on the corner of such-and-such." I would reply with, "Oh, they had such a nice garden." I didn't know them. I might not even have known their names. But they were members of our extended family. Our interactions were limited, but they were pleasant, and while I couldn't tell you any details of their being, I knew they were one of us.

The five stages of grief (denial, anger, bargaining, depression, acceptance) have proved to be fairly appropriate with my recent loss. However, there are other phases I've grown accustomed to falling back on when actual grief overwhelms me. I choose to remember. Much like the neighbor's garden, each death forces me to recollect the many or few exchanges, to dissect how they've influenced me and my life. Most often I find that knowing the person impacted who I am, even if it is as simple as being able to identify a particular flower in the garden. These memories are what the adage "Gone but not forgotten" or "they will live on in our memories" speak of.

It wasn't until after I moved out that my grandmother's health took a turn for the worse. The woman who helped raise me had slipped away over the years, consumed by dementia. I found it uncomfortable to face this stranger during my infrequent visits. One moment we would tell tales from long ago, and the next she'd struggle to discern me from my father or brother. When she died, I was, in part, relieved. Not thankful for myself, but because I knew that a younger, sharper version of herself would be sad to see her last days spent in a haze.

I arrived at my parents' house the day before the funeral. My bags hadn't landed on the floor when the first knock came. I didn't know the woman's name, but she had been a friend to my grandmother over the years. Casserole in hand, she offered her condolences. This scene repeated throughout the evening. Some were fishing for information, but mostly, they offered snippets of memories about a woman who had spent most her life in Brownville Junction. Some of their stories I knew, others I heard for the first time. Each one displayed a lasting impact that wouldn't be put to rest with death.

I wanted to be angry, to scold them for not visiting while she was alive. I hadn't confronted my own feelings of the situation, and as I laid in bed that night, it finally made sense. Much like walking down Main Street, to pay my respects to a classmate I never knew, they were making their own march. I might have lost my grandmother, but they too had lost one of their ranks, a commander of her generation.

In a world where our kin die frequently, we choose to remember as much as we mourn. This is magnified in a small town where your neighbors are treated as extensions of your immediate family. I might not have a specific memory, but my mother would remind me that she worked with them, or that my dad went to school with their son. Our interconnectedness is one of our biggest strengths, but it also cuts the other way. When one of us hurts, we all hurt.

This is another layer of what it means to be a Mainer.

SURVIVING MAINE

When we talk about survival in Maine, the images conjured are of continuous snow falling, white covering our roads, homes and fields. There is a romance to seeing undisturbed snow as far as the eye can see. During the summer, there is a fear of ticks, or drinking tainted waters. But these harsh realities thrust upon us by Mother Nature don't come with a romantic twist. Maine is dangerous mistress, and she tests us during all four seasons.

We've learned to co-exist with snow, but the rains? We never suspected the dangers.

Water in Maine is a different type of dangerous. During the summer months, with ice melting from our mountains and raising the level of our rivers, we are greeted with a new set of problems. Our drinking water, supplied from these lakes and rivers, has an increase in mercury, requiring us to boil any water we consume. Melting ice causes the rivers to crash over our dams and flood our roads and cuts entire towns off from civilization. We should have seen this disaster coming, but like always, we assumed we could weather the storm.

The rain came down in sheets. It would pause, to create a perpetual mist in the air, and then came the second volley of torrential downpour. Throughout New England, we are accustomed to the rapid changes in weather. One day we suffer through ninety-degree heat with extreme humidity, and we endure rolling blackouts. The next day, we're watching golf ball sized pieces of ice strike the pavement and we rush to protect our cars. In the Northeast, Mother Nature is a temperamental bitch, and we are at her mercy.

Brownville Village consists of one main road that cuts through town and a small intersection in the middle of town known as "Four Corners." There was a tree cutting business, a small gift shop, a gas station and a mechanic's garage occupying each of the corners. Between the gas station and gift shop, a road crossed the bridge to town hall. In our small community, this was about as bustling and vibrant as the area got. The rain started, rolling down the hill, draining off into the river as it had done a thousand times before. However, it was what we couldn't see that would create a disaster.

Main Street had vanished. Not simply washed away by the rain, but devastated, collapsing in on itself in the middle of the Four Corners. The pavement crumbled, dropping a dozen feet into a sinkhole. The metal of the railroad tracks stuck into the air, twisted and torn. Even the buildings were clinging to their foundations, ready to slide into the hole or worse, the river. The reports were on display on social media, warning travelers to find alternate routes, but this far North, options were slim. For many, the state had been split in two by an impassable crater.

I had to see it with my own eyes.

Closed roads are a familiar sight in Maine. As the ice thaws and corrodes the edges of our pavement, two lanes quickly drop to one. There are often signs redirecting us. For a passenger vehicle, if you know the dirt roads well enough, you can navigate around the closures. Every trip instantly goes from twenty minutes to an hour or more, but it is doable. However, our lumber and paper industry doesn't have the luxury of taking questionable roads. Trains were being redirected, trying to compensate for one of the most essential methods of shipping vanishing. Route 11, Main Street in Brownville Village, is a critical element to our lifeblood, and that limb had been severed.

The reality far surpassed the photographs I had seen. The hole easily stretched one hundred feet, surrounded by other smaller patches of missing pavement. The railroad tracks were struggled to remain intact, looking more like a roller coaster ride. The crowds gathered, standing at the edge, trying to grasp what this meant for the tiny community. The rows of cars grew longer as people tried to return home, reach vacation destinations, or venture to work.

We have often felt isolated by the state in which we live. The denser populations of Bangor, Augusta or Portland get the attention they need to thrive. But this far north, we are an afterthought, often ignored. As we stood there, the speculation started, how long would it be before the state came to our aide. Would they send the department of transportation to secure our buildings and lift our roads? Would the railroad send repair crews? How long would it be before the divide between our communities were stitched together?

Despite the fact the disaster left us in a difficult state of mind, it didn't deter us from our community obligations. Once the onlookers had established that it wasn't a piece of media sensationalism, they got to work. They stopped the cars seeking passage and offered alternate routes known only to the locals. Workers were already establishing a perimeter, assessing the damage and attempting to ensure no further damage came to our buildings. There was no point in dwelling on questions with no answers; we are people of action. Much like shoveling our neighbor's walkways, we pitched in where we are able.

As I climbed over the rubble I caught sight of a woman running to her house. At first I thought she was running to answer the phone. While I snapped photos, documenting the destruction, she came back out with a giant red cooler, heaving it along as she approached the workers. She stopped to talk to the men, covered in sweat and caked with dirt from working for God-only-knows how long. She reached into the cooler and pulled out bottled water for the workers, and then moved along to the next.

While I finished, heading back to my car, I overheard an elderly couple assessing the situation. She was worried about how it would make it difficult to reach the city for supplies. He ended it with a simple, "We'll survive." His matter of fact words warmed my hearts. This is the essence of Maine, the sheer determination to push forward despite the obstacles set in our way. He gave me a nod and a smile as I passed by, acknowledging a bond created by our hometown.

It's these moments that make me long for this small community. Where, despite all our differences, we have a common thread uniting us. This is what it means to be from Maine.

"IF THE STARS SHOULD APPEAR…"

"If the stars should appear but one night every thousand years, how man would marvel and stare."
- Ralph Waldo Emerson

I often talk about the isolation or the dangers of being a Northerner in Maine, but truthfully, we endure because of the beauty of our surroundings. During the day, we have our lakes and rivers, with the sun reflecting in a way that lights up the ground. The movement of our trees and grass create a rustle that is more captivating than any song I can imagine. The land on its own is a reason to visit.

However, I think there is something even more magical about nature in Maine. It's subtle, and if you don't take a moment to understand the vastness of it, you might very well miss out on one of the most majestic aspects of the state. When the sun has set, and the world slows, settling in for the night, we have the darkness.

For a while, I've been living in a small suburban town in Massachusetts, far away from any major cities. It holds a bit of that small town charm, a little slice of the magic I remember. But at night, when you step outside and look to the sky, you can see the light from Boston. It pollutes the sky. For those unfamiliar with the world where I grew up, you'd say it is beautiful that you can see the stars. But it offers me a bit of melancholy, a reminder of what I have left behind.

When I visit my ancestral home, there are always a round of locations I have to see, to make sure they're still standing. I stop by the cemetery where my great-grandmother, grandmother, and brother are resting. Then it's traveling the back roads until I'm standing on the landing in Lakeview Plantation. I pull into the train yard and wait to see if I might catch one of the steel monsters arriving across the black trestle bridge. Ultimately, as the day ends, and I finish my tour, I travel the back roads to return to my parents' home near the city.

Cutting through Charleston, there is a hill that tops off at the correctional facility where my father once worked. Just before that, there is a massive field, clear of pine trees, overlooking the valley below. Pulling off the to the side of the road, I flip off the lights on my truck and start walking through the high grass. Hidden in the field, a large boulder is barely visible. I sit there as the sun sets, transforming the tops of trees into a sea of warm tones of orange and red.

When it finally vanishes, there is a dark blanket that settles over Maine. In most places, the sky, still illuminated, remains slightly brighter than the darkness of the tree line. Here, the black of the trees is married to the emptiness of the sky. The only difference, on a clear night, tiny burning balls of gasses appear by the tens of thousands. As the light of the sun pulls back, the stars have a chance to shine.

As the wind blows across the field, there is a rustling, punctuated by the crickets. The peepers cut in, determined to be the louder melody. Lying back on the rock, it reminds me of my bedroom as a kid, with tiny glowing stars stuck to the ceiling. The immensity of the scene leaves me feeling small, a speck of dust in the universe. But sitting there, I feel as if I can see the far corners of all that is. I am humbled, but thoroughly satisfied, to be part of this grandeur.

My parents have moved to their forever home, a small cabin far enough into the county that the locals are as much French Canadian as they are Mainer. The houses become scarce, replaced by single homes, large barns and copious amounts of crops and cows. People grow just as rare and the closest city is an hour away. You've entered what we affectionately call, "The County."

Aroostook, where on average, there are only ten humans per square mile.

My parents' home is exactly what comes to mind when you think of a camp on the lake. It hides away from the road, surrounded by trees and almost impossible to see neighbors. Twenty feet from their porch, you're standing on the edge of a lake and on most days, it seems as if you might be the only person in town breathing the crisp air. It is a sight to see, but it's only as the sun sets that you can understand the splendor.

With my phone in hand, I flip on the flashlight and stumble my way across their yard. Down the rocky path and over a small drop, I'm standing on the edge of the lake. It's similar to the experience on the hill, the inability to differentiate the landscape from the sky. But unlike before, there isn't a single light to be found. Even my parents' home, with the living room lights on, seem unable to penetrate the darkness.

The water is quietly splashing on the rocks, as if they are being made with a white noise machine. The insects are more than happy to fill the air with their sounds, while a loon sounds as if it is being tortured. There isn't a breeze to rustle the nearby trees. Even with my feet in the freezing surf, the world has come to a dead halt. After a day of adventure, it offers a respite, a chance to breathe and gather energy for the next day.

Then I look up.

It's as if the stars burn brighter, to the point where you can see them pulse with life. It's not the usual set of blinking lights, not the planets that break through. There are millions, more than I ever imagined were possible. Big and small, there is almost no spot in the sky without a tiny light breaking through. The moment you realize that each of those tiny dots are surrounded by their own planets, everything gets small. Then something unexpected happens. There is a sense of belonging, a happy accident that has made you part of this infinite space. On this particular night, as if to accentuate the splendor of nature, stars zip across the sky.

Offering this description to friends, they will try to compare it with their own homesteads. With cities nearby, it is a poor substitution and I find it impossible to explain. It's not a trait unique to Maine, but it is a quality only experienced by those detached from civilization. For us, we can pause and stop looking forward and experience the world from a new angle. For those of us who left this world, it is a chance to connect with a memory.

After all, we haven't seen so many stars since we left home.

A MAINE MOBSTER

Despite our twelve towns coming together for middle and high school, there remained smaller town elementary schools. Brownville Elementary served both Brownville and Brownville Junction, housing somewhere around one hundred and fifty students from Kindergarten to 5th grade. It's a chance for us to socialize with neighbors and meet kids we could bike to see on the weekends.

It had the added benefit of being a new school, a shining gem in the community. For the kids, it wasn't important that the building was new. What really mattered was the new playground, with new swings, smooth basketball court, and copious equipment to keep us entertained. When I returned in 5th grade, I recognized a few of the faces, but mostly, I was an outsider. Having moved half a dozen times, I recognized the signs of being ostracized. Being a social butterfly wouldn't work for me. It required drastic measures.

In 5th grade, I became the Kingpin of Brownville Elementary.

It wasn't enough to fit in and make friends. No, I needed to storm through those doors and establish myself at the top of the social ladder. Using my astounding business skills, I knew I could cut through the hierarchy and assert my rightful place as ruler of the playground. I waded through a racketeering business, putting me on the fast track to being the underworld lord of organized crime in the Junction. Unfortunately, acquiring a fedora, suit and stylish cane proved harder than I anticipated. I'd have to settle for a Simpson's t-shirt and sweatpants.

We lived a short walk to Stymiest, a small store with two rows of shelves, two gas pumps and, at the time, a recycling center. The store was more for a quick soda, grabbing a loaf of bread, or stocking up on a variety of snacks for the afternoon. While you wouldn't do your grocery shopping there, it was the only store my parents felt comfortable letting me visit on my own. Armed with spare change found between the couch cushions, it was like rolling into a seedy bazaar.

While the store had little in the way of staples, it offered a wide variety of candy at the check-out counter. During a routine stop to pick up Maine's infamous Humpty Dumpty potato chips, I spotted candy cigarettes. They had two varieties of these delightful treats. One was a chalky tasting thing that may have had sugar in it. The other was a chalky chewing gum shaped like a cigarette. I'm sure my father's smoking habit spurred it, but I decided they were the perfect way to fast track my reign over Brownville elementary.

While it was questionable enough for a 5th grader to develop a candy cigarette habit, I had to take it one step further. I scrounged all the money I could in the house, roughly three dollars, and made an investment. I bought two dollars' worth of the chalk cigarettes. The entire stock: two hundred of the little buggers. The gum sticks were more expensive at five cents a smoke, so I only brought a handful, a premium product for my master scheme.

With my backpack filled with the confectionary treats, it was time to begin my life as a gangster.

Mrs. Hill, my 5th grade teacher, didn't take lip from any student. I knew that if she found my stash, I'd never rake in my fortunes. My operation required secrecy; I was very aware that my underhanded dealings somehow violated a rule in the school. I wasn't entirely sure if it was handing out sugar treats, appearing to be smoking, or some mix of the two. Leave it to the school administration to squash a fledgling entrepreneur.

Like any good business owner, I put a two hundred percent markup on the goods, and waited for the droves of clients to come my way. It started with one student, obviously impressed with the candy I tucked behind my ear like a suave pre-teen. During snack time, I lured over unsuspecting students, curious about the clandestine meetings taking place behind my cubby. By lunch time, I had sold out of my inventory, having to turn away would-be customers. They offered crackers, bags of chips, and whatever else their mothers had packed for them. I knew my school-wide ascension was underway when the kids offered me their milk money.

I also suspected my dealings were drawing unwanted attention. As half the class puffed away on their gum, it was without a doubt Mrs. Hill grew aware of a shift in the power dynamic. Thankfully, selling out by lunch allowed me to lie low and let the heat die. It wouldn't do well for my empire if they dragged me to the principal's office on my first day. I was already plotting how I would take my profits and reinvest. As soon as I stepped off the bus, I'd drop my backpack on the kitchen table and journey to the store, now referred to as my "supplier". I had created a demand, and I couldn't allow my sugar-dependent clients to go without product.

Unfortunately, the backend of my mob empire was slow to acquire new product. The cashier raised an eyebrow as I acquired the remaining cigarettes. She probably feared that I was heading toward childhood obesity or a diabetic coma. I considered offering her a cut of the profit, but for now, our arrangement allowed me to continue peddling.

The next day, I ran out of product before our first snack period ended.

Unfortunately, every mob story ends, a standoff of epic proportions. My clients grew belligerent, drunk on candy cigarettes. With her iron fist, Mrs. Hill crushed my empire as she issued a blanket warning to the class. She confiscated their illicit substances, tossing them into the trash. I then considered offering *her* a cut, more than enough to buy an additional milk come lunch time, but I refused to share the limelight.

I suspected she knew I was the mastermind, given my pockets were lined with nickels. If it hadn't been for her crackdown, I'm sure I would have been selling fermented juice boxes within the month. It wasn't enough to conquer the 5th grade classroom, there was an entire school of would-be clients, just waiting to be converted.

In hindsight, I don't think Stymiest ever got more stock in the store. Which makes me ponder, how long were the original ones on display? There is a chance the same cigarettes had been sitting there since my parents were kids. I'm surprised students didn't die from stale sugar overdose. My life as an adventurous mob boss lasted for two whole days, and to a kid, that is a lifetime.

I might not have ruled Brownville Elementary, but it did side-step the ostracization, and begin my life as one of the "cool kids."

QUESTIONABLE FIRST JOB

Employment is one of the ongoing struggles of living in an isolated town. Our parents started each morning with an hour commute, heading off toward the more populated portions of Maine. There were ten or twenty people for every available position at our local hardware or car parts store. While the adults in town held tightly to their jobs, it was near impossible for younger people to find positions. A few of my classmates occupied the handful of positions bagging groceries, but most of us found spare change in mowing lawns or babysitting younger siblings.

I wish I could say this was a story proving that even a small-town boy could find a position in the big city. However, my first job was more comical than triumphant.

Spending the vast majority of my time in coffee shops working on this novel, I am reminded that my first position wasn't teaching, nor an admin job in college. No, my first official paycheck came from a small coffee shop in Dover-Foxcroft. While this should be reason to celebrate, in my naivety, I should have questioned the fact it was named the Kristian Korner Cafe.

During my high school years, I spent a good portion of my money on the upkeep of my saxophone. Between reeds, fresh pads, or having the joints oiled, it added up. Once I joined community band, I decided I wanted to experiment with new instruments. I suspected this would be my major in college so it seemed smart to invest in my future. Thankfully, through my connections, I was introduced to a gentleman who owned a small music shop in Dover-Foxcroft and he frequently discounted any repairs I needed.

Walking into his store was like a kid walking into a candy store. While his clients typically ran more the way of percussion or guitar, he kept an entire wall stocked with brass instruments. I managed with a "beginner" level saxophone most of my life, but the professional model always struck me as a beautiful piece of metal. But knowing I wanted to expand my background and not wanting to carry something heavy during marching band, I inquired about one of the flutes. Much to my surprise, they're not priced based on size. Knowing there was no way my parents could swing the hefty price tag, I asked if there would be some method of paying in labor. Much to my dismay, he didn't need help, at least not in *this* store.

Outside of community band, I knew of the owner through a friend. They attended the same church, and while I have no opinion on those who express their faith, he had a reputation. Where some might put their faith on display, this man was a zealot, a fanatic to a degree I had never encountered before. I hesitated when he offered me the position, hand held out, ready to shake on the arrangement. I frequently made bad choices in my teen years; what was one more? With a shake, I sealed my fate and became an indentured servant to Dover-Foxcroft's only cafe.

It is difficult to tell if his not-so-witty name was for the sake of alliteration, or that he counted bigotry as one of his many traits. Being sheltered, and a bit on the dense side, I didn't even notice until one of my friends visited, pointing out the suggestive A-frame sign in front of the establishment. Knowing that we credit my home town as the first daylight march of the KKK, in hindsight, I think I know the answer to this question.

I had no training as I went into this job. He opened the door for me one day and threw me to the wolves. Thankfully, the business was unbelievably slow. I think at best I had one or two patrons come in during my daily shift. They would grab a quick cup of coffee and vanish. Despite boasting a lengthy menu of food, the decor inside didn't tempt people to take their chances on ordering food from a clueless teenager.

Only once did somebody come in to discuss theology. Having attended Sunday school for the entirety of my youth, and a frequent church-goer with my grandmother, I am well versed on the subject. However, his conversation quickly turned to the more violent passages in the Bible. Since the customer is always right, I nodded and held back any scathing remarks I might offer in reply. Easily my size, this bald man, dressed in a sleeveless denim jacket and ass-kicking boots, tried to spur a conversation that treaded into dangerous territory. Looking back, I believe his views had little to do with religion and more to do with the visual cue from the name of the cafe. It took a few decades before the lightbulb came on and I understood the clientele.

I held my tongue, an act of God on its own, while I worked there. I paid off my service and in exchange I received the flute the owner had set aside. While wrapping up my duties for the man, I overheard his exchange with another customer. With conviction, he explained how God had put him on this Earth to make money. He tried to explain how finding "riches" was less figurative and more of a literal journey. When the customer left, eyes rolling back in his head, the owner, with reckless abandon, delved into his dating life. Through a pen pal website for incarcerated women, he was determined to show one lucky lady the error of her ways and make an honest woman out of her. I was convinced he was going to get shanked in his sleep.

The coffee shop folded shortly after we went our separate ways. Apparently God hadn't offered to pay the bills. Only months after that, the music store closed as well and nobody heard from the owner. I have a theory that he met his prison bride, she broke him and is now serving another term for matricide. It would be a fitting end.

So yes, while over the years I have had many jobs, many with accolades and prestige, it started here. On Main Street in a neighboring town, I spent my days slinging coffee, drowning my woes in caffeine, all in the pursuit of a flute. Only in Maine can fact be stranger than fiction.

THE SURF OF MAINE

Maine – a tourist destination in the Northeast. We are well known for our mountains, our forests, and our lakes. People come to partake in a rustic way of life and enjoy the beauty of a slower lifestyle. Much of this takes place in the northern reaches of the state, but southern Maine does their fair share of tempting "out-of-staters" to visit Vacation Land. With their rocky beaches, outstanding seafood, and posh seaside communities, they help balance out our offerings. In Maine, there is a vacation destination for every person.

Ogunquit, Maine in one of the many towns that provide direct access to the ocean.

The plethora of small hotels mixed with countless bed-and-breakfast establishments make it the perfect weekend escape. When one of my friends suggested we venture north from Massachusetts to the southern stretches of Maine, I didn't hesitate. I have to remind people that Maine is larger than many countries, and despite living there throughout my youth, there is much I have yet to explore. Each trip to my parents requires me passing by the exit for the tourist destination, but never had I stopped to explore. For me, the surf along Ogunquit Beach was uncharted territory, and I looked forward to the experience.

I packed my bag, and with a traveling companion, we headed north. The first thing that struck me on this drive is that Ogunquit is south of Portland. I am always reminded about how easily I get lost and how quickly I forget the geography of this massive body of land. A fact that only exacerbated this particular case, as I think everything south of Portland is New Hampshire, much the way people of Portland consider everything to the North as Canada.

We had barely checked into the hotel when I found myself in an alien world. The land itself is flat. At almost any point you can look down the road and watch as it vanishes into the ocean. The air itself was different; damp and smelling of salt. The people are as different as the landscape. With the countless run down motels, it was obvious visitors preferred to spend their time outdoors, continuing a theme that runs throughout Maine.

Unlike their northern kin, the southerners of Maine are used to dealing with the public and have a more civil disposition to the tourists who invade their hometowns. Even more than us, they rely on the money of tourists to continue their way of life. Not once during our stay did we see a sneer or hear a comment about being flatlanders. In the North, we would have led with that.

There are only two "real" roads in Ogunquit. The primary road cuts through the town, offering a scenic view of the ocean while the other leads directly to the water. The downtown is like many New England towns; there are a variety of shops selling locally made products and sweatshirts for those chilly nights. But mostly, it clings to its small town charm, with small bistros, cafes, and fine dining, all overlooking beautiful vistas.

Nobody in my caravan of out-of-staters knew anything about Ogunquit before coming there. For those in the know, Ogunquit has a reputation as being a heavily gay-friendly town, and the gay bars or pubs promoting drag queen karaoke show this. Of course, this is a tightly held secret and my friends did not know the fabulousness in store that evening.

The first inkling that they knew something was "different" came when a friend phoned us, hunting for our hotel. As he slowly drove through town, he belted out, "There's a whole lotta gay here." This band of misfits is theater folk, so gay is nothing new. I promptly explained we were standing in Maine's answer to "P-Town," a gay mecca. It fascinated them.

For the first night, we spent our time wandering through town, darting in and out of the shops. With several people in the group unfamiliar with Maine and its delicacies, we demanded an initiation. From one restaurant to the next, we sought out any place offering boiled whole lobsters. For those unaccustomed to eating lobster, there is a method that is difficult to explain. Between the bibs, the stainless steel cracker and explaining what is and isn't edible, there is brief lecture before you can begin. As our New Yorker stared at the two pounds of sea crustacean, we held back our laughter. Watching an outsider experience one of our staples quickly turned into hysterics. His messy, messy, messy approach was a riot all on its own.

Our journey eventually brought us to the local gay bar. In one night, I bumped into the majority of the men I once dated in Maine and even a few from Massachusetts. There is something about the scenario that would normally frighten me, but in true Maine fashion, it was like visiting long-lost friends. Once beers were in hand, embarrassing stories were told. We walked down memory lane and parted company with, "We should do this more often." I was shocked and delighted. In my youth, this culture was the same one pushing me out of Portland and into southern New England.

With the music thumping and it nearly impossible to hear, we moved to a tamer setting. Even the idea of Maine having a nightlife astounded me. This small seaside town was unlike anything I had ever experienced. Once we reached the next pub, it warmed my heart as a drag queen greeted us asking if we wanted to step on stage and sing. The local patrons sounded dreadful, but it was less about accuracy and more about having fun. We cheered on every Sonny and Cher song.

None of this is the typical scene I would expect of Maine. While we are one people, our geography is large enough that each region of Maine boasts its own culture. I was happy to see the commonalities, but I was even more excited by the diversity.

Refreshed and with show tunes stuck in our head, we started our next day ready to tackle the real reason we went to Maine. We drove to a local spot known for surfing and walked past the dunes to a beach that extended for miles in either direction. It was chilly, but well within bathing suit weather for any Mainer. My friend slipped into her thermal wetsuit and took to the waves. Being one of Maine's woods people, I'm not much of a beach goer and avoid the ocean as a rule. But as Mother Nature created a sandstorm, the waves topped with a white crest, and my friend took to the water, determined to experience the surf. Periodically, she required breaks, her hands reminding me of freezer-burned chicken. But after a few moments' respite from the icy waters, she charged back into the surf, ready for another round through the gauntlet.

As the weekend concluded, we packed up the car. My seats were covered in sand and the smell of salt filled the air. We passed through downtown, a new collection of memories to satisfy our taste for adventure. As we exited, boarding the interstate that would lead us to Massachusetts, the signs along the road bid us farewell, welcoming us back should we need another opportunity to step away from the hustle and bustle of life.

Any reason to set foot back on the soil, or sand, of Maine.

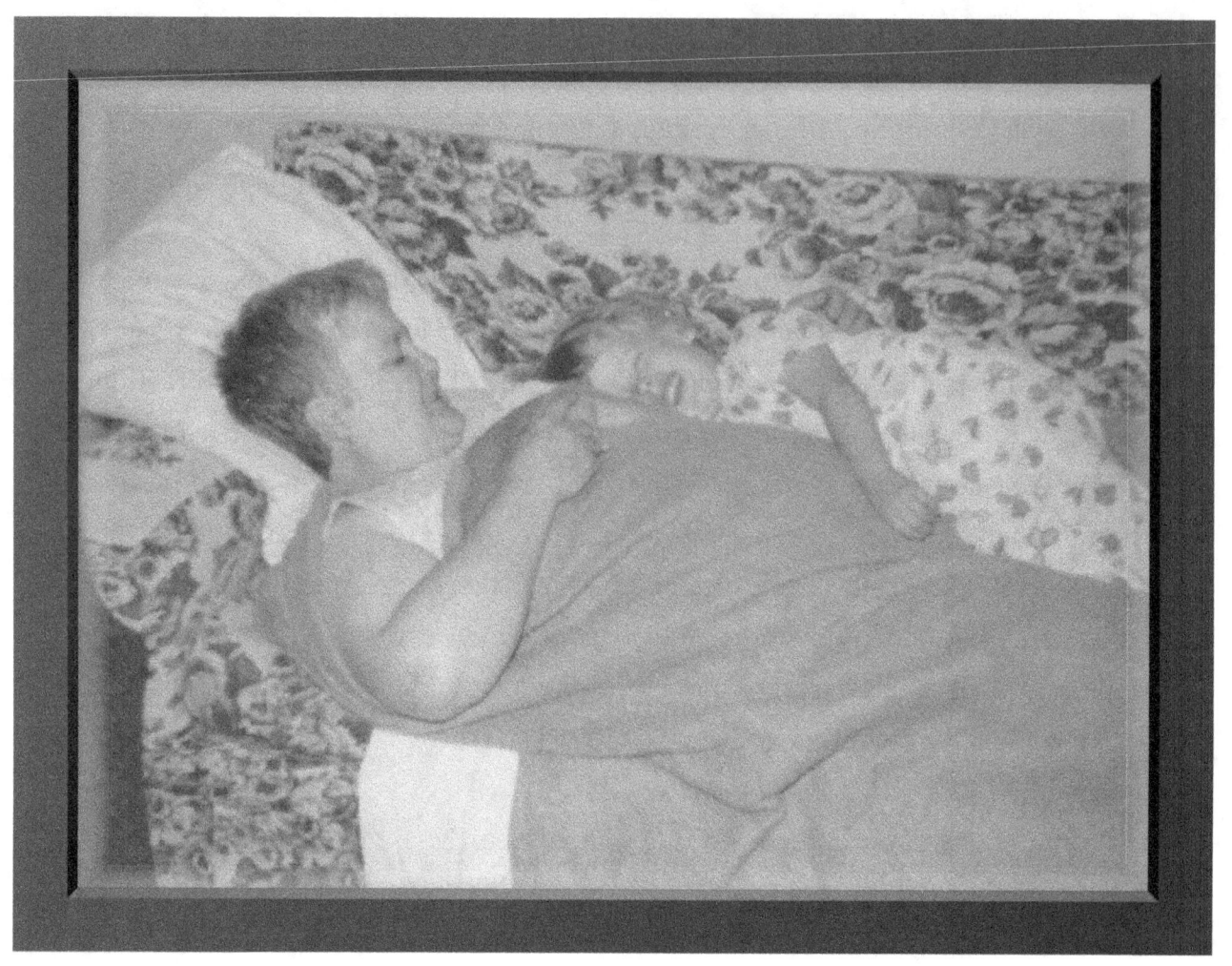

HER WATCHFUL EYE

Once we moved to Maine, our family grew by one. Our house came with problems for our extended family, but eventually, we modified it to better suit our needs. I took the attic as my own, my mother and father occupied the second floor, and my grandmother moved to an attached in-law suite. We shared the kitchen and living room, but mostly, we settled on the common ground of a four-seasons porch.

My grandmother had very few requests while we conceived the construction, but she demanded a window looking out onto our yard. At the time, I thought it an awkward request. Our yard on that side of the house basically showed our sidewalk, a street, and then the neighbor's yard. There was little worth seeing, but my grandmother insisted. After moving in and upsetting her routine, it was the least we could do.

She got her massive window.

During my teen years, my father worked during the day and my mother attended university. My grandmother served as my third parent, and mostly, we led a peaceful coexistence. However, unlike the fast-paced lives my parents led, driving toward their goals, my grandmother had already achieved them. Her life had slowed as she entered her twilight years. For a teenager, this is an entirely unique perspective. While I attempted to pack my life full of activities, friends, and experiences, she spent her time unpacking her collection of memories.

Our porch housed a china hutch filled with my mother's precious moments, a stool for the dog so he could see out the window, and a rocking chair. It served as the entry into our home, and anybody on the porch could see guests parking their car before they made for our house. Most days, my grandmother spent her days on the porch, soaking up the sunshine and watching the world pass by.

Over time, she became a fixture, the watchdog for our home. From her perch, she waved our guest through, doing a quick inspection before they entered our home. But what I remember the most are the small touches added by my grandmother to turn this space into her own. Outside, a flower box spread the length of the window, filled with her favorite flowers. Mimi spent her days plucking the dying blooms, making sure it remained pristine from spring to fall. She also insisted on a bird feeder, a little excitement as the squirrels attempted to steal seed each time she filled it.

She was particular, to say the least. While the yard always had a smattering of seed, her true goal was to create a sanctuary for the humming birds. Filled with sugar water, she planted these tiny feeders on the window. At any given moment, you could see three or four of the tiny birds hovering in the air, waiting for their turn to feed. Whenever they appeared, my grandmother would look up from her word search book and admire the colorful creatures. I have to imagine that much of my appreciation for nature, or even my desire to take a moment to step back and take it all in, came from watching her. She would catch me watching and give me a smile before going back to her puzzles.

During the summer, she managed a carefree approach to life. But as the leaves changed and snow quickly coated the ground in a blanket of white, her demeanor changed. Much like our home, she had weathered the worse that Maine offered. We spent more time indoors, avoiding the frigid temperatures. Her T-shirt became a sweatshirt, and eventually she'd have a blanket crossing her lap. Even as the porch grew cold, she refused to give up her sentry, determined to persevere.

We were separated by sixty years and had little in common at this point. But there were many days, when the television had nothing worth watching, that I would join her. I'd pull out the dog's makeshift perch and sit, or sometimes I'd lean over her shoulder and take part in her word searches. When she grew annoyed at the speed in which I could finish them, we'd share gossip. She was a master at gathering intelligence, either through the neighbors who visited or from church, and more often than not, I had no idea who she was speaking about. But she was my Mimi, and I'd listen.

One wintery day, the snow fell. I was on the living room couch reading something for a class, one of the few times I ever did homework in school. With no electronics on in the house, you could hear grumbles of age in the frame. I could hear through the kitchen, the familiar creaking of my grandmother's rocker. I'm not sure if it's by design or by illusion, but falling snow creates a void of sound. The house got eerily quiet. I went to the kitchen for food, and from the angle, I could see the reflection of my grandmother in a window. I remember being perplexed by what she was doing, just staring off into space. She held her knitting needles, but she had abandoned knitting, fixated on something happening on the other side of the window.

I stared for a while, trying to understand what she watched with such diligence. I was baffled by what could be so captivating. Eventually, the snow became a spectacle as it fell with ferocity. The heat in the house kicked off, and it grew cold. As time passed, I could hear her rocking stop and start-up again as she returned to her room to grab a sweatshirt, sliding it over her house coat.

It had gotten dark, and she remained watchful as ever, following the flakes as they fell. I admired the woman, and her ability to be at peace with herself. I made hot chocolate, two cups. Handing her one of our brown mugs, I asked what was up. She pointed with her chin, telling me to watch the storm outside. By the street light on the corner, it was apparent the storm was picking up speed, covering the street. I pulled up a stool, and we sat in silence, watching the heavy snowfall as comrades in arms. I jokingly said, "Making sure the snow is doing its job?"

She continued rocking as she answered. "If I don't do it, who will?"

THE ICE COVERED ROADS

When the snow is falling, it is easy to identify who is and is *not* from Maine. We describe the roads using words like, "slick" or "slow moving," but you'll never hear us say they're too dangerous for driving. Many to the North have heavy-duty trucks, with thick treads, capable of driving in any condition. Even those with small four-door sedans have learned to ride the grooves, tail the plows, or navigate through the wilderness using only the best roads. Those unaccustomed to our determination can be found, knuckles turning white as they drive at a crawl. You'll find Mainers passing them, barely slowing.

Though I describe it like a scene from Mad Max, this is a skill we gain over time. With damaged roads or no roads at all, there is a checklist of items we have to overcome before we get our Winter Expert License. Because of the danger, our parents often urge us to take Driver's Education in the winter, to help give us the skill set to handle a vehicle in the worst of conditions. It sounds like a pragmatic approach, but for me, I was impatient and decided to take my driving lessons in the fall.

When the snow fell, I realized I had made a grave error.

The first time I faced the ice covered roads, the day after a heavy snowfall, I discovered that a teenager's invulnerability doesn't extend to their vehicle. My parents didn't have issues with me driving during or after a storm, but there were particular roads they forbid me from traveling. Of course, I ignored their warnings when a friend needed a ride home. To reach Lakeview Plantation from my house required cutting through three towns who were diligent about plowing their roads. However, as I crossed from Milo into this small lake community, it was obvious they didn't take the same care. Because of the frequent logging trucks that traveled the road and the underground springs, they considered it dangerous in the best of conditions.

Side note: Had I listened to my parents more often, life would have been much easier.

We drove towards his house, reaching an area where the road becomes a series of twists and turns. The radio was blaring, most likely set to some hardcore radio station as we continued to fight for control of the dial. The back wheels slipped from one set of grooves to the next. Since they were created by logging trucks, my car didn't quite fit, causing it to slide back and forth. A few slides turned into fishtailing. I could hear Mr. Oakes, my once-upon-a-time driving instructor, screaming in my head, "Turn into the skid."

I turned the wheel back and forth, thinking I had the situation under control. It grew worse, and as I tapped the breaks, I found I had to admit the truth; I lost control of the car. The car made its first rotation, the backend swinging around. One turn wasn't enough; we achieved five hundred and forty degrees of spinning. I planted my hands firmly on the wheel, knuckles white as I pushed myself into the seat and prepared for the impending crash. The world became a blur and I couldn't make out the road. I feared an oncoming vehicle smashing into my car, at best destroying it and at worst, killing its passengers. As a last resort, I closed my eyes as I prayed we survived the disaster.

Now, let's discuss the goings-on in the passenger seat. While I feared for my life, my companion was being treated to the best amusement park ride of his life. He screamed like it was the first dip on a roller coaster, hands firmly planted against the roof. While I wrote a mental will, he was already planning to take a second ride for no admission. Even as the car stopped, his hooting and hollering continued. If I could have removed my hands from the steering wheel, I'd have strangled him.

The whole incident couldn't have lasted more than a few seconds. The car came to an abrupt stop as we slammed into a bank of powdered snow. My car compressed five feet of fluff into the eighteen inches of space underneath my car. Once the adrenaline flowed from my hands, allowing me to inspect my body for injury, we got out and assessed the damage. While many would think the danger was over, Mainer's know that the accident itself is only the beginning. On a chilly afternoon, the countdown started, and we needed to get my car free before the sun set.

Without shovels, we used our hands to pull the snow free from around the wheels. We rocked the car back and forth, trying to give it enough momentum to break free, but after several attempts, we admitted defeat. Miles from the nearest house, we plotted our next course of action. We had just settled on walking toward Lakeview when, in true Maine fashion, we experienced a bit of trail magic. A man with his large truck came around one of the twists in the road. Slowing, he rolled down his window and asked if we needed assistance. In a well-rehearsed move, he pulled the chains from his bed, latched onto my car and within minutes, he pulled my car free of the bank.

I was relieved that I wouldn't have to call my parents and receive a tongue lashing for driving one of the forbidden roads. With no damage, we were home free of consequence. But when my mom came home that night, without a moment's notice, she asked, "Have some car troubles?"

It amazed me. Had she inspected the car and found a new scratch amongst the many littering our family vehicle? Had she calculated the mileage and knew the exact distance to and from my friend's house? Or had the man who saved us turned out to be my family's insurance provider and called my grandmother to let her know we were safe and would be home soon?

Yeah, just my luck.

DEMOLITION DERBY: MAINE STYLE

Having a license in Maine is one of the most important rites of passage for a teenager. With this small sheet of plastic, we can traverse the state, break the borders of our towns and, for some of us, see friends living an area code away. The small laminated rectangle had barely formed a dent in my wallet. Matter of fact, the only reason I owned a wallet was to provide my license a home. Otherwise, it was void of money, social security card, or even the condom you'd normally find. No, the experience of being able to get behind the wheel and drive to all points in Maine was still fresh.

My license was used most often to view movies. I frequently visited the "cheap seat" movies with a buddy to waste away our evenings. It had become a ritual, and this was like any other night. It was bleak and stormy on a dismal road in the backwoods of Orono. The sheets of rain coated the pavement, making it hard to see beyond the bumper of my 1991 Dodge Spirit. Clouds swirled above the small city, threatening to create a vortex and cleanse the college town.

The kids in my town were a conundrum. We could barely afford the gas in our cars, but somehow, we always managed to buy ourselves a three dollar movie ticket and an order of nachos. No popcorn; we weren't rich. I had dropped off my companion at the theater, and since a nearby friend had asked to join, I made the quick trip to campus to retrieve them for our second-rate blockbuster.

Barely a mile from the theater, I found myself in a perilous situation.

I had yet to accomplish the extended driver's course, "Driving for the Offense: A Road Rager's Guide to Aggressive Maneuvering." I found myself in the wrong lane, put there by a frustrated, lost driver. The lane forced me to turn left and cross traffic at a busy intersection. As I did, I could see a large truck coming straight towards the passenger side corner of my car. My life flashed before my eyes, and only being seventeen, I found the reel to be even more lackluster than the movie we hoped to watch. Time slowed as the truck approached, leaving my mind to stray from the impending collision.

Did I study for my upcoming test? Did I forget to save money for a school lunch tomorrow? Who will tape Buffy for me? Holy shit, if I die, how will I ever find out what happens in the recent issue of X-Men? Yes, I had spare time. I'm pretty sure there was a point where I started reviewing a chemical equation. Somewhere in my heightened sense, I am sure I solved world hunger and discovered the cure for cancer. And then I found myself fixated on the need to change the oil in my car. My upcoming encounter with a giant truck would remove that as a priority.

The truck struck, folding my tin can underneath itself. The car crumpled. I could hear the sound of metal being crushed. The car spun, and I remember gripping the wheel so tightly I ripped it from the steering column. My seatbelt slowed my impact but ripped free from the side of the car, doing little to protect my body. The airbags forgot their invite to the party. My car was no longer a rectangle; it was a misshapen piece of debris crowding the road.

I'm not sure how many times the tinfoil ball spun about. When it stopped, it happened with a jolt. It had shaken all logic from my body, and my only thought was to get free of the wreck. I attempted to open the door to my car. It was firmly latched in place and wouldn't budge. Thinking it was the perfect time to take a nap and regroup, my world turned black. Either from fear or the flood of adrenaline, I continued to fade in and out of reality. I snapped to when a lady tried to pry the door away from the vehicle. My senses were on fire, sending me into shock.

Seconds or minutes passed, and I woke to find myself on the pavement.

This woman, my angel, stood over me, repeatedly saying, "I was a nurse." I ran my hands along my body, battered and bruised. I searched for broken bones, unsure if I should be moving. As I finished, she reached down and heaved me to my feet. The two gentlemen in the truck had gotten out and were swearing about their broken grill. Yes, only the grill was broken, and the driver stormed toward me. He cursed, pointing at me as my angel acted as my second set of legs.

I hit him.

There was no logic behind my actions, just that I was operating without higher brain function. He had made his threats, and I decided the next course of action would be to protect myself. I pulled away from the nurse. My fist connected with his teeth. I'd like to say I continued to pummel the man who felt my life was less than the cost of a new grill, but no. After one hit, I collapsed, the pavement ready to say hello to my face.

The world blinked in and out of existence.

The next moment of clarity allowed me to see they had loaded me onto a gurney in an ambulance. Every time my eyes open, a paramedic explained he was preparing to prick me with a needle. I'm convinced I saw the grim reaper, sitting next to the medic, cackling every time I closed my eyes. The wounds weren't nearly as severe as I thought, but of course, I needed to add a teenage flare to my fight for survival. Through this, each time I opened my eyes, I spotted the medic hovering over my body. For all the flurry of emotions and worry, I remember him having kind eyes. If they were the last I'd see, it'd be a fitting end.

Like I said, I was melodramatic.

I got to the hospital and was stabilized, and they repeatedly told me I was going to make it. It was only when the nurse said, "We've called your parents," I realized I would rather deal with the grim reaper. My mother was pissed. Not pissed that her car was broken but pissed because she thought, with it being April 1st, I had concocted a masterful a prank. I love that my mom thought highly enough of me to believe I was capable of a scheme involving traffic reporters, a medical staff, and the EMS folks in central Maine.

She arrived. I'm not sure if she was crying, but I do remember she swore like a sailor. My brush with death may have unsettled me, but the wrath of my mother is a scorn no man wants. Thankfully, I was only on crutches for a few weeks, and everything returned to normal. The reaper left without my soul. I left without the paramedic's phone number, and a truck driver left without a tooth.

NEXT DOOR, A WORLD AWAY

We are not all farmers.
There is a stereotype for those living in my region of Maine. It is said that cows outnumber us and our land is nothing more than acres of potato fields that span in every direction. We don't all ride tractors and I'm not sure I've ever seen a man in overalls chewing on a bit of wheat. No, while we lived next to these institutions that provided many families their livelihood, very few of us were part of the farming community.

However, a childhood friend, through a series of family incidents, inherited a farm. When we reconnected a decade later, he suggested I come up and experience his world. Within an hour of where I grew up, I drove down a long dirt road heading toward a farm house straight from a postcard. The massive barn sat back from the house, the doors thrown open wide, revealing a tractor inside. I couldn't have imagined a more idealized version of a farm if I tried.

The sun had set almost an hour ago, and as I pulled in, he was still wearing his work clothes. Sitting at the kitchen table, I waited for him to shower and wash away the dirt. In true Maine fashion, he put on a pot of coffee, settling in for a night of catching up. He quickly told me about a runaway cow he had to retrieve from an adjacent farm and how it put him an hour behind his usual schedule. When he confessed to the stress of dealing with crops and the livestock, I found myself surprised. I assumed most farms only dealt with one or the other, and considering the trucks carting milk from northern Maine, I assumed livestock was the default.

I realized I had more questions than answers. While I talk about my people being one with the land, he showed me that perhaps that relationship is more distant than I thought. I confessed to only knowing one or two families in school that worked on their family farms, but then I am reminded that farming wasn't the only occupation that worked the land. During school, we had two weeks of optional vacation time, where students who worked could take it off. This followed harvest time for potato picking and blueberry raking.

One year, I decided to pick blueberries on the weekend, thinking this would be much preferred to an hour long class of geometry. It was the perfect day, a light breeze and the sun shining but not hot enough to be considered sweltering. Joining a friend, he handed me a box where I would put the berries and a metal rake used to pull them from the bushes. After spraying a generous layer of bug spray, we ventured into the field. I think I lasted an hour, bending at the waist, scooping berries, before I prayed that heatstroke killed me. I had barely collected enough berries for a child's snack, but it felt as if I had single-handedly cleared the entire field.

As we finished the pot of coffee, it had reached prime time when he said he needed to be heading to bed. My evening had barely started, and he was ready to turn in for a night so he could rise before the roosters crowed. From the kitchen we could hear the cows mooing loud enough that he decided they needed an inspection. He slid on his boots and invited me along. A chance to see the interior hidden from the casual viewer.

One of his herd had been injured (not the cow who escaped) and it was expressing its discomfort. He flipped on the overhead lights. The barn was far larger than I could have ever imagined. Stalls lined the side, housing dozens of cows as they came in from the chill. When I asked about milking them, he laughed at my ignorance. He explained there was a machine to do this, so I had to scrub the image of him on a stool, pulling at the cows' utters, from my mind. Okay, at this point it was abundantly clear that I might live nearby, but I'd never make it as a farmhand.

I like to think, as a people, Mainers appreciate the land we inhabit. But it's few who have a direct connection. This man had a symbiotic relationship where he cultivated the land for his survival. I admired his endurance in the backbreaking work. In a world filled with dot-com businesses, when we have become reliant on retail outlets, he has maintained a family tradition of providing the resources that make our state is famous. He does this with such a strong sense of pride you can't help but look at him and his way of life with envy.

It's one of those instances where I believe the outside world views us as a stereotype. We're cast into an imaginary role as the Mainer. The more I explore, and the more I dig through what makes us who we are, I see we are a community of diverse individuals spanning from white collared administrators to blue collared field workers. While the outside world might think this creates a caste system amongst our residents, we treat it as a level playing field; each of us fulfilling these roles and respecting the many differences between us. Out-of-staters might think it derogatory to paint me as a farmer, a potato picker, or lumberjack. I'd be proud to be any. After all, each of these is one of many images of a true Mainer.

THE PRESTIGE OF SCIENCE FAIR

There are a few things my school is known for. In sports, we boast one of the top basketball programs in the state, proven over and over by our performance in the state tournament. But in academics, we aren't a school filled with prestige. Even though we might not have an exemplary track record, our science department filled a wall with signatures of students who competed in Maine's statewide science fair.

Mr. Valente was one of the most demanding teachers I had during my tenure at Penquis Valley High School. The same man had taught my mother and gone to school with my grandmother. Teaching chemistry and physics, it was impossible to dodge his classroom and still graduate. The man's reputation preceded him, to where even my mother chuckled when she saw my class list for sophomore year.

I loathe chemistry.

Math has never been my strongest subject. While I had my best year academically in geometry, I floundered in chemistry. Between needing to memorize the periodic table, balancing equations, and understanding chemical properties, I found myself sinking. To this day, I still don't understand endothermic versus exothermic or how to balance a chemical formula. I was near failing until he mentioned an opportunity for extra credit. Desperate, I was prepared to jump through burning hoops if necessary.

The parameters were simple; we had to develop a hypothesis and test it. At the end of our experiment, we would give a presentation and if it made the cut, then we would move onto the state competition. There was a bonus for participants: we would get a trip to Boston to the Museum of Science. Leave it to a teenager to put more effort into their extra credit than they ever did the original assignment.

My hypothesis: plants grow faster when they are exposed to violent, cell membrane breaking frequencies.

The assumption is that plants grow faster to music, and I was curious. If we could speed the process up with classical music, then perhaps thrash metal would do wonders. While my parents weren't thrilled with the constant noise coming from our spare bedroom, I did indeed prove my hypothesis. When it came time to present, I did well enough that Mr. Valente gave me that rare approving nod. From there, I was one of the few chosen to take my experiment and continue in preparation for the state competition.

I reached University of Maine Orono with my little experiment. We had prepared speeches, visuals, and even brought in elements of our project. Walking down the aisle, it was obvious that my concept was beneath many of my competitors. As the judges walked toward my setup, I debated if a fog machine, some flashing lights, and a microphone blaring epic music would help me land the win. I did my best, and as I discussed the application for rapid acceleration in vegetation and the impact on farming culture, the judges quickly jotted down notes. I received more approving nods. Later, when they announced the winners, I had accepted my impending defeat. To my surprise, I took silver in the category of Environmental Sciences.

I had never been an outstanding student. For the first time, I enjoyed the experience and the rewards it provided. I spent days pouring over the minimum five-page paper, perfecting my use of MLA format and writing in third person past tense. Now, as I write, I remember thinking, "I can't go over twenty pages for this paper?" Mr. Valente's voice taunts me as I have to edit down my word count. I enjoyed this one project enough, that when selecting classes for my junior year, the only one I demanded was physics. Despite my poor grades in chemistry, I was determined to prove myself.

My junior year, during physics, a friend and I decided we'd join forces and tackle science fair together. We wanted to make a small land rover equipped with cameras used to research caverns. We received outstanding grades on our papers; however, we quickly learned we were idea men. Our technical skills fell incredibly short, to the point that Mr. Valente made the comment we shouldn't have waited till the day before to work on it. I was annoyed. We spent hours cannibalizing parts and just didn't have the resources to bring our vision to fruition. We might rule the world someday, but we'd need henchmen to carry out our plans. Despite this epic level failure, I finished the year with surprisingly good grades.

In my senior year, I found it impossible to squeeze advanced physics into my class schedule. I had a grudge and needed to prove myself. Not being in Mr. Valente's class, the only way I could participate was by partnering with one of his students. Thankfully, Chris Jay, a friend from band, offered and I was back in the game. With our mutual love of music and his future goal of majoring in psychology, we found the sweet spot. We enter into the psychology category.

Our hypothesis: Music can influence and alter human emotions.

We easily assume this topic. However, the studies of the impact of music hadn't become widespread in 1999. After selecting a variety of songs void of lyrics, we started the experiment. During a party, one-by-one we asked our friends to listen through the soundtrack while talking in a steady stream of consciousness. They told stories, recounted memories, and described their surroundings. With hundreds of pages of data, we ventured to my future college to speak with a doctor of Music Theory where we explored the merits of music, our particular selection, and the influence of the medium on mankind.

We were ready. Armed with one of the best papers in the school and a presentation that proved our understanding of the scientific method, we received permission to compete. On my second trip to the University of Maine, I came prepared. Our category, Psychology was one of the largest, and we moved through the aisles, studying our competition. When it was our turn, we navigated the presentation with gusto. As the heads of the psychology department moved on, we high-fived, awaiting our impending victory.

Of the nearly hundred psychology experiments, I wasn't sure we had made enough of an impact to win. In the presentation hall, we waited, second guessing our choices. As they announced our names, there was a strut to our step as we accepted our medals. While we didn't take the gold, or even the silver, the bronze medal served as a reminder that Mr. Valente's demanding and often brutal approach to teaching had been effective.

Mr. Valente retired after my senior year. There were times when I cursed his name. However, now I can see he was more than willing to be the villain to get his point across. I've had teachers like him in college and on the list of teachers who I respect most, they were all the ones I hated when I was in their classroom. I still can't balance a chemical formula to save my life, but thanks to Mr. Valente, I developed new criteria for success. My senior year, I would be amongst the list of high honors for the first time. It would not be the last.

THROUGH THE GAUNTLET

"Mr. Flagg, you must have been crazy when you were in high school." Because of my non-conventional teaching methods, I hear this frequently from my students. Yeah kid, let's go with that story. The truth, as a kid, I was incredibly boring. While my parents and I were always at odds, it's funny to look back and think, why? I never drank, I only started smoking because I was trying to remove my goody-two-shoe image, and I rarely violated my curfew. Mostly, I was a saint.

My mother frequently warned me about hanging around the kids with a reputation for being corrupt influences. She would add, "You need to learn to make your own fun." In a world where there is little extracurricular entrainment for teenagers, many turned to drugs or alcohol to fill the time. Amongst my group of friends, we actively sought adventure. With the mountains circling our town, inevitably, we'd find ourselves lost in the woods.

It finally happened my junior year. In a streak of boredom, we decided to do a communal camping trip. I had gone countless times before with my father, but never with friends. When I explained the plan to my parents, they shrugged and offered a simple, "Be safe." Despite venturing twenty miles into uninhabited trails, my parents knew that our definition of shenanigans would involve skinny dipping before booze.

After acquiring my license, I discovered a majestic spot near the Katahdin Ironworks known as Gauntlet Falls. After presenting it as an option, the organizers quickly agreed that it offered more than enough entertainment for our band of misfits. Armed with tents, sleeping bags and coolers filled with bacon, we started our mass exodus into the forests. While many of us were accustomed to "roughing it," it was obvious by the number of creature comforts that we were traveling with an inexperienced group of Mainers.

Much like any other planned camping trip, it was dreary for most of our stay. We pitched our tents and tucked away our gear. It wasn't long before we built a fire, determined to cut through the chill of the damp weather. We had nearly twenty people gathering as the day continued. As the night approached, I watched our group of friends, a diverse collective for our school, split into small groups. Much like myself, each person on this excursion brought with them expectations.

***

The Lovers - I can't remember how long they had been dating, but they had become a success story amongst our circle. He, the younger man, dating the older woman. An innocence and curiosity about them provided our group of friends hope. I recall walking over the ledge that led down to the waterfall, to find him sitting on the rocks below, cradling her as they watched the wilderness together. While the sight of the woods spanning as far as the eye can see was impressive, seeing the two lovers finding solace in each other's embrace was the beautiful sight. Watching them, it was clear that there was a magic radiating from the splashes of the river.

* * *

The Departed Lovers - While we had one couple in a torrid romance, we had another that had once been sweethearts. Watching the familiarity in which they responded to one another, you couldn't help but see they had been each other's first loves. At night, I shared a tent with them and, at some point, I could hear her whispering about the cold. Without asking, he crawled into her sleeping bag. I thought it would get awkward, but seconds later, they fell asleep. What was beautiful about it was waking up before them to see him wrapped around her while they slept. Because of that act, I have used it as my definition of intimacy for years.

* * *

The Almost Lovers - Amongst such a tight-knit group there were plenty of crushes and heartbreaks. For a while, every other weekend somebody was either crushing, confessing, or breaking hearts. I always knew who it was; the perk of being the gay confidant is a lady tells every secret. On this trip, one of my friends was using the opportunity to confess his feelings to a girl he had pined over for years. I don't believe he ever did, but she knew his intentions. While we gathered around the campfire, there was a magic in the possibilities of what may happen. I could see the way she casually laughed at his jokes, resting her hand on his knee. The coy manner in which she flirted suggested she was assessing the potential of right now, tomorrow, and a distant future as she explored possibilities.

* * *

The Friends - Mostly we were all friends. In a school where the population is small, this outing represented a significant percentage of our student body. There was something different about being on our own, in the unknown. We had some expectation of "trail magic" to make the event memorable. For a weekend, we set aside our differences. Our catty comments, age-old grudges, and sideways glances vanished. Underneath the stars, twenty miles from the nearest paved road, we forgot our transgressions. It wasn't that we offered a truce, it was as if the moment we inhaled the mountain air, we transformed, forgetting everything from before. I had been close to everybody in this crowd and, surrounding the campfire, I could only recall the best of each of us.

* * *

The Almost Friends - Many of us were inseparable, but on this particular trip, strays accompanied us. These were friends of friends, but we invited them into our social circle without prejudice. It is a small community, where we're bound to one another through a thousand tightly woven threads. They entered my life, and our lives, and even the faintest impressions could ripple outward and create a lasting effect helping strengthen our foundations. From my perch, a rock sitting high above the swimming area, it was amazing to watch them. For that moment, that weekend, we were like brothers and sisters. We chased each other on the landing, dunked one another in the river, and told tales by the campfire. We were a family, some close, some not, but we mingled as if we were blood.

* * *

The Jokers - The first morning, I heard maniacal laughter peppered with the occasional snort. It was rich, and as the voice bellowed, you couldn't help but to join. He was being goaded into adding a newly discovered container of garlic to the camp's eggs. I emerged from the tent to see our joker, his infectious laugh spreading through the camp. His face was as far from serious as one could imagine; the mad scientist, experimenting with breakfast and his cackling drove his machinations onward. Despite the angst and hardship burdening us as teens, this is what I remember the most. We endured hardships, some more than any teenager should be asked to bear, but I remember we laughed. Even with our part-time companions, we laughed, fought, and forgave. We ate garlic filled eggs, and even though our food tasted wretched, we continued until our jaws hurt.

* * *

After that first trip, we ventured to Gauntlet Falls several more times throughout high school. There would never be camping, and the number of attendees would be small compared to "the excursion." We would find ourselves recounting the tale over and over again. We talked about how our tents leaked or how we nearly died being pulled under the water. There were frequent talks about returning, about reliving the experience. But it never happened. I believe we all knew that no planned recreation would ever surpass the first.

I was lucky to have that moment, that weekend, with the people I cared about. They stepped into my world, a world in which we ventured beyond our comfort zones and found a place that forced our thoughts inward. While I'm sure it's me injecting an experience with far more romance than the reality, I feel as if it was quantifiable just how much we each grew during those forty-eight hours.

Gauntlet Falls offered me solace, a space away from the complexities of life. While I didn't know it at the time, I needed this to help quiet an internal war being waged. It worked, and later in life, I would return seeking to recreate the magic of that weekend.

RETURN TO THE GAUNTLET

I fled the state of Maine. When I dropped out of college and couldn't leave fast enough. The next few months were spent traveling the East coast looking for something, anything that would give me an excuse to not return. I had endured all a small town could throw at me, and I thought the state owed me an exit plan. Wandering, I was lost and unsure of what the future held. I had followed the expectations thrust upon me, and as they crumbled, I didn't know what to do. Worse than that, I didn't know who I was in the bigger world. Depression made any forward momentum come to a standstill. I rallied against the darkness, but try as I might, I couldn't find a path offering the freedom I craved.

Eventually I escaped. Through a long list of freak occurrences, I attended Salem State College. While I had a new environment, I continued to stray. My psyche was fractured, and I walked through life aimlessly, with no goals or ambition. While some might attribute this to being a young adult, for me, it bordered on catastrophic and the fear of being hospitalized for this inability to step outside myself was real. This lack of self had already brought life to a crashing halt, resulting in a broken human and forcing me to drop out of college at one point. I found the same sensations brewing, ready to surface and destroy my new sense of reality.

Once again, I ventured north to reconnect to my soul.

I find stability in memories, and returning to the land of my childhood home, I hoped to find something that helped me shake this uncomfortable dread. I stopped at my parents' house, grabbed my camping gear and borrowed my father's pickup truck. Then it was onward, saying farewell to civilization as I entered the mountains and the valley beyond. North on Route 11, the road connects Brownville Junction to Millinocket while passing through the unknown territory of T5R9. I drove until the pavement gave way to deeply grooved tracks in dried mud. The road into Katahdin Ironworks was traveled more by loggers than by car and the iron-rich ground makes the road the color of red clay.

For those who favor their creature comforts, there is a campground where trailers and campers litter the landscape, complete with a small hut for showers and bathrooms. I kept going, not interested in maintaining any level of comfort on this trip.

The only signs of human life were the logging trucks carrying their goods from the forest to the mills. I arrived at the split in the road, decorated by a massive orange snow plow. I feared I'd have forgotten the way, a dilemma that can quickly result in being lost in the wilderness. I slowed, remembering a trip years prior, with a car full of misfits ready to find themselves an adventure. As I hoped, the memories came in bursts, reminding me of the nights of laughter we had while staring up at the stars.

Confident, I pushed onward.

The moment I got out of the truck, the smile broke out across my face. Years earlier we had parked here and started unloading our camping gear quickly so we could begin swimming. My tent went up in record time, and I gathered the wood I'd need for the evening. Once the chores were done, I climbed the rocks overlooking the waterfalls. The air smelled like freshly dried linens mixed with an edge of moisture from the fall's mist. The sound of water smashing into water drowned out any other sound from the forest. I pulled the hoodie over my head, to ward away the cold. Sitting on the rocks, I settled in for a night of getting lost in my own thoughts.

Unmoving, I sat there for hours. The sun dipped behind the trees, causing the sky to turn the colors of fire. The birds had quieted, no longer cawing in an attempt to be heard over the splashes beneath. Even the stone under my butt had gone from providing a radiant warmth to draining it from my body. I watched as hawks returned to their perches and a pair of beavers left a fallen tree for the next day. My hands pressed against the surface of the rock. It was rejuvenating. Somewhere in these observations I found myself at peace. In a moment of clarity, I saw through the uncertainty of life and focused on the potential of what might be.

I tried to stand, but my legs had grown numb. Toppling, I slammed onto the ground. I laughed. My inability to control my limbs spoiled the moment of pure serenity. My chin bumped the rock, and I feared I might have cracked a tooth. While I assessed the damage, with my face close to the stone, I could see a carving in the rock. It was littered with people signing their names, attempting to leave a legacy exceeding their finite lifespan. Of all the etchings, the one closest was from the lovers who joined me years ago in an attempt to find a romantic weekend. On that trip, he had carved their initials into the rock, a permanent "I love you".

Their relationship had flourished and faded. They would find it awkward to be near one another and eventually found comfort in being friends again. They would part ways, and their friendship would grow distant as they married and began their own families. Years ago, in that very spot, there had been a simplicity in our lives and with a small rock, they had captured it inside a carving. The memories of an adventure we undertook as a family came rushing back, playing in slow motion. It overwhelmed me with how beautiful things were and how despite all the struggles we faced, those moments remained locked away in a special place meant for safe keeping.

Life had moved on. I had not.

For years, I had lived with a hole in my chest, small at first, but slowly widened by anxiety, depression and fear. Where my heart had once been, where I felt joy, there was only this absence. I had thought my life had come to an abrupt halt, shattered and crumbling. I thought about how each of the people on that trip had moved on to lead their lives, now almost distant and unfamiliar faces. As they shook away their adolescence and emerged as adults, I had become fixated on holding onto these memories. I fought hard to escape a world that never felt entirely my own, and when I had been presented with what I truly wanted, I returned to a memory.

I cried.

Much like the lovers, it was time to look to the future. One by one, I worked through the events of a weekend spent at Gauntlet Falls, where we bonded as kin. I was confronted with the most amazing moments of my life, and while they were special, it was time to tuck them away and make room for more. I said goodbye to who they were, and acknowledged that in their place, new versions had emerged. It was a farewell to my younger self, ready to be done with my childhood and take the next, bold, and frightening step into the person I would someday become.

These uplifting memories would support, but they would not define me. It would be the last time I visited the falls.

I left with no idea of what challenges lay ahead. But for all the trials and tribulations, I had to remind myself; I am a Mainer. Born to a wild world, we find ourselves with our feet firmly planted and moving forward. With the hole a little smaller, and my heart a little fuller, I would drench my fire in the morning and return to a life that had barely started. Should I need a compass to guide me, I only needed to remember the carving in the rock.

I am who I am, not who I was.

FROM THE ASHES, WE RISE

A member of my writing group asked, "Is I.Am.Maine a story about where you lived, or is it about you growing up there?" At the time, I couldn't answer the question. When this project started, I wanted to tell tales filled with heart that revolved around a small community. Some of these tales talk about the evolution of a town nestled in the heart of Maine. Others talk about my family and coming into my own within its borders. The stories, for me, weave together creating a single beautiful tapestry.

It took years, but I finally have my answer.

I.Am.Maine is about a memory of what we once were and how a small town forged us into the people we are today. It is about the longing for the best of our origins and coming to grips with the truths coloring our pasts. Many of these stories pull back the curtain of nostalgia and often give way to dark themes. They are laced with melancholy, as even the fondest memories are frayed by an underlying sense of sadness.

For me, I.Am.Maine was and will always be a journey. This project started as a humorous walk down memory lane, and as I dug deeper, I discovered that despite its flaws, Maine remains my home. It has little to do with my destination; instead, it reflects on the experiences that shaped my path. I.Am.Maine has become less about explaining my birthright to flatlanders, and more about connecting with a piece of my heart that I closed years.

I.Am.Maine is battle cry.

I've woven the tales with humor because that's how my memory works. But by the end of this journey of self-reflection, I found something that I hope is evident in every chapter: I am a proud Mainer. It's impossible to define what it means to be from this magical world where the people exist within nature. It took dissecting my childhood to see how these two things entwine.

Through I.Am.Maine I have rediscovered former teachers, aunts, uncles, cousins, friends, and even the townsfolk for who I only know by surname. Alone, they might be individuals, but together they form the backbone of what it means to be from a small town cut off from the rest of the world. I think of the woman behind the counter at the post office, the man running the general store, or the people sipping coffee at Stymies and feel we are family, sharing a common ancestry created by a village we call home.

It was years in the making, but I found my way home.

Thank you.

FICTION BY JEREMY FLAGG

The Night Quartet
Nighthawks
Night Shadows
Night Legions
Night Covenants
Morning Sun (Prequel)

The Dawning of Superheroes
Awaken the Daughter
Anoint the Daughter
Ascend the Daughter

Suburban Zombie High
Suburban Zombie High
Suburban Zombie High: The Reunion
Suburban Zombie High: Final Class

www.ingramcontent.com/pod-product-compliance
Lightning Source LLC
Chambersburg PA
CBHW081343070526
44578CB00005B/711